UNCASTE

UNDERSTANDING UNMARRIAGEABILITY: THE WAY FORWARD TO ANNIHILATE CASTE

A.B.KARL MARX SIDDHARTHAR

Endogamy is the key to the mystery of caste system.

Caste and Endogamy,
according to our analysis of the various definitions of caste,
are one and the same thing.

-Dr.Ambedkar, in 'Castes In India- Their Mechanism, Genesis And Development'.

TABLE OF CONTENTS

PREFACE

CHAPTER 1

INTRODUCTION TO CASTE AND UNTOUCHABILITY FROM DR.BABASAHEB AMBEDKAR'S WRITINGS AND SPEECHES.

CHAPTER 2

DEPRESSED CLASSES: THE TRUE UNMARRIAGEABLES WITHIN THE HINDU SOCIAL ORDER.

IVb. Endogamy– the synonym of Caste.

IVc. Graded Inequality- the obstacle that fortifies Caste System.

IVd. Caste System- a closed form of Stratification.

IVe. 'Social Inequality' in the context of Caste System and to the cause of studying Unmarriageability.

IVf. The peculiarity of the Social Inequality within Hindu society.

IVg. The Final Inference- the right understanding of Social Inequality in accordance with the Hindu Social Order.

V. Conclusion: Unmarriageability is the spearhead against the Caste System.

CHAPTER 6

UNMARRIAGEABILITY: WHY THE STIGMA SHOULD BECOME THE SPEARHEAD?

I.   Confronting the Dissenters beforehand- the Significance of Unmarriageability.

II.   Rationale One: The long hiatus of the Unmarriageables in reviving Buddhism.

III.   Rationale Two: Unmarriageability has the resistance to thwart the anti-Reservation outlooks and efforts.

IV.   Rationale Three: Unmarriageability exposes the present Young Generation's submissiveness before the Caste System.

CHAPTER 7

UNMARRIAGEABILITY: HOW TO WIELD THE SPEARHEAD?

PREFACE

HOW THIS BOOK SHOULD BE CONSTRUED

This book should never be understood as a prescription for exogamy over endogamy by the Unmarriageables in their desire to assimilate within the Hindu society. None of the words in this book and the meaning they carry are meant in that way. Nor should they be understood in that connotation.

Through the concept of Unmarriageability, I intend to make two distinct and direct appeals to the Unmarriageables and the caste Hindus:

To the Unmarriageables by indicating the stigma of Unmarriageability, I try to light their consciousness that they are never a part of the Hindu society and in fact form a separate element in the national life. The Unmarriageables should construe the stigma of Unmarriageability purely as a strategic spearhead to enlighten themselves to denounce Hindu religion and embrace Buddhism. This should be their primary concern. Apart from this, they should realise that the concept of Unmarriageability provides strong rationale against anti-reservation endeavours, questioning the conscience of young generation remaining dormant to the caste prejudices, and laying out the path to annihilate caste. The Unmarriageables should resist the caste Hindus by bringing Constitutional amendment to abolish caste and banning the caste matrimonies- thereby centre-staging the stigma of Unmarriageability prevalent within the Hindu society. In any way, if my reiteration to amend the Constitution to include abolition of caste appears to be utopian to anyone, it does not undermine my arguments. Rather what we are reminded of is the dystopian state in which we are living at present that makes us even to think of abolition of caste as a utopian or fairy tale concept.

My appeal to the caste Hindus via the stigma of Unmarriageability is if at all there is any intention among them to reform the Hindu religion- socially and religiously, it can be done only through the superposition of exogamy over endogamy. This would be a hard task for them to initiate and even harder to have their thoughts inclined in that direction. They should undo what they have done for centuries. Caste system is eternal because endogamy has made it to be so and if the caste Hindus do not wish the Hindu society to remain rotten for eternity, they should superimpose exogamy over endogamy and purge the stigma of Unmarriageability. Definitely, this prescription would be indigestible to them. But if they no longer wish to remain as sunken humanity, they must realise this as the 'only' right prescription that they have to choose.

Having said this much about the purpose of the book, there is an altogether different question that I would like to entertain briefly- Does the term 'Unmarriageables' and the concept of Unmarriageability intended to infuse inferiority complex among the Depressed classes in any manner? The readers would independently answer the question in negative if they grasp the purpose of the book that I have aforesaid. Also, each and every idea expounded in this book negates the necessity of such a question to arise. However, I can completely understand why such a question could arise. Though I have presented the stigma of Unmarriageability from the standpoint of Unmarriageables, this entire book is a critique on the caste

Hindus and their Brahminical Hindu society. As each caste unit is endogamous i.e. the members of each caste being Unmarriageables to the rest of the castes, it is up to the caste Hindus to continue embracing it as a practice or realise it as a stigma and shun it. Also, I do not wish to ignore this question on account of being an outcome of shallow understanding. Because, the question, if wrongly answered, has enough potential to reduce the authenticity and the noble intentions of my book itself. It is for this reason I have included 'The Unmarriageables- Why the Name is Essential?' as chapter 3 in this book. The readers would find that the book can survive without this chapter yet I have taken the trouble to intrude into the dialectical construction of the book by inserting this chapter only to nip in the bud the criticism of infusing inferiority complex among the Depressed classes via the term 'Unmarriageables' and the concept of Unmarriageability.

The ultimate fight of the Unmarriageables should be the fight against Unmarriageability. But the purpose behind it should never be to make themselves marriageables. Rather, the motive should be explicit and clear- to denounce Hinduism. It is in this inclination I am pronouncing the fight against Unmarriageability as the spearhead against the caste system.

There might be challenges in embracing Buddhism but the Unmarriageables should not forget that the social reform of prescribing exogamy to the Hindu society will be seen by the Hindus only as an unacceptable and ludicrous endeavour. Instead of trying to reform the endogamous Hindu society, the Unmarriageables must realise that the path to Buddhism would unfold a silent revolution among them. Embracing Buddhism is a lot easier than achieving exogamy.

The foundation and inspiration for this book is undoubtedly BAWS (Dr. Babasaheb Ambedkar Writings And Speeches). The beginning chapter which solely consists of his writings is intended to familiarize anyone with the right understanding about the subject of the caste system and the Hindu society before introducing to her or him the concept of Unmarriageability. *The works of Dr.Ambedkar reproduced throughout the book is fondly highlighted in Italics to gather the attention of Readers.*

At ample places in the book, I have made repetitions to bring in Emphasis which might bother the intellectuals and scholars but much required for the masses and reformers who are my constant concern in the process of crafting a positive social change.

The stigma of Unmarriageability offers wide scope for the Feminist thinkers to ponder upon. This book is an invitation to them to explore the subject further.

A. B. Karl Marx Siddharthar

CHAPTER 1

INTRODUCTION TO CASTE AND UNTOUCHABILITY FROM DR.BABASAHEB AMBEDKAR'S WRITINGS AND SPEECHES

Essential and unessential features of Caste

The basic conception of social organisation which prevails among the Hindus starts with the rise of four classes or varnas into which Hindu society is believed to have become divided. These four classes were named: (1) Brahmins, the priestly and the educated class, (2) The Kshatriyas, the Military Class, (3) The Vaishyas, the trading class and, (4) The Shudras, the servant class. For a time these were merely classes. After a time what were only Classes (Varnas) became Castes (Jatis) and the four castes became four thousand. In this way the modern Caste System was only the evolution of the ancient Varna System.

No doubt the caste system is an evolution of the Varna System. But one can get no idea of the caste system by a study of the Varna System. Caste must be studied apart from Varna.

An old agnostic is said to have summed up his philosophy in the following words:

"The only thing I know is that I know nothing; and I am not quite sure that I know that".

Sir Denzil Ibbetson undertaking to write about caste in the Punjab said that the words of this agnostic about his philosophy expressed very exactly his own feelings regarding caste. It is no doubt true that owing to local circumstances there does appear a certain diversity about caste matters and that it is very difficult to make any statement regarding any one of the castes absolutely true as it may be as regards one locality which will not be contradicted with equal truth as regards the same caste in some other area.

Although this may be true yet it cannot be difficult to separate the essential and fundamental features of caste from its non-essential superficial features. For easy approach to this to ascertain by asking what are the matters for which a person is liable to be excluded from caste. Mr. Bhattacharya has stated the following as causes for expulsion from caste: (1) Embracing Christianity or Islam, (2) Going to Europe or America, (3) Marrying a widow, (4) Publicly throwing the sacred thread, (5) Publicly eating beef, pork or foul, (6) Publicly eating *Kaccha* food prepared by a Mahomedan, Christian or low Caste Hindu, (7) Officiating at the house of a very low caste Shudra, (8) By a female going away from home for immoral purposes and (9) By a widow becoming pregnant. This list is not exhaustive and omits the two most important causes which entail expulsion from caste. They are (10) intermarrying outside caste, (11) Interdining with persons of another caste, (12) Change of occupation. The second defect in the statement of Mr. Bhattacharya is that it does not make any distinction between essentials and unessentials.[1] Of course when a person is expelled from his caste the penalty is uniform. His friends, relatives, and fellow men refuse to partake of his hospitality. He is not invited to entertainment in their houses. He cannot obtain brides or bridegrooms for his children. Even his married daughters cannot visit him without running the risk of being excluded from caste. His priest, his barber and washer man refuses to serve him. His fellow caste men sever their connection with him so completely that they refuse to assist him even at the funeral of a member

---

[1] The original word in the MS was 'essentials'. The editors felt it to be 'unessential 'and therefore corrected it accordingly. — Ed.

of his household. In some cases the man excluded from caste is debarred access to public temples and to the cremation or burial ground.

These reasons for expulsion from caste indirectly show the rules and regulations of the caste. But all regulations are not fundamental. There are many which are unessential. Caste can exist even without them. The essential and unessential can be distinguished by asking another question. When can a Hindu who has lost caste regain his caste? The Hindus have a system of *Prayaschitas* which are penances and which a man who has been expelled from caste must perform before he can be admitted to cast fellowship. With regard to these *Prayaschitas* or Penances certain points must be remembered. In the first place there are caste offences for which there is no *Prayaschita*. In the second place the *Prayaschitas* vary according to the offence. In some cases the *Prayaschita* involves a very small penalty. In other cases the penalty involved is a very severe one.

The existing of a *Prayaschita* and its absence have a significance which must be clearly understood. The absence of *Prayaschita* does not mean that any one may commit the offence with impunity. On the contrary it means that the offence is of an immeasurable magnitude and the offender once expelled is beyond reclamation. There is no re-entry for him in the caste from which he is expelled. The existence of a *Prayaschita* means that the offence is compoundable. The offender can take the prescribed *Prayaschita* and obtain admission in the caste from which he is expelled.

There are two offences for which there is no penance. These are (1) change from Hindu Religion to another religion, (2) Marriage with a person of another caste or another religion. It is obvious if a man loses caste for these offences he loses it permanently.

Of the other offences the *Prayaschitas* prescribed are of the severest kind are two: (1) Interdining with a person of another caste or a non-Hindu and (2) Taking to occupations which is not the occupation of the caste. In the case of the other offences the penalty is a light one almost nominal.

The surest clue to find out what the fundamental rules of caste are and what caste consists in is furnished by the rules regarding *Prayaschitas.* Those for the infringement of which there is no *Prayaschita* constitute the very soul of caste and those for the infringement of which the *Prayaschita* is of the severest kind make up the body of caste. It may therefore be said without any hesitation that there are four fundamental rules of caste. A caste may be defined as a social group having (a) belief in Hindu Religion and bound by certain regulations as to, (b) marriage, (c) food and (d) occupation. To this one more characteristic may be added namely a social group having a common name by which it is recognised.[2]

Understanding Caste

To this subject, I suggest the readers to study in detail 'Castes in India- Their Mechanism, Genesis and Development', a paper read by Dr.Ambedkar on 9th May 1916 before the Anthropology Seminar of Dr.Goldenweizer during his stay at the Columbia University for the Doctoral studies. This classic will throw the much-needed understanding about caste.

Class-Caste System

The Caste system is a system which is infested with the spirit of isolation and in fact it makes isolation of one Caste from another a matter of virtue. There is isolation in the Class system but it does not make isolation a virtue nor does it prohibit social intercourse. The Class system it is true produces groups. But they are not akin to Caste groups. The groups in the Class System are only non-social while the Castes in the

---

[2]BAWS, Vol. 5 p.156

Caste system are in their mutual relations definitely and positively anti-social.[3]

... class and caste, so to say, are next door neighbours, and it is only a span that separates the two. *A Caste is an Enclosed Class.*[4]

For a static conception of the Hindu Social Organization an idea of the caste and the caste system is enough. One need not trouble to remember more than the facts that the Hindus are divided into castes and that the castes form a system in which all hang on a thread which runs through the system in such a way that while encircling and separating one caste from another it holds them all as though as it was a string of tennis balls hanging one above the other. But this will not be enough to understand caste as a dynamic phenomenon. To follow the workings of caste in action it is necessary to note one other feature of caste besides the caste system, namely class-caste system.

The relationship between the ideas of caste and class has been a matter of lively controversy. Some say that caste is analogous to class. Others hold that the idea of caste is analogous to class and that there is no difference between the two. Others hold that the idea of caste is fundamentally opposed to that of class. This is an aspect of the subject of caste about which more will be said hereafter. For the present it is necessary to emphasis one feature of the caste system which has not been referred to hereinbefore. It is this. Although caste is different from and opposed to the notion of class yet the caste-system as distinguished from caste recognises a class system which is somewhat different from the graded status referred to above. Just as the Hindus are divided into so many castes, castes are divided into different classes of castes. The Hindu is caste conscious. He is also class conscious. Whether he is caste conscious or class conscious depends upon the caste with which he comes in conflict. If the caste with which he comes in conflict is a caste within the

---

3BAWS, Vol. 9 p.423
4BAWS, Vol.1 p.15

class to which he belongs he is caste conscious. If the caste is outside the class to which he belongs he is class conscious. Any one who needs any evidence on this point may study the Non-Brahmin Movement in the Madras and Bombay Presidency. Such a study will leave no doubt that to a Hindu caste periphery is as real as class periphery and caste consciousness is as real as class consciousness.

Caste, it is said, is an evolution of the Varna System. I will show later on that this is nonsense. Caste is a perversion of Varna, at any rate it is an evolution in the opposite direction. *But while Caste has completely perverted the Varna System it has borrowed the class system from the Varna System.* Indeed the Class-Caste System follows closely the class cleavages of the Varna System.

Looking at the caste system from this point of view one comes across several lines of class cleavage which run through this pyramid of castes dividing the pyramid into blocks of castes. The first line of cleavage follows the line of division noticeable in the ancient Chaturvarna system. The old system of Chaturvarna made a distinction between the first three Varnas, the Brahmins, Kshatriyas, Vaishyas, and the fourth Varna namely the Shudras. The three former were classes as the Regenerate classes. The Shudra was held as the unregenerate class. This distinction was based upon the fact that the former were entitled to wear the sacred thread and study the Vedas. The Shudra was entitled to neither and that is why he was regarded as the unregenerate class. This line of cleavage is still in existence and forms the basis of the present day class division separating the castes which have grown out of the vast class of Shudras from those which have grown out of the three classes of Brahmins, the Kshatriyas and Vaishyas. This line of class cleavage is the one which is expressed by the terms High Castes and Low Castes and which are short forms for High Class Castes and Low Class Castes.

Next after this line of cleavage there runs through the pyramid a second line of class cleavage. It runs just below the Low Class Castes. It sets above all the castes born out of the four Varnas i.e. The High Castes

6

as well as the Low Castes above the remaining Castes, which I will merely describe as the 'rest'. This line of class cleavage is again a real one and follows the well defined distinction which was a fundamental principle of the Chaturvarna System. The Chaturvarna System as is pointed out made a distinction between the four Varnas putting the three Varnas above the fourth. But it also made an equally clear distinction between those within the Chaturvarna and those outside the Chaturvarna. It had a terminology to express this distinction. Those within the Chaturvarna high or low, Brahmins or Shudras were called *Savarna* i.e. those with the stamp of the Varna. That outside the Chaturvarna were called Avarna i.e. those without the stamp of Varna. All the Castes, which have evolved out of the four Varnas, are called Savarna Hindus—which is rendered in English by the term Caste Hindus. The ' rest ' are the *Avarnas* who in present parlance spoken of by Europeans as Non-Caste Hindus i.e. those who are outside the 4 original castes or Varnas.

Much that is written about the Caste System has reference mostly to the Caste-System, among the Savarna Hindus. Very little is known about the Avarna Hindus. Who are these Avarna Hindus, what is their position in Hindu Society, how are they related to the Savarna Hindus, are questions to which no attention has so far been paid. I am sure that without considering these questions no one can get a true picture of the social structure the Hindus have built. To leave out the Class cleavage between the Savarna Hindus and the Avarna Hindus is to relate Grimm's Fairy Tale which leaves out the witches, the goblins and the ogres.

The Avarna Hindus comprise three divisions (1) Primitive Castes, (2) Criminal Castes and (3) The Untouchable Castes. The total population of persons comprising these three classes is by no means small. The population of the Primitive Tribes in India according to the Census of 1931 is stated to be about 25 millions. The total population of persons listed as Criminal is somewhere about 4 1/2 millions. The total population of Untouchables in 1931 was about 50 millions. The grand total of these three comes to 79 1/2 millions.[5]

The division between classes who are within the Chaturvarna and those who are without it though real and fundamental is undoubtedly archaic in its terminology. The system of Chaturvarna is no longer operative as law. It is therefore somewhat academic to speak of classes being within Chaturvarna and without Chaturvarna. The question will be asked, what are the modern counterparts of these ancient classes? The question is perfectly legitimate especially as I have to explain how the ancient law of Manu is responsible for the present day lawlessness of the Hindus. Although I am using archaic language, two things will show that my thesis is true. The first is that the ancient social divisions of Manu are not without their counterpart in modern times. The modern counterparts of those ancient divisions are Hindus and untouchables. Those whom Manu included within the Chaturvarna correspond to the modern composite class called Hindus. Those whom Manu called Bahayas (outside the Chaturvarna) correspond to the present day untouchables of India. The dividing line between the four classes—Brahman, Kshatriya, Vaishya and Shudra—included within Chaturvarna have in modern times become some what blurred and there has been some degree of amalgamation between them. But the line which Manu drew between those within the Chaturvarna from those outside the Chaturvarna is still clear and is not allowed to be effaced or crossed. That line is the line which at present separates the Hindus from the untouchables. The first thing that is clear is that the ancient divisions have descended to modern times. The only change is the change of names.

The second question is, has the law as laid down by Manu for the Bahayas any counterpart in the present day social relationship between the Hindus and the Untouchables?[6]

---

[5]BAWS, Vol. 5 p.163 or BAWS, Vol.3 p.146
[6]BAWS, Vol. 5 p.278

It may well be asked how much of this Dharma of Manu now remains? It must be admitted that as law in the sense of rules which a Court of Judicature is bound to observe in deciding disputes, the Dharma of Manu has ceased to have any operative force-except in matters such as marriage succession etc.- matters which affect only the individual. As Law governing social conduct and civic rights it is inoperative. But if it has gone out as law, it remains as custom.

Custom is no small a thing as compared to Law. It is true that law is enforced by the state through its police power; custom, unless it is valid it is not. But in practice this difference is of no consequence. Custom is enforced by people far more effectively than law is by the state. This is because the compelling force of an organized people is far greater than the compelling force of the state.

Not only has there been no detriment to its enforceability on account of its having ceased to be law in the technical sense but there are circumstances which are sufficient to prevent any loss of efficacy to this Dharma of Manu.[7]

Caste is Endogamy

... This critical evaluation of the various characteristics of Caste leave no doubt that prohibition, or rather the absence of intermarriage—endogamy, to be concise—is the only one that can be called the essence of Caste when rightly understood. But some may deny this on abstract anthropological grounds, for there exist endogamous groups without giving rise to the problem of Caste. In a general way this may be true, as endogamous societies, culturally different, making their abode in localities more or less removed, and having little to do with each other are a physical reality. The Negroes and the Whites and the various tribal groups that go by name of American Indians in the United States may be cited as

---

[7]BAWS, Vol. 5 p.283

more or less appropriate illustrations in support of this view. But we must not confuse matters, for in India the situation is different. As pointed out before, the peoples of India form a homogeneous whole. The various races of India occupying definite territories have more or less fused into one another and do possess cultural unity, which is the only criterion of a homogeneous population. Given this homogeneity as a basis, Caste becomes a problem altogether new in character and wholly absent in the situation constituted by the mere propinquity of endogamous social or tribal groups. Caste in India means an artificial chopping off of the population into fixed and definite units, each one prevented from fusing into another through the custom of endogamy. Thus the conclusion is inevitable that *Endogamy is the only characteristic that is peculiar to caste,* and if we succeed in showing how endogamy is maintained, we shall practically have proved the genesis and also the mechanism of Caste.[8]

Origin of Caste

The question of origin is always an annoying question and in the study of Caste it is sadly neglected; some have connived at it, while others have dodged it. Some are puzzled as to whether there could be such a thing as the origin of caste and suggest that " if we cannot control our fondness for the word 'origin', we should better use the plural form, viz. 'origins of caste' ". As for myself I do not feel puzzled by the Origin of Caste in India for, as I have established before, endogamy is the only characteristic of Caste and when I say *Origin of Caste* I mean *The Origin of the Mechanism for Endogamy.*[9]

---

[8]BAWS, Vol. 1 p.8
[9]BAWS, Vol. 1 p.14

Understanding Untouchability

Psychologically, caste and untouchability are one integral system based on one and the same principle. If the caste Hindus observe untouchability it is because they believe in caste.

Looked at from this point of view, the idea of hoping to remove untouchability without destroying the caste system is an utter futility. The underlying idea that caste and untouchability are two different things is founded on a fallacy. The two are one and are inseparable. Untouchability is only an extension of the caste system. There can be no severance between the two. The two stand together and will fall together.

There is another reason why untouchability cannot disappear by a stratagem, legal or rational. As has already been pointed out, the Hindu social order is based on the principle of graded inequality. It may not be an exaggeration to say that not many people understand the significance of this principle. The social system based on inequality stands on a different footing from a social system based on graded inequality. The former is a weak system which is not capable of self-preservation. The latter on the other hand, is capable of self-preservation. In a social system based on inequality, the low orders can combine to overthrow the system. None of them have any interest to preserve it. In a social system based on graded inequality the possibility of a general common attack by the aggrieved parties is non-existent. In a system of graded inequality, the aggrieved parties are not on a common level. This can happen only when they are only high and low. In the system of graded inequality there are the highest (the Brahmins). Below the highest are the higher (the Kshatriyas). Below the higher are those who are high (Vaishya). Below the high are the low (Shudra) and below the low are those who are lower (Untouchables). All have a grievance against the highest and would like to bring about their down fall. But they will not combine. The higher is anxious to get rid of the highest but does not wish to combine with the high, the low and the lower lest they should reach his level and be his equal. The high wants to over-throw the higher who is above him but does not want to join hands with the low and the lower, lest they should rise to his status and become equal to him in rank. The low is anxious to pull down the highest, the higher and the high but he would not make a common cause with the lower for fear of the lower gaining a higher status and becoming his equal. In the system of graded inequality there is no such class as completely unprivileged class except the one which is at the base of the social pyramid. The privileges of the rest are graded. Even the low is a privileged class as compared with the lower. Each class being privileged, every class is interested in maintaining the social system.

Untouchability may be a misfortune to the Untouchables. But there is no doubt that it is a good fortune to the Hindus. It gives them a class which they can look down upon. The Hindus do not want a system in which nobody will be anybody. They also do not want a system in which everybody may be somebody. They want a system in which they will be some bodies and others will be nobodies. The Untouchables are nobodies. This makes the Hindus some bodies. The system of untouchability sustains the natural pride of the Hindus and make them feel as well as look big. This is an additional reason why the Hindus are not likely to give up untouchability particularly those large majority who are small men.

Untouchability will vanish only when the whole of the Hindu Social Order, particularly the caste system will be dissolved. Is this possible? Every institution is sustained by some sort of a sanction. There are three kinds of sanction, which supply life force to an institution. They are legal, social and religious. The vitality of the institution depends upon the nature of the sanction. What is the nature of the sanction behind the caste system? Unfortunately, the sanction behind the caste system is the religious sanction, for, the caste as a new form of the Varna system derives its sanction from the Vedas which form the sacred book of the Hindu religion and which are infallible. I say unfortunately because anything which has a religious sanction becomes by virtue of it sacred and eternal.

To the Hindu, caste is sacred and caste is eternal. If caste cannot vanish what hope is there for untouchability to disappear?[10]

The 3 Principles of Hindu Social Order

If the Hindu social order is not based on equality and fraternity, what are the principles on which it is based? There is only one answer to this question. Though few will be able to realize what they are, there is no doubt as to their nature and effect on Hindu society. The Hindu social order is reared on three principles. Among these the first and foremost is the principle of graded inequality.

That the principle of graded inequality is a fundamental principle is beyond controversy. The four classes are not on horizontal plane, different but equal. They are on vertical plane. Not only different but unequal in status, one standing above the other. In the scheme of Manu, the Brahmin is placed at the first in rank. Below him is the Kshatriya. Below the Kshatriya is the Vaishya. Below Vaishya is the Shudra and below Shudra is the Ati-shudra or the Untouchable. This order of precedence among the classes is not merely conventional. It is spiritual, moral and legal. There is no sphere of life which is not regulated by this principle of graded inequality.

One can substantiate this by numerous illustrations from the Manu Smriti. I will take four illustrations to prove the point. They will be the law of slavery, law of marriage, law of punishment and law of Samskaras and law of Sanyas.[11]

---

[10]BAWS, Vol. 5 p.101

[11]BAWS, Vol. 3 p.106

The second principle on which the Hindu social order is founded is that of fixity of occupations for each class and continuance thereof by heredity.[12]

... The principle does not stop with fixity of occupation. It grades the several occupations in terms of respectability.[13]

The third principle on which the Hindu social order is founded is the fixation of people within their respective classes. There is nothing strange or peculiar in the fact that the Hindu social order recognizes classes. There are classes everywhere and no society is without them. Families, cliques, clubs, political parties, nay communities, gangs engaged in criminal conspiracies, business corporations which prey upon the public are to be found in all societies in all parts of the world. Even a free social order will not be able to get rid of the classes. What a free social order aims to do is to prevent isolation and exclusiveness being regarded by the classes as an ideal to be followed. For so long as the classes do not practise isolation and exclusiveness they are only non-social in their relations towards one another. Isolation and exclusiveness make them anti-social and inimical towards one another. Isolation makes for rigidity of class consciousness, for institutionalizing social life and for the dominance of selfish ideals within the classes. Isolation makes life static, continues the separation into a privileged and underprivileged, masters and servants.

Not so much the existence of classes as the spirit of isolation and exclusiveness which is inimical with a free social order. What a free social order endeavours to do is to maintain all channels of social endosmosis. This is possible only when the classes are free to share in an extensive number of common interests, undertakings and expenses, have a large number of values in common, when there is a free play back and forth, when they have an equable opportunity to receive and to take from others. Such social contacts must and does dissolve custom, makes for an alert

---

[12]BAWS, Vol. 3 p.111
[13]BAWS, Vol. 3 p.113

and expanding mental life and not only occasion but demand reconstruction of mental attitudes. What is striking about the Hindu social order is its ban on free inter-change and inter-course between different classes of Hindu society. There is a bar against inter-dining and inter-marriage. But Manu goes to the length of interdicting ordinary social intercourse.[14]

... The Hindu social order is opposed to fraternity. It does not admit the principle of equality. Far from recognising equality it makes inequality its official doctrine. What about liberty? So far as choice of occupation goes, there is none. Everyone has his occupation determined for him. Only thing left to do is to carry it on. As to freedom of speech it exists. But it exists only for those who are in favour of the social order.[15]

What about liberty of action? In the sense of effective choice, there is no room for it in the Hindu social order. The Hindu social order leaves no choice to the individual. It fixes his occupation. It fixes his status. All that remains for the individual to do is to conform himself to these regulations.

The same must be said with regard to political liberty. The Hindu social order does not recognise the necessity of a representative government composed of the representatives chosen by the people. Representative Government rests on the belief that people must be governed by law and law can be made only by the representative of the people. The Hindu social order recognises the first part of this thesis which says that people must be governed by law. But it denies the second part of the thesis which says that law can be made only by the representatives chosen by the people. The tenets of the Hindu social order is that the law by which people are to be governed is already made and is to be found in the Vedas. Nobody has a right to add to and subtract from it. That being so, a representative assembly of the people is unnecessary.

---

[14]BAWS, Vol. 3 p.113

[15]BAWS, Vol. 3 p.114

Political liberty which is liberty to frame laws and to make and unmake Government is futility for which there is no place in the Hindu social order.

To sum up, the Hindu social order is an order based on classes and not on individual. It is an order in which classes are graded one above the other. It is an order in which the status and functions of the classes are determined and fixed. The Hindu social order is a rigid order. No matter what changes take place in the relative position of an individual his social status as a member of the class he is born in relation to another person belonging to another class shall in no way be affected. The first shall never become the last. The last shall never become the first.[16]

Unexplored Arena: Anuloma and Pratiloma Marriages

A society is not to be condemned as body because there are groups in it. It is to be condemned if the groups are isolated, each leading an exclusive life of its own. Because it is this isolation which produces the anti-social spirit which makes co-operative effort so impossible of achievement.

This isolation among the classes is the work of Brahmanism. The principal steps taken by it was to abrogate the system of intermarriage and interdining that was prevalent among the four Varnas in olden times. This has already been discussed in an earlier section of this chapter. There is however one part of the story that remains to be told. I have said the Varna system had nothing to do with marriage. That males and females belonging to the different Varnas could marry and did marry. Law did not come in the way of inter-varna marriage. Social morality was not opposed to such marriages. Savarna marriage was neither required by law nor demanded by Society. All marriages between different Varnas—irrespective of the question whether the bride was of a higher Varna than the bride-

---

[16]BAWS, Vol. 3 p.115

groom or whether the bride-groom was of the higher Varna and the bride of the lower Varna—were valid. Indeed as Prof. Kane says the distinction between Anuloma and Pratiloma marriage was quite unknown and even the terms Anuloma and Pratiloma were not in existence. They are the creation of Brahmanism. Brahmanism put a stop to Pratiloma marriages i.e. marriages between women of a higher Varna and men of lower Varna. That was a step in the direction of closing the connection between the Varnas and creating in them an exclusive and anti-social spirit regarding one another. But while the inter-connecting gate of the Pratiloma marriage was closed the inter-connecting gate of Anuloma marriage had remained open. That was not closed. As pointed out in the section on graded inequality Anuloma marriage i.e. marriage between a male of the higher Varna and the female of the lower Varna was allowed by Brahmanism to continue. The gate of Anuloma marriage was not very respectable and was a one way gate only, still it was an interconnecting gate by which it was possible to prevent a complete isolation of the Varnas. But even here Brahmanism played what cannot but be called a dirty trick. To show how dirty the trick was it is necessary first to state the rules which prevailed for determining the status of the child. Under the rule existing from very ancient times the status of the child was determined by the Varna of the father. The Varna of the mother was quite unimportant. The following illustrations will place the point beyond doubt:

Father's name	Varna of father	Mother's name	Varna of mother	Child's name	Varna of child
1 Shantanu	Kshatriya	Ganga	Shudra (Anamik)	Bhishma	Kshatriya
2 Shantanu	Kshatriya	Matsyagandha	Shudra (Fisher)	Vichitra Virya	Kshatriya
3 Parashar	Brahmin	Matsyagandha	Shudra (Fisher)	Krishna-Dwaipayana	Brahmin
4 Vishvamitra	Kshatriya	Menaka	(Apsara)	Shakuntala	Kshatriya
5 Yayati	Kshatriya	Devayani	Brahmin	Yadu	Kshatriya
6 Yayati	Kshatriya	Sharmishta	Asuri (Non aryan)	Druhya	Kshatriya
7 Jaratkaru	Brahmin	Jaratkari	Nag (Non aryan)	Asita	Brahmin

The rule was known as the rule of Pitra Savarnya. It would be interesting to consider the effect of this rule of Pitra Savarnya on the Anuloma and Pratiloma systems of marriage.

The effect on Pratiloma marriage would be that the children, of mothers of the higher Varnas would be dragged down to the level of the lower Varnas represented by their fathers. Its effect on Anuloma marriage would be just the contrary. The children of mothers of the lower Varnas would be raised up and absorbed in the higher Varnas of their fathers.

Manu stopped Pratiloma marriages and thereby prevented the higher from being dragged to the status of the lower. However regrettable, not much damage was done by it so long as the Anuloma marriage and the rule of Pitra Savarnya continued in operation. The two together formed a very useful system. The Anuloma marriage maintained the interconnection and the Pitra Savarnya rule made the higher classes quite composite in their make up. For they could not but help to be drawn from mothers of different Varnas. Brahmanism did not want to keep this gate of intercommunication between the Varnas open. It was bent on closing it. But it did it in a manner which is disreputable. The straight and honourable way was to stop Anuloma marriage. But Brahmanism did not do that. It allowed the system of Anuloma marriage to continue. What it did was to alter the rule of determining the status of the child. It replaced the rule of Pitra Savarnya by the rule of Matra Savarnya by which the status of the child came to be determined by the status of the mother. By this change marriage ceased to be that means of intersocial communication which it principally is. It relieved men of the higher Varna from the responsibility to their children simply because they were born of a mother of lower Varna. It made Anuloma marriage mere matter of sex, a humiliation and insult to the lower Varnas and a privilege to the higher classes to lawfully commit prostitution with women of the lower classes. And from a larger social point of view it brought the complete isolation among the Varnas which has been the bane of Hindu Society.[17]

---

[17]BAWS, Vol. 3 p.306

Inter-caste Marriages: Tendency towards Anuloma i.e Hypergamy

Each caste is engaged in nothing but establishing for itself a status superior to that of another caste. This is best illustrated by rules of hypercommensality and rules of hypergamy.

> ... Speaking of hypergamy, Mr. Blunt[18] says:—
> "The custom of hypergamy introduces an important modification into the marriage laws of many castes. Where it prevails, the exogamous groups are classified according to their social position; and whilst a group of highest rank will take brides from it, it will not give brides to a group of lower rank. The law is found most highly developed amongst Rajputs but it is observed by many other castes..... Indeed amongst all Hindus there is probably a tendancy towards hypergamy."

What is it that has behind these rules regarding hyper-commensality and hypergamy? Nothing else but the spirit of high and low. All castes are infested with that spirit and there is no caste which is free from it.[19]

---

[18]'The Caste System of Northern India' pp.89–90

[19]BAWS, Vol. 3 p.105

CHAPTER 2

DEPRESSED CLASSES: THE TRUE UNMARRIAGEABLES WITHIN THE HINDU SOCIAL ORDER

I. Unseeables, Unapproachables, Untouchables, and Unmarriageables.

II. The Social transition of Untouchables and Unmarriageables– How they differ?

III. Ascending scale of reverence and Descending scale of contempt.

IV. Inter-caste Marriages- the contradiction within.

V. Inter-caste Marriages- a relaxed Descending scale of contempt.

VI. Descending scale of contempt- elastic at the start and rigid when descends.

VII. Depressed Classes: Unmarriageables in the truest sense.

VIII. The Social transition- yet to begin.

IX. Parents- the real kingpins.

I
Unseeables, Unapproachables, Untouchables, and Unmarriageables

When Purusha sukta mandala of Rig Veda (tenth mandala) remained the general will of the Indian society, condition of the Depressed Classes were- unseeables, unapproachables, Untouchables and Unmarriageables. As the needs and luxuries of the society increased, the compulsion to have social intercourse with the so long isolated servile classes (Depressed Classes) became imminent. Servileness was imposed upon them. Thus the unseeables became seeables. As the service rendered by the servile classes increasingly had to be done in the close vicinities of caste Hindus, the seeables also became approachables. About these two social changes- the transformation from unseeables to seeables and the transformation from unapproachables to approachables, when given a thought, it is easily evident that both the transformations were not driven by the reformative attitude or the goodwill of the caste Hindus. Nor the change was driven by the outrage of the Depressed Classes to uplift themselves. The Depressed Classes became seeables and later also as approachables simply to meet the needs of the caste Hindus. So, for centuries together, these servile classes remained as seeables, approachables, Untouchables and Unmarriageables. There was no social upliftment in their condition until the 20th century. Mind of brilliance is not required to understand this stagnancy in their social position. The reasons are very simple:

(1) With the servile class remaining as seeables, approachables, Untouchables and Unmarriageables, the caste Hindus were able to usurp and exploit their services to the fullest.

(2) With more than two and a half millenniums of continuous subjugation and the feeling of indignation completely shaved off from their traits, the servile class never revolted together to claim their dignity. Nor even were they aware of their right to claim dignity.

Some might be intrigued by the use of the terms 'unseeables' and 'unapproachables'. They might feel it as fictional. Of course, the terms appear to be so in its sense. But, to stick to the fact, it reflected the scenario of Hindu Social Order. The following extract from Dr.Ambedkar's writings tells the relevancy of these terms until a few decades before:

... Untouchables are those who cause pollution only by a physical touch. There are people who cause pollution if they come within a certain distance. They are known as unapproachable. Again there are people who are in a worse position than the unapproachables. They cause pollution if they come within sight. They are known as unseeable. It is said of the Nayadis—a people who fall into the category of the unapproachable, "that they are the lowest caste among the Hindus— the dogeaters. They are the most persistent in their clamour for charity, and will follow at a respectful distance, for miles together any person walking, driving or boating. If any thing is given to them, it must be laid down, and after the person offering it has proceeded a sufficient distance, the recipient comes timidly forward, and removes it." Of the same people Mr. Thurston says "The subject (i.e. the Nayadis) whom I examined and measured at Shoranur, though living only about three miles off had, by reason of the pollution which they traditionally carry with them to avoid walking over the long bridge which spans the river, and follow a circuitous route of many miles".

In the Tinnevalley District of the Madras Presidency, there is a class of unseeables called Purada Vannas. Of them it is said, "that they are not allowed to come out during day time because their sight is enough to cause pollution. These unfortunate people are 'compelled' to follow the nocturnal habits, leaving their dens after dark and scuttling home at the false dawn like the badger, hyaena, aordvark.[20]

Turning to the issue of the Depressed Classes remaining as Untouchables, with the crusaders of caste rising from the mid 19th century

---

[20]BAWS, Vol.5 p.139

and awakening the Depressed Classes, anti-untouchability movement gained its momentum and reached its peak in the first few decades of 20th century.   Temple entry and water fetching movements became the spearheads to abolish untouchability and to assert the minimum human rights of the Depressed Classes. Vaikom Satyagraha(1924), the case of Chawdar Tank(1927), Kala Ram Temple entry(1927) were prominent few. The Depressed Classes fought for their rights to the use of public utilities and institutions, such as schools, wells, roads, buses, trams, railways, public offices, etc. They burnt the Manu Smriti and refused to lift the dead cattles belonging to the Hindus and to skin them. Those who held the view that caste is a mere social distinction- one among them being Mr.Gandhi, were even contended that Untouchability is a sin. After independence, abolition of Untouchability has been incorporated under the fundamental rights (Article 17) into the Indian Constitution. Put into practise, though Untouchability has not ceased completely, seeing and judging the whole picture, it can be said that the Depressed Classes 'during their lifetime' are now seeables, approachables, touchables but continue to be Unmarriageables.   But a caution has to be made at this point. Like separate wells and separate tea tumblers[21], if separate graveyards for the Depressed Classes is also an extension of Untouchability being practised, then most of the Depressed Class in villages 'after their death' are buried only as Untouchables. The law which attempts to make a person touchable during her lifetime does not succeed in preventing the society turning her into an Untouchable after her death. Graveyard being separate for the Depressed Classes and the rest of the community is the condition existing in most of the Indian villages. Anyone who enters a village can recognize this very easily.

Thus the social change involving the transformation from Untouchables to touchables not been completed yet, inter-caste marriage involving the Depressed Classes is also occurring as a rarity.   Before dealing the core consideration of this chapter- whether the social

---

[21] Two tumbler system practised in the tea shops- one for the caste Hindus and another for the Untouchables.

transformation of Depressed Classes from Unmarriageables to marriageables has started or not, the need to understand the big difference between the social transformation from Untouchables to touchables and the social transformation from Unmarriageables to marriageables becomes essential.

II
The Social transition of Untouchables and Unmarriageables– How they differ?

A. The yardstick that can tell the social transition of the Depressed Classes from Untouchables to touchables are:

i) they having access to the interior of the ordinary Hindu temple;

ii) when they no longer live in the separate quarters away from the habitation of the Hindus;

iii) when they are allowed to use palanquin and to take a procession of their idols through the village instead of specific routes during festival times;

iv) when the procession carrying the idols of the caste Hindus is taken through their streets;

v) when the two tumbler system in the tea shops, one for the caste Hindus and another for the Untouchables, cease to exist;

vi) when there is no separate graveyards, one for the caste Hindus and another for the Untouchables, in each village etc;

vii) when they are no longer forced to exhibit odd gestures of deference in front of caste Hindus like taking off one's headgear, standing with bowed head, carrying footwear in the hand, not wearing clean or 'white' clothes, not riding two wheelers through the streets of upper castes and so on.

The peculiar thing in all the above cases is that the site of practise happens to be a public place.

<u>B. The yardstick that can tell the social transition of the Depressed Classes from Unmarriageables to marriageables are:</u>

> i) inter-caste marriage taking place between a bride of a Depressed Class and a bridegroom not belonging to the Depressed Class.
> ii) inter-caste marriage taking place between a bridegroom of a Depressed Class and a bride not belonging to the Depressed Class.

Considering the case A, the play of three forces is required to propel the change and to remove the stigma of Untouchability inflicted on the Depressed Classes:

> i) Notional change in the mindset of the caste Hindus to put to an end to the inhuman practice associated with Untouchability.
> ii) Authority of law in abolishing Untouchability and its coercion on the caste Hindus not to practise Untouchability.
> iii) A sense of indignation on the part of Depressed Classes to fight against Untouchability whenever and wherever if practised.

The site of practise where Untouchability happens, when studied, is predominantly public and being such, it becomes easier to evince Untouchability. So, an aggrieved individual from the Depressed Class can utilise the authority that law exerts to end the practice happening in the places connected. The chances of caste Hindus in bringing down the efficacy of law being there, still such possibility could be confronted with the mobilization of Depressed Classes to fight for their dignity and against Untouchability. Even if it becomes impossible to change the notion of caste Hindus who sanctify Untouchability with their Vedic logic, a unified Depressed Class with the law to support their cause can halt the Vedic logics to come into practise. It must be however said that such attempts by the Depressed Class while resisting the tyranny of caste Hindus though might turn out to be tiresome and time consuming, they should not lose the hope and halt their resistance.

Summing the argument, the point I intend to say is - the Depressed Class themselves have the needed means to drive the social change that will transform them from Untouchables to touchables. The law helps them to retrieve their dignity from the caste Hindus. It is absurd to expect that caste Hindus will abolish the caste based separate graveyards. Rather, the Depressed Class should strive for it. The caste Hindus can slow the pace but that has to be complemented with the disunited Depressed Class lacking self-respect.

Considering the case B, unlike the three forces that could change the social fate of the Depressed Classes in case A, there is only one force that can propel the change and remove the stigma of Unmarriageability inflicted on the Depressed Classes- the notional change in the mindset of the caste Hindus and they going for inter-caste marriage with the Depressed Classes.

The Law and Depressed Classes capable of playing a part in case A are tied together in this case. It will be absurd if the law is made to compel caste Hindus to opt for inter-caste marriages with the Depressed Classes. Law cannot enlighten the caste Hindus that caste is nothing but endogamy and advise them to go for exogamy in order to abolish caste. Also, no individual from the Depressed Class has claimed herself to be an Unseeable or an Unapproachable or an Untouchable or an Unmarriageable. Caste Hindus stigmatized them to be so. Being stigmatized as Unmarriageables, all that the Depressed Classes could do is to marry within their community. The Depressed Classes practise endogamy because the option for exogamy was not open to them. Caste Hindus practise endogamy because with their Vedic mind they do not prefer exogamy. So, unless the caste Hindus are inclined to exogamous marriages with the Depressed Classes, the social change of transforming the Depressed Classes from Unmarriageables to marriageables is not bound to happen.

To conclude, for the Depressed Classes to become touchables, the ball lies in their court too. They at least have some role to uplift themselves. But for the Depressed Classes to become marriageables, all they could do is to wait and watch as the ball lies in the court solely comprising of caste Hindus.

III
Ascending scale of reverence and Descending scale of contempt

No community other than the Depressed Classes were referred as Unseeables, Unappraochables and Untouchables. Such references were made exclusively to the Depressed Classes. Although the term Unmarriageables, while considering the pulse of the Hindu society can be applied only to the Depressed Classes, the term with a casual and careless literal interpretation might wrongly connote to include the rest of the caste communities too within its ambit. After all, from the Brahmins' perspective, the Kshatriyas, Vaishyas and Shudras are Unmarriageables. From the Kshatriyas' perspective, the Vaishyas and the Shudras are Unmarriageables. For the Vaishyas, the Shudras are unmarriagebles. Even for the Shudras who are placed at the bottom of the Varna system, the Depressed Classes are Unmarriageables. I make all these statements keeping two things in mind:

(1) Touching only the ambit of Chaturvarna- the four Varnas(castes) being Brahmins, Kshatriyas, Vaishyas, and Shudras. The innumerable sub-castes each Varna hold are not touched. Otherwise, for a member of a sub-caste, the rest not belonging to his sub-caste are all Unmarriageables. Do remember that I am considering Varna in synonymous with caste and the numerous divisions each Varna has as sub-castes.

(2) I have considered the ascending scale of reverence. Otherwise, for a Varna placed below, even the Varnas above it become Unmarriageables. To exemplify, Brahmins, Kshatriyas and Vaishyas become Unmarriageables to the fourthly placed Shudra, if the ascending order of reverence is not considered.

So before scrutinizing the question whether the social transformation of Depressed Classes from Unmarriageables to marriageables has started or not, the question that has to be answered is- Are the Depressed Classes the only Unmarriageables in the present Hindu society?

For this, understanding the two dictates of caste hierarchy becomes essential. Before going for a crystal clear study about the same, I provide the relevant extracts of Dr.Ambedkar:

... the gradation of castes in India, founded as it is in theology, forms an ascending scale of reverence and a descending scale of contempt. The effect of this gradation is to create in the minds of the lower orders a preference for the members of the higher and in the minds of the higher orders a repulsion for the members of the lower.[22]

IV
Inter-caste Marriages- the contradiction within

What sustains caste is endogamy. Caste is nothing but endogamy. Caste as a notion regulates the endogamous marriages of the Hindu society. Same caste marriage or the custom of endogamy has been passed on from generation to generation like the genes of parents get naturally transmitted into their children. But for inter-caste marriage to happen the rule that caste is endogamy has to be violated. Even after this violation, no caste group is free to have marriage alliance with any other caste group as it wishes. At this junction, another notional belief, which is the byproduct of caste itself, lays the rule for inter-caste marriages, in a similar manner caste laid its rule of endogamy. The notional rule that comes into play is the ascending scale of reverence and the descending scale of contempt in the graded caste hierarchy.

---

[22]BAWS, Vol. 17 part 3 p.28

In the graded system of caste,

(a) for the caste placed higher, the rest graded below it are Unmarriageables to it;

(b) for the caste placed at the middle, the rest placed below it are Unmarriageables to it;

(c) for those placed at the bottom, except to their own community, for the rest they remain Unmarriageables.

These tendencies of treating certain castes as Unmarriageables reflect the descending scale of contempt present in the caste hierarchy.

With endogamy (marriage within the same caste) being the norm of the Hindu society, only under the circumstantial bend, exogamous marriage (inter-caste marriage) is permitted in a caste group. Even in this case, the readiness to permit varies depending upon the position of the other caste group with whom the alliance is entertained. The consent of a caste group is tough to get if the other caste group with whom the alliance is entertained is placed at the lower position than its own in the graded hierarchy of caste. The consent of a caste group is easy to obtain if the other caste group with whom the alliance is entertained is placed at the higher position than its own in the graded hierarchy of caste. The higher the position of the other caste from itself easier is the consent to be obtained from it.

Seen from this angle,

(d) to the caste placed at the top, no caste except its own can become marriageables since it is the one at the top of the graded hierarchy;

(e) to the caste placed at the middle, if circumstances bend, those at the top are revered as marriageables. After all, it will be an alliance with the castes placed above them in the graded hierarchy of caste;

(f) to the caste placed at the bottom, if circumstances bend, those at the middle and top are readily considered as marriageables. After all, it will be an alliance with the castes placed above them in the graded hierarchy of caste.

These tendencies of accommodating certain castes as marriageables reflect the ascending scale of reverence in the caste hierarchy.

So, in the cases of (d), (e) and (f), the consent from the caste placed lower than the other involved in the alliance talk is possible. But seeing from the angle of the caste group placed higher in the same cases of (d), (e) and (f) respectively, for them the alliance being negotiated is the case of descending scale of contempt. From their perspective, it is the case of (a), (b) and (c) accordingly. For them, those who have given the consent to have marriage alliance with them are to their caste status bound to be Unmarriageables.

Now I can safely say as a statement that whenever an inter-caste marriage alliance happens, which is nothing but a marriage negotiation entertained between two caste group placed at different positions in the graded hierarchy of caste, an unavoidable contradiction arises- caste placed lower considers the higher caste as marriageable and the caste placed higher considers the lower caste as Unmarriageable. To say the same in other words, inter-caste marriage is nothing but an attempt to join two castes having confronting beliefs about the exogamy involving both- the higher caste seeing the lower caste with contempt and the lower caste seeing the higher caste with reverence. In this tangled situation, how does the law of ascending order of reverence and the law of descending order of contempt which lays the guidelines for inter-caste marriages untangles the knot? The burden to answer this crucial question falls on me, if I had to further my other arguments.

V

Inter-caste Marriages- a relaxed Descending scale of contempt

It must not be forgotten that endogamy is the norm of the Hindu society. Only under circumstantial bend, exogamy is opted.

In the matter of marriage the regulation lays down that the caste must be endogamous. There can be no intermarriage between members of different castes. This is the first and the most fundamental idea on which the whole fabric of the caste is built up.[23]

Hence, it must be remembered always that the logic of ascending scale of reverence towards higher castes and descending scale of contempt towards lower castes is subordinate and secondary only to the rule of endogamy i.e. the bondness an individual has to her own caste. This scheme of Manu is exposed by Dr.Ambedkar in 'The Hindu Social Order: Its essential principles':

Manu is of course opposed to intermarriage. His injunction is for each class to marry within his class. But he does recognise marriage outside the defined class. Here again, he is particularly careful not to allow inter-marriage to do harm to his principle of inequality among classes. Like slavery he permits inter-marriage but not in the inverse order. A Brahmin when marrying outside his class may marry any woman from any of the classes below him. A Kshatriya is free to marry a woman from the two classes next below him, namely, the Vaishya and Shudra but must not marry a woman from the Brahmin class which is above him. A Vaishya is free to marry a woman from the Shudra class which is next below him. But he cannot marry a woman from the Brahmin and the Kshatriya class which are above him.[24]

I have been mentioning the term 'circumstantial bend' often. I must connote at this stage, in what sense I am using the term. When a typical caste Hindu family is considered, under the normal circumstances, norms and traditions, the marriage affair of all its members is seen as a family affair. The liking of the parents about the girl who will become their daughter-in-law or the boy who will become their son-in-law becomes a

---

[23]BAWS, Vol.3 p.144

[24]BAWS, Vol.3 p.108

prerequisite for the marriage talks to proceed. The mutual liking between the two individuals going to be married also becomes essential but for sure it has to be complemented with the consent of both their parents. Even if the two individuals do not have an affinity towards each other with regard to their marriage, they could be persuaded, with or without difficulty, if both their parents decide to marry them. It must not be forgotten that the family being of caste Hindus, the rule of endogamy plays not just a prominent role but it is the basic rule that has to be confirmed with. Naturally, only within the closed circle of the caste, the match-making effort of the parents lies. But under the 'circumstantial bend' that I am referring, a girl and a boy, coming from different caste Hindu families, whose caste is dissimilar and unequal, decide to marry each other. So the first thing they had to do is to break the governing rule of marriage being followed in their respective families- the rule of endogamy. They had to get rid of the affinity of caste from the minds of their parents. In this regard, how far it is possible to get rid of the affinity of caste is very crucial. Because, it is only to that extent the ambit of space for the inter-caste marriages to the consented could be created. When the circumstances bend, i.e., when the children opt for exogamy, how far in the mingling of caste to occur could the parents be persuaded? To what extent would the parents allow inter-caste marriages? What are the castes to which they will nod their heads? What are the castes to which they will even bargain their child's head to be chopped off than to allow her to intermarry? To answer these questions, the law of ascending order of reverence and descending order of contempt, which dictates the marriage when a girl and a boy coerce their decision to marry each other exogamously on their parents, has to be given a serious consideration. Also, it is not hard to understand that it has to be considered only from both of their parents' perspective, as the girl and the boy already desire to have their exogamous marriage. The dissent coming from the parents, naturally it has to be explained how the law dictating inter-caste marriage derives their assent.

In the graded scale of caste hierarchy, the caste of the girl and the boy are not placed at the same level. This being so, the consent from the parents of the girl or the boy, whosoever caste is placed below the other, is easier to get and even if there arises a need to coax them such a job is not strenuous. The law of ascending scale of reverence is the rationale behind this. So half the knot being untangled easily, how the remaining knot gets removed? How the parents of the girl or the boy, whosoever caste is placed higher than the other, agree to have a marriage alliance with the caste placed below theirs, when the law of descending scale of contempt prevents them to do so? Before going into this question, let me remind you about the choice that the dissenting parents do not have. The choice to get their child married within their own caste is not with them. Though they desire an endogamous marriage for their child, the child is pressing them for her/his inter-caste marriage. So, how the parents with their caste-filled mind fulfil their child's wish? The only way out is- to relax the logic of caste existing in their minds. So, to give a statement at this juncture, an inter-caste marriage is the persuaded acceptance of a relaxed descending scale of contempt an upper caste has towards the lower caste. But how far an upper caste relaxes the contempt towards the lower caste? The answer to this question is very significant as it will answer the question of whether the social transformation of Depressed Classes from being Unmarriageables to marriageables has begun or not. For, if the relaxation goes down till the bottom of the caste order, then it is bound to make Depressed Classes as marriageables.

VI
Descending scale of contempt- elastic at the start and rigid when descends

With regard to marriage under circumstantial bend, a Brahmin parent will have her hatred for Kshatriya, Vaishya and Shudra and it manifolds in the order mentioned. In the same manner, a Kshatriya's contempt for her daughter-in-law or son-in-law will be natural if she/he is a Vaishya and it will be much more if she/he is a Shudra. A Vaishya too will exhibit her contempt if she has to get her child married to a Shudra. Though the circumstantial bend forces a Brahmin parent to relax her contempt towards the three castes below hers', her notional relaxation of contempt is not likewise with all. When persuaded, she might relax her contempt towards a Kshatriya, but it becomes very difficult for her to do the same towards a Vaishya and if the case happens to be a Shudra, it will be impossible for her not to see that person of the lastly placed caste without any contempt. The pattern in her behaviour, if needed to be theorized goes like this- the law of descending order of contempt which directs her hatred towards lower castes is quite elastic (i.e. hatred could be pacified) when she encounters the immediate caste placed below hers' but the law's rigidity (i.e. hatred becomes intense and immune to persuasion) increases further and further as she moves down the caste pyramid further and further from her own caste. Susceptibility to have marriage alliances with other castes reduces proportionately when she travels downhill away from her own caste position.

Therefore, though Vaishya has one caste below it, Kshatriya has two castes below it, Brahmin has three castes below it, none will be accepting all the castes that are under them. Each caste could be persuaded to descend for a short distance and only to that extent their descending order of contempt could be relaxed. To explain the same with Class-Caste theory which was briefed in Chapter 1, a caste Hindu Brahmin parent who is at the top in the gradation of caste system, nods for the caste that comes under the same class category of her caste and rejects to have marriage alliance with the caste that does not fall under her caste's class category. Nod is given when class similarity is felt even at the cost of caste differences. When class difference occurs, the issue of Unmarriageability arises. To still explain the same in another manner, she nods for those castes that are close to her caste status. *Status is a dual matter, a matter inter se between two persons and unless both move from their position there can be no change.*[25] *So,* how far will she move from her position? Well, it depends upon the depth of her affinity towards the caste to which she belongs. The possibilities are:

a) If she nods for a marriage alliance only with the sub-castes coming under the Brahmin caste, then, her class-caste

---

[25]BAWS, Vol. 5 p.470

consciousness is so strong and restricted as her class consciousness is in synonymous with the Brahmin caste alone.

b) If she accepts a marriage alliance only with the sub-castes coming under the Brahmin, Kshatriya or Vaishya caste but not with the Shudra caste, then, her class-caste consciousness is quite relaxed but nonetheless restricted as her class consciousness operates at the difference level of Regenerate classes (the Brahmin, the Kshatriya and the Vaishya caste) and the Unregenerate class (the Shudra caste).

c) If she accepts a marriage alliance with any caste belonging to the Chaturvarna but not with the Untouchables, then, her class-caste consciousness is very much relaxed but nonetheless restricted as her class consciousness operates at the difference level of Savarna (the Brahmin, the Kshatriya, the Vaishya and the Shudra caste) and Avarna (the Untouchables).

A significant inference to be made at this point is— when two Brahmins are considered, it should not be assumed that the class consciousness of both is inclusive of the same castes and sub-castes. From the system of caste, one might sieve only for the Regenerate class while the other might sieve by the differences of Savarna and Avarna. The pore criteria that each adopts to sieve the castes of same Class from the caste system need not be the same. It is because the definition of Class each individual holds varies and therefore the castes each individual sieve in and sieve out differs. The porousness of a caste Hindu will tend to include the castes placed far below hers' only when she relaxes her caste's Class consciousness. The more affinity if she has for her caste alone, in other words, the more prejudiced if she is towards other castes, less is the chance of she considering the castes placed below hers' to be within her caste's class. If she does not share the class consciousness with a caste then she will not be ready to have a marriage alliance with that caste, when the circumstances bend. I remind here again that in normal circumstances, a caste Hindu always prefers to have marriage alliance with an individual belonging to her sub-caste alone. In other words, she treats her sub-caste in synonymous with her class when it comes to marriage. The consideration of Class-Caste theory comes in only when circumstances bend.

In reality, it must be noted that the caste law operates at the level of sub-caste and not at the caste level. Therefore, though there are only four castes, the number of sub-castes these four incorporates sums up to more than four thousand. One must not forget that not only castes but sub-castes are also hierarchical. This being so, none of the two sub-castes are coequal. Therefore, though Vaishya has only Shudra below it and Shudra has none below it, when both are considered again with their sub-castes, it will be very much evident that the law of descending order of contempt and the Class-Caste theory has more space for themselves to play in both these castes' numerous sub-castes.

Having said about the four castes and how they allow inter-caste marriages under the circumstantial bend, it is right time to study about how far the Depressed Classes form a part in the inter-caste marriages.

VII
Depressed Classes: Unmarriageables in the truest sense

Understanding the position of the Depressed Classes in the caste system becomes a prerequisite for studying the inter-caste marriages involving the Depressed Classes:

A relationship of touchables against Untouchables may cause surprise. Such a surprise will not be altogether without reason. The touchables are not one uniform body of people. They are themselves divided into innumerable castes. Each Hindu is conscious of the caste to which he belongs. Given this heterogeneity it does seem that to include all the touchable castes into one group and put them as forming a block against the Untouchables is to create a division which can have no meaning. But although this division of touchables against Untouchables may require explanation, the division so far as modern India is concerned is real and substantial.[26]

> *... the case of the Untouchables is different. There is positive injunction against their incorporation in Hindu Society. There is no room for reform. They must remain separate and segregated without being a part of the Hindu Society. The Untouchables are not a part of the Hindu Society. And if they are a part they are a part but not of the whole. The idea showing the connection between the Hindus and the Untouchables was accurately expressed by Ainapure Shastri the leader of the orthodox Hindus at a Conference held in Bombay. He said that the Untouchables were related to the Hindus as a man is to his shoe. A man wears a shoe. In that sense it is attached to man and may be said to be a part of the man. But it is not part of the whole for two things that can be attached and detached can't be said to form parts of one whole. The analogy though is none the less accurate.*[27]

Quoting the extract in chapter 1 again,

> *The Chaturvarna System as is pointed out made a distinction between the four Varnas putting the three Varnas (the Brahmin, the Kshatriya and the Vaishya) above the fourth (the Shudra). But it also made an equally clear distinction between those within the Chaturvarna and those outside the Chaturvarna. It had a terminology to express this distinction. Those within the Chaturvarna high or low, Brahmins or Shudras were called Savarna i.e. those with the stamp of the Varna. That outside the Chaturvarna were called Avarna i.e. those without the stamp of Varna. All the Castes, which have evolved out of the four Varnas, are called Savarna Hindus—which is rendered in English by the term Caste Hindus. The 'rest' are the Avarnas who in present parlance spoken of by*

---

[26]BAWS, Vol. 5 p.192

[27]BAWS, Vol. 5 p.169

Europeans as Non-Caste Hindus i.e. those who are outside the 4 original castes or Varnas.[28]

When one understands the position of the Depressed Classes in the caste system, it becomes difficult to refute the following arguments:

All the four Varnas- the Brahmins, the Kshatriyas, the Vaishyas and the Shudras, when circumstances bend and throw the choice of exogamy before them, they rethink whether to relax or be rigid on the descending order of contempt they have on the other caste(or sub-caste) involved in the marriage negotiation. The inter-caste marriage is possible if they are convinced that the other caste(or sub-caste) is closer to their position. But when circumstances make them to encounter a marriage alliance with a Depressed Class, unanimous is all the four castes' decision in not relaxing even to the slightest the contempt they have on the Depressed Classes. The contempt, the lastly placed Shudra have on the Avarnas is the same as the contempt a Brahmin placed at the top, have on the same Avarnas. An Untouchable might be rich in both character and wealth, but since she/he is an Avarna, to the Savarnas(the four castes) she/he becomes Unmarriageable. To the Savarnas, with their senseless logic, even the worst of humankind will be marriageable if both share the same Varna but they will not hesitate to term a principled individual as Unmarriageable if she/he is an Avarna. The Depressed Classes have always been outside the purview of Caste System and the Class System it creates. This being the reality, I can safely conclude that to the four Varnas(castes and it sub-castes), higher or lower, the Depressed Classes remain as the Unmarriageables. Each Varna and its sub-castes become marriageable or Unmarriageable in relation to other varnas and their sub-castes. But this is due to the sense of reverence or contempt prevalent among them. While Depressed Classes become Unmarriageables not because of the mere contempt all the Varnas collectively have on them but specifically because of the notional defilement these Varnas have stigmatized on them.

---

[28]BAWS, Vol. 5 p.164

Hence I conclude that Savarnas become Unmarriageable at some situations because of the unavoidable inherent hierarchy in the caste system. While Avarnas become Unmarriageable because the caste system labelled them as such (Remember, Avarnas means those outside the Varna system i.e. the caste system).

Therefore, the word 'Unmarriageables' when used devoid of its careless literal interpretation and referred by its truest intent, it would denote one and only the Depressed Classes and not any other castes or their sub-castes.

VIII
The Social transition- yet to begin

With the Depressed Classes being the only Unmarriageables, the question to be considered is whether the social transformation of the Depressed Classes from Unmarriageables to marriageables has started or not? In other words, how far do the Depressed Classes form a part in the inter-caste marriages?

I bifurcate the inter-caste marriage in which either the girl or the boy belongs to the Depressed Class into the following category:

(A) Such an inter-caste marriage dissented either by the girl's or the boy's parents or both their parents but taking place in deviance to the dissented parents' wish.

(B) Such an inter-caste marriage occurring with the support and consent of the parents of the girl and the boy.

Considering the category (A), though the girl and the boy will live the same life of wife and husband that the world has seen so far, can their marriage be considered as the marriage of the usual kind happening in the

Hindu society? Can their marriage be considered as an indication sent to the Hindu society that the social transformation of the Depressed Classes from Unmarriageables to marriageables has begun? The repercussion of their marriage will provide the answer to these questions. Well, what is the repercussion then? Social excommunication of the newly married couple by the family and community of either who belongs to the upper caste is what the usual outcome of such an inter-caste marriage is. The girl if she belongs to the upper caste or the boy if he belongs to the upper caste will be losing the ties of her/his family as a consequence of the marriage tie she/he formed with the Depressed Class. Unchanging hatred from the parents for choosing the loved one of one's liking, losing the old ties for creating a new tie, casted away from one's own community for forming bonds with a suppressed community is what the consequences will be of. So what do these mean? Are the Unmarriageables becoming marriageables? Definitely not.

Instead, what the social excommunication implicates is the undying hyperbolic enthusiasm of the caste Hindus in ensuring that the stigma of Unmarriageability imposed on the Depressed Classes is retained. By socially excommunicating their own children, the caste Hindu mother and father send a strong warning to their caste community about the dire consequences that will be arising if any of their members intermarry a Depressed Class individual.

Some might start from the same argument that I am dealing right now and try to refute my statement by claiming that despite the threat to be ostracized always present, many are going for the inter-caste marriage with the Depressed Classes and therefore, hurriedly they may conclude that Depressed Classes are becoming marriageables. I do not wish to allow such shallow thinking to weaken the existing truth- Depressed Classes are still considered as Unmarriageables.

Upper castes having marriage alliances with the Depressed Classes, which is in fact a social transition within the caste determined

Hindu society, needs to be well analysed before terming the state of the Depressed Classes. Such inter-caste marriages are possible when,

(1) The General Will of the caste Hindus,
a) to consider the marriage in synonymous with their caste;
b) their concept of notional defilement in connection to the Depressed Classes; and
c) their theory of infallibility of Vedas guarding the caste system fades together.

(2) The deviant (either the girl or the boy) go against the General Will and marry the individual belonging to the Depressed Class.

Even while understanding the case (2), such deviancy, superficially, cannot be considered as an attempt to change the General Will of the Hindu society. The deviant's intent is not to change the General Will of the caste system. The deviant's intent in actuality is not to become a deviant of the Hindu society. Her deviancy is not aimed to remove the blots of the Hindu society. She became a deviant simply because the person she chose to marry happened to be an Unmarriageable. She became a deviant from the society's perspective and not from hers'. Therefore, her deviancy is not aimed to alter the General Will but to marry the person she loved. Though she married an Unmarriageable, her marriage is not going to sermonise the Hindu society that Unmarriageables are also marriageables. Though hers' is a marriage between an upper caste(herself) and an Unmarriageable, the marriage is not going to alter the practice of Unmarriageability as it is not attacking the General Will which imposes Unmarriageability on the Depressed Classes. The marriage does not cure or curse the caste system but is successful to the extent of a girl, who lacks the feeling of caste, marrying the boy whom she loved, against the wishes of her caste prejudiced parents. Inter-caste marriage mentioned in the category (A) of this section is of this kind. Such marriages do not effect a social change that removes the stigma of Unmarriageability imposed on the Depressed Classes. There is no social transition of Depressed Classes from Unmarriageables to marriageables through such inter-caste marriages based on love.

Then, what kind of marriages can bring the needed social transition for the Depressed Classes? It is the inter-caste marriage as mentioned in the category (B) which occurs with the support and consent of the parents of the girl and the boy. But this is possible only when the General Will of the caste Hindus as mentioned in the point (1) fades away. So, the ball lies in the court, solely comprising caste Hindus whose caste feelings and attachments are difficult to be weakened. Hence the marriages under category (B) would not occur often. Though this statement is a normative one, anyone who is aware of the marriages in the Hindu society will not demand an empirical evidence to prove that marriages of category (B) are few. In fact, such marriages are the rarest of rarity and even if happens is insignificant because of their stray occurrences failing to initiate and sustain a social change that could transform the Depressed Classes from Unmarriageables to marriageables.

To conclude this section, an inter-caste marriage between an upper caste and a Depressed Class should not be construed as caste consciousness disappearing from the minds of caste Hindus. Rather such marriage are the triumph of the love marriages happening between the girls and boys of the present generation who do not care about their caste background and who do not pay heed to their parents' caste mindset. Their deviancy is to get united and not to protest against caste. They may be united but at the cost of their caste driven parents socially boycotting them. Their marriage might have happened but not with the consent of their parents. Gaining the parents' acceptance and the absence of ostracism after their marriage are the two indicators of the social transition of the Depressed Classes becoming marriageables from Unmarriageables. Both being rarity, such a transition has not started yet.

IX
Parents- the real kingpins

I had indicated that an inter-caste marriage in which either the girl or the boy belongs to the Depressed Class, if occurs with the support and consent of the parents of the girl as well as the boy, then the marriage can be considered as the pathway to the Depressed Classes becoming marriageables. Is the consent from the parents alone in favour of such inter-caste marriages enough to alter the Hindu society? Analysing how the Hindu marriages are decided will provide the answer to this question. Within the Hindu society, an individual alone does not decide who should be her/his life partner. The marriage affair of the individual in fact is looked after by her/his family. Hindu marriages are family affairs. The term 'arranged marriage' indicates the pivotal role played by the family not only within the Hindu society but overall when the Indian society is considered. But who in the family plays the prominent role? This question has to be answered keeping in mind the social change that happened to the Hindu/Indian families- the transition from joint families to the nuclear families. In a joint family, apart from the parents of an individual whose marriage is being arranged, the other elders of the family also have a say in deciding the marriage alliance. In a nuclear family, the parents have a greater say. The family being patriarchal in both the cases, the male members have a stronger say. Also, whatever kind the family is, the likes of the individual to be married is duly considered. In such a setup, when an individual belonging to an upper caste likes a person who is labelled as an out-caste and she expresses her desire to marry that person, naturally, she has to face the resistance from her family. The members of the family whom she has to persuade in order to obtain the consent for her marriage are the ones who alone can spearhead the social transition of the Depressed Classes in becoming marriageables. Unfortunately, it is the notional solidarity of such members, present in every caste Hindu family, who collectively reaffirm the status of the Depressed Classes as Unmarriageables. Well, who are the kingpins that the girl has to persuade? It is the elders of the family. Not the siblings, but her father and mother. When she gets her parents convinced even her caste community doubts its prerogative of condemnation against such inter-caste marriages. The community might bark but cannot roar. Even if it barks, it can bark only like those lonely mongrels we see in the streets. No one will care for the cry it makes. For sure, the deviant girl will not care. Those kith and kin who dissent to her marriage could be pacified through her parents. The parents become effective pacifiers. In fact, they are. But in reality, when the girl fails to obtain the consent from her parents in accepting a Depressed Class individual as their son-in-law, how the situation turns? Her parents' disapproval provides the authority for her caste community to roar. It roars with the passion for its caste men, to prevent an out-caste joining with them. Even if the girl convinces some of her kith and kin, the effort is fruitless. In fact, her attempt to convince them itself becomes impossible when her parents are the dissenters. Dishonour killings are the best examples. Behind every Dishonour killing, the dissent of the parents is the impetus. What provides the authority for Khap Panchayats is the parents' disapproval in allowing their children going for inter-caste marriages.

To conclude, with regard to the inter-caste marriages, parents merely are not a part of the society. In fact, they are the greater society who can remove the stigma of Unmarriageability of the Depressed Classes. Their consent alone in favour of the inter-caste marriages will not alter the Hindu society. But it is potent enough to weaken all the caste forces that come in the way of removing the Unmarriageability of the Depressed Classes.

CHAPTER 3

THE UNMARRIAGEABLES: WHY THE NAME IS ESSENTIAL?

Bound to be Unmarriageables within the Hindu Social Organization, how are the Untouchables being referred? Not by a standard term, to say. Dr.Ambedkar himself, in the preface of his book 'What Congress and Gandhi have done to the Untouchables' has mentioned about the difficulty in resorting to a common name:

The readers will find that I have used quite promiscuously in the course of this book a variety of nomenclature such as Depressed Classes, Scheduled Castes, Harijans and Servile classes to designate the Untouchables. I am aware that this is likely to cause confusion especially for those who are not familiar with conditions in India. Nothing could have pleased me better than to have used one uniform nomenclature. The fault is not altogether mine. All these names have been used officially and unofficially at one time or other for the Untouchables. The term under the Government of India Act is 'Scheduled Castes'. But that came into use after 1935. Before that, they were called 'Harijans' by Mr Gandhi and 'Depressed Classes' by Government. In a flowing situation like that it is not possible to fix one name, which may be correct designation at one stage and incorrect at another. The reader will overcome all difficulties if he will remember that these terms are synonyms and represent the same class.[29]

In this chapter, I put forward my argument towards the need to have a common name for the Depressed Classes and how the nature of such a name should be. I start with the latter i.e. how the nature of the name referring to the downtrodden community should be, for that will eventually explain the necessity to have a common name for them.

What can a name's nature be of? In the first category, it can be simply for the purpose of denoting without signifying any meaning behind it. Like a 'tree' simply means a tree, a name need not have any special meaning behind it. In the second category, a name can reveal some details about which it refers. The different names denoting the Untouchables can be taken to illustrate this:

> Avarnas- those outside the fold of Varna System; Depressed Classes- the classes in our society that is under the depressed state; Suppressed community- the victims of suppression; Untouchables- the degraded humans whom should not be touched, and so on.

Well, why these names are in negative connotation? Like depressed, suppressed, Untouchables etc. The terms would have sounded nicer if it has been coined positive like how Mr.Gandhi referred the Depressed Classes- Harijans, Sons of God! But the names are not negative in its real sense. In fact, it is more positive than Mr.Gandhi's Harijan. Reason one, the terms express the simple truth- of their deplorable condition. Reason two, to the Depressed Classes the terms have connoted the intended meaning, later on, only to achieve the contrary. What is positive has not been positive in effect and what is negative has turned out to be positive instead. 'Harijan' pacified the Depressed Classes and had the effect of ripping off the feeling of indignation from them. Referring by

---

[29]BAWS, Vol.9 p.(vi), preface

that name acted like a candy given to a crying child just to stop her from crying. On the other hand, the name 'Untouchables' though was intended by the caste Hindus derogatorily, the term had its part in uplifting the Untouchables as touchables. The Depressed Classes indeed perceived the term in a positive manner, though not at the very beginning itself. The term 'Untouchables' only kindled the thought as to why Untouchability exists and made the way to go against it. The terms 'Depressed Classes', 'Suppressed Classes', 'Oppressed Classes' for sure made awareness among the Untouchables about their condition and created a sense of indignation. In fact, the term 'Dalit' which means 'broken men' has turned out to be the reminder of the identity of Depressed Classes, their pride and as a unifying term to exhibit their resistance against the caste system. That realization is the purpose in a name, I would say. And for a name to meet this purpose is very much a pre-requisite in the context of a social problem. For to move towards a social change, conceiving the issues to be changed in the right way is a must, which in turn depends on the connotation of social terms used.

And when it comes to caste, the name just being a descriptive one has been not enough so far. For how effective will it be in a nation that preserves the caste system like a precious and sacred heritage? For sure, the term 'Untouchables' has kindled the thought to go against Untouchability but the question is, has it kindled the people other than the Depressed Classes? For sure, the caste Hindus will not bother about the annihilation of caste. They meant the term with disparagement. Their lives thrive on the superiority that they have within the caste system. When every Indian village practise Untouchability even in its graveyards, what purpose have these terms achieved?

To handle the caste system better and deeper, the name being a descriptive one is just not enough. It should be comprehensive in bringing out the very root of caste system. It should strip the essence of caste. The term 'Dalit' is a revolting word and is aggressive by nature. But still, much more is expected from the term that antagonises the caste system. For this, the name's nature should be of its third kind- the kind that defines the very crux of what it denotes, the kind that compels the listener to conceive exactly the needed understanding of the term, deterring her from grasping its secondary details. Considering this should be the nature of a name in the context of caste, then, what are the terms that meet this criterion? Before moving to this, understanding what the caste is becomes necessary. For, without being aware of the right meaning of the caste, finding the right terms to reflect it will be an exercise of irrationality.

Though much has been said and written against caste, still the general conscience of this nation stays rotten in being favour of it. This fate could be attributed to, though only partially, to the voluminous speeches and writings made on caste without giving the foremost emphasis on what caste is. We have talked a lot about caste without bothering to realize even a bit about the cause and effect of caste.

So what is caste? Is it the dividing wall that isolates a downtrodden class from the rest? Or is it the Khap Panchayats conducted in the Indian villages? Is it the festivals of each caste group celebrated for their Kula Theivams (mythical deities of each caste)? Or is it the graveyards debarred to specific castes? Is it the pride in having a caste surname? Or is it the pride of wearing a sacred thread? What is caste? None of the above and none like the above, to say. The expressions of caste system like the above should not be confused with what defines caste. To question further will make it clear. Why is there a dividing wall? What the Khap Panchayats are for? Why is there a custom in many caste groups to celebrate festival for their Kula Theivams? All these expressions of the caste system in a way or another are intended solely to regulate the kinship within a caste. There is no priority behind these expressions as the purpose is always same and specific- to strengthen the fencing that separates one caste from another. The dividing wall isolates the Untouchables from the rest. The Khap Panchayats ensures the isolation by checking the interaction among different castes. The festivals for Kula Theivams is to reiterate the solidarity within a caste. The separate graveyards humiliate the corpses of the excluded castes. It enforces the superiority of one caste and the inferiority of another. The surname, sacred thread etc. exhibiting the caste pride assists in identifying men and women of the same caste so that they can empathize their common caste feeling together- anywhere, anytime. Thus, these expressions safeguard the system of caste. It is essential to understand here that these expressions only safeguard the system of caste and are not the causes to sustain caste. The question of what is caste and what sustains caste should not be considered as two different ones. They are one and the same. For what sustains caste explains what caste is about and of what it is made of.

Well, what sustains caste? Seeing the caste in a particular perspective will help to answer this. It is essential to understand that caste is nothing but restriction of kinship. Seen from this angle, the answer to what sustains caste is the answer to another significant question- what sustains kinship? Well, what other than marriage sustains kinship? It is the marriages that alone sustains kinship. The bloodline is nothing but the follow-up of the regulation followed in the marriages. After all whom to marry and whom not to marry decide the bloodline. It can be quoted the other way too. The bloodline decides whom to marry and whom not to marry. Either way, it is marriage that sustains kinship. And to consider specifically in the context of caste, it is the endogamous marriages.

So, if endogamy is what caste is, are the terms referring to the servile classes comprehensive enough to reflect the poignancy of caste's meaning. It should be said No. To start with, the term 'Untouchables' touches the issue of Untouchability. But it does not extend itself beyond that. It does not touch caste. Untouchability is considered as a social evil. But it does not pinpoint the evil of caste further. There are still many sociologists and academicians, who are accepted to be so, considering Untouchability and caste as separate issues. The term 'Depressed Class' describes that a class is in the state of unhappiness. While 'Suppressed community' gives a hint that a community has been kept aloof from progressing, 'Servile class' suggests a detail that there is a particular class whose only duty is to serve the remaining classes. 'Avarnas' indicates those outside the fold of Varna system. All these terms- Untouchables, Depressed Class, Suppressed community, Servile Class, Avarnas etc.

describe the state of the downtrodden community. While they describe their state they do not state the reason for it. It should be kept in mind that description is always less in effectiveness than reasoning. While the reasoning also describes, the description need not reason every time. Reasoning is very much important in the context of terms denoting the downtrodden community. For, to know why they remain downtrodden is the most essential part than getting acquainted with mere adjective descriptions about them like depressed, suppressed etc. Proper reasoning about the state of downtrodden community means providing the correct definition of the downtrodden community in relation to the system of caste. And it is not possible to derive a correct definition without touching the poignancy of caste- its endogamous prescription.

Though caste consciousness is the reason for their state, the reason that anchors them in that state is Unmarriageability. A little contemplation is enough to understand that Unmarriageability is only a synonym of endogamy. So, what makes caste poignant? It is endogamy. Endogamy makes the caste poignant. Endogamy is the venom of caste system. Endogamy makes the caste a monster hard to be tackled against. Endogamy makes the caste system impossible to be altered. Caste exists because endogamy persists. Caste is defined by endogamy. Endogamy defines caste. So dealing caste is nothing but dealing the custom of endogamy.

So what is endogamy? Marrying within one's own caste. As simple as that. But to reason the downtrodden state of the Depressed Classes, considering endogamy within the limited realm of caste is inadequate. Rather it should be studied alongside the system of caste. Of course, caste means embracing endogamy. This, otherwise, also means hindering exogamy. Endogamy should be studied alongside its contrast- the possibility of exogamy among the castes. Ascending order of reverence and descending order of contempt that dictates the exogamous marriages under circumstantial bends should be considered. How these dictates ploy in the cases of Depressed Classes must be taken into account to know where they are positioned within the caste system.

To say that Depressed Classes remain as Unmarriageables within the Hindu society stands in the line of fact. The functionality of ascending order of reverence and descending order of contempt can be considered only when the option of marriageability prevails. When the stigma of Unmarriageability exists, these two dictates becomes consequently dysfunctional. Though endogamy is the thumb rule of caste, in reality, castes do intermingle when the situation bends. But it must be noted that the Depressed Class does not form a part in this interaction. The Savarna-Avarna dichotomy explains this. Labelled as Unmarriageables, the caste system ensures that they are always kept aloof from the rest. It is this aloofness that ensures the unalterable stagnant fate of the Depressed Classes. Though caste consciousness is the reason for the pitiable state that the Depressed Classes have been subjected to, it must be understood that it is the curse of Unmarriageability that has sealed their destiny. It is this curse that has stigmatized their lives and is stigmatizing their lives. The curse of Unmarriageability has made them forever as Untouchables, servile, downtrodden, depressed, suppressed and everything that they are.

The issue of Unmarriageability is not ripe enough to be handled before weakening the prevalence of Untouchability. It is impossible to expect from a caste Hindu to accept a downtrodden as marriageable before she/he is convinced of the Untouchable as touchable. Unmarriageability would fade off only after Untouchability. But it is very much essential to mind that Untouchability became prominent only due to the belief of Unmarriageability. A stronger evil created a strong evil. Unmarriageability paved for Untouchability. A poltergeist created a goblin. To ensure that an Unmarriageable does not become marriageable, she was stigmatized to be an Untouchable. Untouchability got derived from the premise Unmarriageability. Thus, referring the Depressed Classes as 'Unmarriageables' reflect them better alongside the issue of caste than calling them as Untouchables.

'Unmarriageables' is the name belonging to third kind- the kind that defines the very crux of what it denotes, the kind that compels the listener to conceive exactly the needed understanding of the term, deterring anyone from grasping its secondary details. Caste is nothing but the issue of Unmarriageability and therefore no other term except Unmarriageables reflects the caste and also the Depressed Classes better. Dragging Unmarriageability brings forth the reason for their state straight away. It comprehensively defines them. The term contains the caste system. Unmarriageables is the term that rightly represents the Depressed Classes. It rightly exposes how the system of caste detained them.

Terms should not be mere terms with regard to caste system. Nor it should be so with regard to any social problem. They have a greater significance. They have a greater significance to reflect and impart some clarity about the issue. They should kindle thoughts about the issue. To the least, they should reveal what the issue is. With regard to caste system, Unmarriageability is the issue and unless the attention is drawn towards it, any effort to act against caste is not complete.

Dr.Ambedkar dealt the issue of name when he argued for the Depressed Classes to come out of the Hindu religion. Let me deal the same again just to deter in advance the unmindful objection that might arise in calling the Untouchables as Unmarriageables. The Doctor writes:

Will conversion raise the general social status of the Untouchables? It is difficult to see how there can be two opinions on this question. The oft-quoted answer given by Shakespeare to the question what is in a name hardly shows sufficient understanding of the problem of a name. A rose called by another name would smell as sweet would be true if names served no purpose and if people instead of depending upon names took the trouble of examining each case and formed their opinions and attitudes about it on the basis of their examination. Unfortunately, names serve a very important purpose. They play a great part in social economy. Names are symbols. Each name represents association of certain ideas and notions about a certain object. It is a label. From the label people know what it is. It saves them the trouble of examining each case individually and determine for themselves whether the ideas and notions commonly associated with the object are true. People in society have to deal with so many objects that it would be impossible for them to examine each case. They must go by the name that is why all advertisers are keen in finding a good name. If the name is not attractive the article does not go down with the people.

The name 'Untouchable' is a bad name. It repels, forbids, and stinks. The social attitude of the Hindu towards the Untouchable is determined by the very name 'Untouchable'. There is a fixed attitude towards 'Untouchables' which is determined by the stink which is imbedded in the name 'Untouchable'. People have no mind to go into the individual merits of each Untouchable no matter how meritorious he is. All Untouchables realize this. There is a general attempt to call themselves by some name other than the 'Untouchables'. The Chamars call themselves Ravidas or Jatavas. The Doms call themselves Shilpakars. The Pariahs call themselves Adi-Dravidas, the Madigas call themselves Arundhatyas, the Mahars call themselves Chokhamela or Somavamshi and the Bhangis call themselves Balmikis. All of them if away from their localities would call themselves Christians.

The Untouchables know that if they call themselves Untouchables they will at once draw the Hindu out and expose themselves to his wrath and his prejudice. That is why they give themselves other names which may be likened to the process of undergoing protective discolouration.

It is not seldom that this discolouration completely fails to serve its purpose. For to be a Hindu is for Hindus not an ultimate social category. The ultimate social category is caste, nay sub-caste if there is a sub-caste. When the Hindus meet 'May I know who are you' is a question sure to be asked. To this question 'I am a Hindu' will not be a satisfactory answer. It will certainly not be accepted as a final answer. The inquiry is bound to be further pursued. The answer 'Hindu' is bound to be followed by another; 'What caste?'. The answer to that is bound to be followed by question: "What subcaste?" It is only when the questioner reaches the ultimate social category which is either caste or sub-caste that he will stop his questionings.

The Untouchable who adopts the new name in a protective discolouration finds that the new name does not help and that in the course of relentless questionings he is, so to say, run down to earth and made to disclose that he is an Untouchable. The concealment makes him the victim of greater anger than his original voluntary disclosure would have done.

From this discussion two things are clear. One is that the low status of the Untouchables is bound upon with a stinking name. Unless the name is changed there is no possibility of a rise in their social status. The other is that a change of name within Hinduism will not do. The Hindu will not fail to penetrate through such a name and make the Untouchable and confer himself as an Untouchable. The name matters and matters a great deal. For, the name can make a revolution in the status of the Untouchables. But the name must be the name of a community outside Hinduism and beyond its power of spoilation and degradation. Such name can be the property of the Untouchable only if they undergo religious conversion. A conversion by change of name within Hinduism is a clandestine conversion which can be of no avail.[30]

So when the name 'Untouchable' repels, forbids and stinks, is not the name 'Unmarriageable' even stinkier than that? Should not be hurriedly construed so. Let me consider 'Untouchable' before perusing 'Unmarriageable'. The term 'Untouchable' indeed had its better effects. This can be realized in Doctor's writing itself. *The social attitude of the Hindus towards the Untouchables is determined by the very name 'Untouchable'. There is a fixed attitude towards 'Untouchables' which is determined by the stink which is imbedded in the name 'Untouchable'.* True it is. But on whom the name has such an effect? The caste Hindus! Can it be said a dignified name as a substitute would have a different influence on them? It cannot be said 'yes' either. Because 'Harijan' promoted by the Mahatma himself failed to do so. The name 'Untouchable' single-handedly do not drive the caste Hindus' attitude.

---

[30]BAWS, Vol.5 p.418

Their heart and mind are in concurrence in the hatred they have on the Depressed Classes. The fulcrum of hatred stems from their attitude. This is not only being complemented but also compounded by the stink in the name 'Untouchable'. But, mind it, all this happens within the sphere of caste Hindus. What the name 'Untouchable' did to the Untouchables? *There is a general attempt to call themselves by some name other than the 'Untouchables'. The Chamars call themselves Ravidas or Jatavas. The Doms call themselves Shilpakars. The Pariahs call themselves Adi-Dravidas, the Madigas call themselves Arundhatyas, the Mahars call themselves Chokhamela or Somavamshi and the Bhangis call themselves Balmikis. All of them if away from their localities would call themselves Christians.* The Untouchables resorted to this kind of protective discolouration. But why they did so? It is because of the name. The name 'Untouchable' repelled them from Hindu society. So to enjoin themselves stealthily, they had to hide their stigma of untouchability. As one's identity straight away is reflected in her name, the Untouchables dignified their names. I would say this as a reflexive thinking of mediocrity than considering it as a thoughtful realization. Because, it is only natural for the Suppressed Classes, in the initial hazy wake of their collective thinking, to try to escape from the stigmas that are imposed upon them. They just attempted to escape from being humiliated. They did not revolt against the humiliation. They tried to escape but not revolt. It happened so as their fear of standing against triumphed over the courage to reinstate their dignity. But the Depressed Class eventually realized that their escape from Untouchability is not possible unless and until the path of revolt is chosen. *The Untouchable who adopts the new name in a protective discolouration finds that the new name does not help and that in the course of relentless questionings he is, so to say, run down to earth and made to disclose that he is an Untouchable. The concealment makes him the victim of greater anger than his original voluntary disclosure would have done.* So what did the name 'Untouchables', derogatorily termed by the caste Hindus, did to the Untouchables? The name reminded their cursed state in Untouchability. Their initial effort of protective discolouration, to conceal their identity, was because of this. Though the effort went futile, the name 'Untouchable' brought eventually a worthy realisation- it made the

Untouchables conscious of being stigmatized and suppressed. I would call it as an immense realization. And immense significance it has. The struggle of Slaves against their Masters and Slavery, Serfs against their Lords and Feudalism, Blacks against the Whites and Apartheid, Proletariat against the Bourgeois and Capitalism, all were not the unavoidable events that the history of mankind had to fetch for itself as it furthered. The realization of the suppressed classes of being dehumanized by the Masters, enslaved by the Lords, discriminated by the Whites and exploited by the Bourgeois mended the history. Human mind and human history cuddle each other. The history had always been of what the mind was conscious of. The realization had always been the seed for revolts and revolutions. So, the name 'Untouchables' though embarrassed the Depressed Classes in the beginning, it did its part in awakening their minds. Anti-Untouchability movements would not have been possible without this clarity brought in the minds of Untouchables. The prime reason why these movements took off was the ever bent Untouchables learnt to stand against Untouchability. And the stinking name 'Untouchable', when every time was spelt out, after a point of time, though delayed, reasoned to them, why their knees should not be bent anymore. The name had the crucifying effect. Though in the beginning, it killed the dignity of the Depressed Classes and devalued them, it prepared them to rise for their self-esteem. 'Untouchable' backfired on the caste Hindus. They coined the name to corner the Depressed Classes forever. But the name instead united the Depressed Classes to crush the fallacious supremeness on which the caste Hindus thrived. The term 'Untouchable' pulled down the Untouchables, kindled their thoughts, moulded and raised them against Untouchability, in the course of time. Stinking though, it did not spread the odour till the end. Instead, the name kindled the urge for their equality with the rest, claimed their dignity and humanity.

But I do believe now that it is time to discard the usage of the reference 'Untouchable'. In fact, long before it should have been made defunct. The name has become a hurdle now. Decades before, the issue of Unmarriageability should have been the main concern of the Depressed Classes. But, here they are, shouting rhetorics still against Untouchability.

The symptoms need to be tackled. But should not diagnosing the disease and finding the cure for it be the main concern? The system of caste exposes itself in vibrant modes. One such is via Untouchability. Unfortunately, the Depressed Classes remain succumbed to the peripheries of the caste system. The menace of Untouchability never favoured them to surpass it and see through the issue of Unmarriageability. The very breath of caste system remains undisturbed- unspoken, untouched, yet to be tackled. It is in this illiterate scenario, the name 'Unmarriageables' acquires its urgency to be familiarized. The Untouchables need to reckon, first and foremost, that they are the Unmarriageables of the Hindu Social Organization. And nothing can remind much better and more often about Unmarriageability than the name 'Unmarriageables'. It enlightens them that they are a separate element and does not form a part of Hindu social life. By reminding them that exogamy can never become the norm of the Hindu religion, the name guides them to embrace Buddhism. As said by the Doctor, *names serve a very important purpose. They play a great part in social economy. Names are symbols. Each name represents association of certain ideas and notions about a certain object. It is a label. From the label people know what it is.* 'Unmarriageables' symbolizes the cause through which the caste system sustains itself. The name represents the scheduled state of the Depressed Classes citing the genuine reason for it. It highlights the notional defilement imprinted on them. Being so, it becomes the precise label to catalyse them to take into their hands this very long neglected issue of Unmarriageability. And mind it, to touch and scrutinize Unmarriageability is to make a hole into the soul of the caste system itself.

To justify the reference 'Unmarriageables' for the Depressed Classes, I believe to have reasoned enough. But still, to convince the unconvinced minds, if any, I put my arguments further. Why should the Untouchables, apart from being demeaned already, demean themselves with the term 'Unmarriageables'? That should be the question, I suppose, to be raised as an immediate objection. A name sounding dignified should not be so much a priority as to the name reminding the Depressed Classes about their long lost dignity, I suggest. The concern should be more about revealing the crux of the caste system than the euphemism needed in a name. 'Unmarriageables' reasons and reflects their state. This alone is adequate to justify the name's necessity. Secondly, to say that the name carries insult is altogether a wrong understanding. How absurd will it be, if the Blacks refuse to consider themselves as Blacks and resort for another name just because the prejudiced human minds equates White as fair? The dark skin to them is as much as their flesh is to their blood. Against the prejudice and not the blackness, is what the Blacks stood. Unmarriageability is very clearly an issue of prejudice. The Hindu religion had made it inseparable from the Depressed Classes. Whether they change their name or not, whether it sounds respectful or not, the stigma of Unmarriageability prevails on them. There is no change in it. The Unmarriageables have to strive against the Unmarriageability and not against their name. The stinking custom of Unmarriageability insults them and not the name 'Unmarriageables' which in fact illuminates them about it. Being an Unmarriageable only means being a victim of Unmarriageability. It brings out the prejudice. It exposes the trick of the caste system. The name does not insult. Rather, it symbolizes the insults being met.

In the wake of annihilation of caste, the issue of Unmarriageability has not been raised so far. The Depressed Classes know that they are the Untouchables within the Hindu society and being so have inclined themselves to remove the blot. The nation has seen anti-Untouchability movements. But they have not quite realized that they too are the Unmarriageables. They have not yet realized that to fight against their Unmarriageability lies their ultimate struggle against the caste system. They are yet to get provoked for remaining as Unmarriageables. Why so is the delay? The reason begins from the references denoting them. The caste Hindus called them as Untouchables and not as Unmarriageables. There existed this term, Untouchable. And not the term Unmarriageable. There is reason for this too. Under the sway of caste system, the acceptance of caste Hindus towards physical association with the Depressed Classes itself was a mighty improbability. When the question of physical proximity with the Depressed Classes itself stood absurd, where is the chance to think of them as marriageables? When it is too much for the Hindu society to accept the Depressed Classes even as touchables where is the question of imagining them as marriageables? Marriageability was too much an issue to be touched. That is why, unlike the term 'Untouchables', no similar term existed referring to the stigma of Unmarriageability associated with the Depressed Classes. Also, the Depressed Classes themselves never went satisfactorily beyond the fight against Untouchability. To be conscious of the fact that Untouchability is just an extension of caste is very important. The existence of Untouchability simply means that the society is diagnosed with caste. Untouchability is just a symptom of caste. The Depressed Classes dealt only with the symptom and not against the disease. Caste is the disease called Unmarriageability. They never put a blow on it.

The term 'Untouchables' had a counter effect. It strived to make the Depressed Classes as touchables. It instilled among them a consciousness to fight against Untouchability. Like so, it is very essential to have the term 'Unmarriageables' for the Depressed Classes. The mere reference of the term 'Unmarriageables' will remind that Unmarriageability exists. No one is conscious of this evil which sustains caste. The term will remind the evil's existence. The term will reason out why Khap Panchayats exist and Dishonour killings happen. The term will bring to light the curse of Unmarriageability. And more importantly, the term will awaken the Depressed Classes to stand against Unmarriageability, to cut the very root of caste system.

There is a chance to nod that the call for the need for inter-caste marriages to abolish caste has dealt the issue of Unmarriageability. A wrong nod this would be if nodded. It would be a greater mistake not to brief about how the two are different. I would like to handle this beforehand. Inter-caste marriage is the binding up of two castes together by marriage alliance. It could be any two castes. Its acceptance is either due to the fading of caste consciousness or because of the ascending order of reverence a caste has for another. While the former reasoning can be called progress, later is an attempt of the caste system to safeguard itself in the next best possible manner when its prescription of endogamy gets breached. Such an acceptance, I have explained earlier, is guided by a relaxed descending order of contempt. This being the case of inter-caste marriage, the issue of Unmarriageability is altogether different. Though the cure for Unmarriageability also involves inter-caste marriages binding up the two different castes, it is not any random two castes. In its case, one caste is always from the Depressed Classes and the other coming from higher castes. The one stamped as Avarna and the other belonging to one of the four Varnas. The one who was stigmatized and the other who stigmatized. The one branded as Unmarriageables and the other being as marriageables. So this kind of marriage in which one of the castes is from Depressed Classes cannot take place unless the consciousness of caste fades away. The thrashing of Unmarriageability is, therefore, a reform for sure while the occurrence of any inter-caste marriage should not be construed so always. An inter-caste marriage that abolishes Unmarriageability creates a change against the existing. For, it converts the Unmarriageables into marriageables. But when the regular inter-caste marriages happening within the Hindu society is considered, it has to be said that the Depressed Classes usually do not form a part in it. Their inclusion in an inter-caste marriage that is devoid of social excommunication happens not that often. Even if they are involved, the new kinships that a marriage usually establishes are denied to them. They are inducted as a blemished member into the family of their spouse and are considered as a stain forever. Though the marriage happens between two individuals of two different castes, the one belonging to the Depressed Class is denied the luxury of marriage by the family of others who belongs to higher caste. Theirs is a distinguished inter-caste marriage. They are accommodated and adjusted with annoyance but not embraced and empathized. The treatment they receive as daughter-in-law or son-in-law is pseudo and not real. Do mind that it is treatment and not a bonding or kinship. They remain as individual instead of getting accepted as a member of the family. In the worst turn out, such an inter-caste marriage faces the blow of Dishonour killings.

So, it is an illiterate's approach to consider that any inter-caste marriage is a blow to the caste system. Caste system itself is a hierarchical conflict of ascending order of reverence and descending order of contempt. Being so, it is not unusual when a lower caste's reverence over a higher caste defeats the higher caste's contempt towards the lower caste eventually leading to an inter-caste marriage between the two. But what is unusual is when the castes not belonging to Depressed Classes form inter-caste marriage alliance with a caste categorized within the Depressed Classes. For, it is coming together of those who are considered as marriageables with those excluded as Unmarriageables. A forbidden marriage happens here. A deviancy occurs. The Hindu Social Order receives a bolt of disobedience. Not just a shocking bolt it is but also a reforming bolt. To the caste Hindus, who dehumanized the Depressed Classes, now to enter into marital relation with them defines what contradiction is. Unless the venom of caste oozes out from their minds completely, such an occurrence is utopian for sure. To not be the one they so far have been demands immense changeover. It demands a notional change. It demands the caste consciousness to be ripped off completely. The Dharma of Manu needs to be thrown away entirely. The effort will topple the Hindu social organization. Such is the significance of inter-caste marriages with the Depressed Classes.

So the inter-caste marriages in which only the four Varnas interact should not be put on par with the inter-caste marriages between one of the four Varnas and the Avarna i.e. the Depressed Classes. To do so is a grave misunderstanding about the caste system and inter-caste marriages. The former is just breaking up of the caste system's foremost rule i.e. endogamy while the latter is leaving out the stubbornly long-held notional defilement with regard to the Depressed Classes. While the former is just a circumstantial bend, the latter is a bend made to the caste system itself. While the former fractures the caste system, the latter annihilates it. While the former disrupts the caste system, the latter puts a death blow to it. Easier to theorise than to drive a change. So true it is in the context of caste system. Is the Hindu society receptive to the inter-caste marriages with the Depressed Classes? This pertinent question drags the Hindu psyche into consideration. No one has explained much better about it than Dr.Ambedkar. The learned Doctor writes in 'The House the Hindus have Built' as follows:

What is the relation of the Savarna Castes to the Avarna Castes? The cleavage between the Savarna Castes and the Avarna Castes is not uniform in its consequences with the result that the position created is not easy to grasp. The line of the cleavage running between the Savarna Castes and the Avarna Castes produces a relationship between the Savarna Castes and the two Avarna Castes—the Primitive and the Criminal Castes which is different from the relationship which it produces between the Savarna Castes and the last of the Avarna Castes namely the Untouchables. This line of cleavage between the Savarna Castes and the first two of the Avarna Castes is a cleavage between kindred and friends. It does not make intercourse on respectful terms between the two impossible. The cleavage between the Savarna Castes and the Untouchables is of a different kind. It is a cleavage between two non-kindred and hostile groups. There is no possibility of friendly intercourse on respectable terms.

What is the significance of this line of cleavage? On what is it based? Although the cleavage is definite the basis of it has not been defined. But it seems that the basis of cleavage is the same as that which exists between the Dwijas and the Shudras. Like the Shudras the Avarna Castes are composed of unregenerate people. They are not twice born and have no right to wear the sacred thread. This also brings out two facts which otherwise are lost sight of. The first fact is that the difference between the Shudra Castes of the Savarna division of castes and the Primitive and the Criminal Castes of the Avarna division is very thin. Both are touchable and both are unregenerate. The difference is one of cultural development. But although the cultural difference between the two sections is great—as great as there is between a highly cultured and the unmitigated barbarian—from the point of view of the orthodox Hindu, the difference between them is one of degree. It is to mark this difference in culture that the Hindus invented a new terminology which recognised two classes of Shudras, (1) Sat-Shudras and (2) Shudras. Calling the old body of Shudras as Sat Shudras or cultured Shudras and using the term Shudras to those comprising the Primitive Castes who had come within the pale of Hindu Civilisation. The new terminology did not mean any difference in the rights and duties of Shudras. The distinction pointed out those Shudras who were fit for associated life with the Dwijas and those who were less fitted for it.

What is the relation of Avarna Castes to one another? Do they exist as mere collection of castes or have they any class cleavages? They are certainly mere collection of Castes. There are certainly lines of class clevages running through this block of Avarna Castes. Whether there is a line of class clevage running between the Primitive Castes and the Criminal Castes may be a matter of some doubt. Perhaps the line is faint. But there is no doubt that there is a very definite a very broad and a very emphatic line of clevage between the Primitive Castes and the Criminal Castes and the Untouchables. The former two have a very clear notion that they are the higher classes and the Untouchables are the lower classes within this block of Avarna Castes.

The discussion carried on so far reveals three characteristic features of Hindu Social Organisation: (1) Caste, (2) A hierarchical System of Castes and (3) A Class System cutting into the Caste System. Undoubtedly the structure is a very complicated one and it is perhaps difficult for one who has not been woven into it to form a true mental picture of the same. Perhaps a diagrammatic presentation may be helpful. I give below one such representation which in my judgment is calculated to give the idea of this social structure of the Hindus.[31]

---

[31] *Part of this diagram is left blank in the MS. —Ed.*

A Caste Hindus Savarna Castes	C Caste Hindus Savarna Castes	E Non-Caste Hindus Avarna Castes	G Non-caste Hindus
Class I	Class II	Class III	Class IV
High Castes Dwijas—Castes evolved out of the three Varnas, Brahmins, Kshatriyas and Vaishyas.	Low Caste Shudras— Castes evolved out of the 4th Varna namely Shudras.	Primitive Castes Criminal Castes	Untouchables
B	D	F	H

This diagram presents a Class-Caste-System of the Hindus and is so drawn as to give a true and a complete picture of their social organisation. This diagram brings out several of its important features. It shows that there are two divisions of Hindus (1) Savarna Hindus and (II) Avarna Hindus. It shows that within the first division there are two classes of Castes (1) Dwijas and (2) Shudras and within the second division there are two Classes of castes (1) Primitive and Criminal Castes and (2) The Untouchable Castes. The next thing to note is that each caste is enclosed and separated from the rest— a fact which is not shown in the diagram— each of the four classes of Castes is grouped together and placed within a class enclosure. This enclosure segregates a class of a Caste and marks it off from another class. A class of Castes is not as organised as a Caste is. But a feeling of Class is there. The third thing to note is the nature of partitions used for the enclosures. They are of various strengths, some are permanent, some are temporary. The partition between the Dwijas Castes and the Shudras Castes is not a partition at all. It is only a curtain. It is not a partition at all. It is intended to keep them aloof. It is not intended to cut them as under. The line of cleavage between the Shudra Castes and the first two of the Avarna Castes is a regular partition. But it is both thin and small. It can be jumped over. The partition separates but does not cause severance. But the partition between these three classes and the Untouchables is a real and irremovable partition. It is a barbed wire fence and its intention is to mark a severance. To express the same thing in a different way the first three enclosures are so placed that they are one within the other. The first partition between the Dwijas and the Shudra Castes may be removed the two become the occupants of one enclosure instead of two separate enclosures. Similarly the second partition may be removed in which case the Castes which are Dwija, Shudra, Primitive and Criminal form one whole—if not a single whole—occupying one single enclosure. But the third partition can never be removed. Because all three Classes of Castes are united on one issue namely that they shall not be one[32] with the Untouchables as one united body of people. There is a bar sinister, which serves the Untouchables from the rest and compels them to be apart and outside.

The diagram shows the different Classes of Castes one above the other. This is done to mark the hierarchy, which is an important feature of the Caste System. I have described the two classes of the Savarna Castes as High Class Castes and Low Class Castes. But I have not described the other two classes of Avarna Castes as lower Class Castes and lowest Class Castes. In a sense this would have been correct. In general social esteem they are no doubt lower and lowest in status. But in another sense this would not be appropriate. The terminology of high, low, lower and lowest assumes that they are parts of one whole. But are the Avarna Castes and the Savarna Castes parts of one whole? They were not. The Primitive and the Criminal Castes were not in contemplation when the plan of the Varna System, the parent of the present caste system, was laid. Consequently nothing is said about their status and position in the rules of the Varna System. But that is not the case with the Untouchables. They were within the contemplation of the Varna System and the Rule of the Varna System with regard to the Untouchables is very clear and very definite. The rule as laid down by Manu the Hindu Law giver is that there are only four Varnas

---

[32] *This space is left blank in the typed copy of MS. The word 'one' is introduced by us.—Ed.*

and that there is not to be a fifth Varna. The reformers who are friends of Mr. Gandhi in his campaign for removal of Untouchability are endeavouring to give a new meaning to the statement of Manu. They say that Manu has been misunderstood. According to Manu there is no fifth Varna and therefore he intended to include the Untouchables into the 4th Varna namely the Shudras. But this is an obvious perversion. What Manu meant was there were originally four Varnas and four they must remain. He was not going to admit the Untouchables into the House the ancient Hindus had built by enlarging the Varna System to consist of five Varnas. That is what he meant when he said that there is not to be a fifth Varna. That he wanted the Untouchables to remain out of the Hindu social structure is clear from the name by which he describes the Untouchables. He speaks of them as Varna—Bahyas (those outside the Varna System). That is the difference between the Primitive and Criminal Castes and the Untouchables. There being no positive injunction against their admission in Hindu Society they may in course of time become members of it. At present they are linked to Hindu Society and hereafter they may become integrated into it and become part of it. But the case of the Untouchables is different. There is positive injunction against their incorporation in Hindu Society. There is no room for reform. They must remain separate and segregated without being a part of the Hindu Society.[33]

Such being the rotten psyche of the Hindus, can they be expected to intermingle with the Depressed Classes? When the Depressed Classes are considered unfit for human association, mockery it would be to expect from the caste Hindus to enter into marital relationship with them. The notion of Unmarriageability is deeply entrenched inside the minds of caste Hindus. To handle it is to handle the caste system. And to handle the caste system is to shake the foundation of Hinduism itself. Any effort against any one of the three- Unmarriageability, caste system or the Hindu religion, tampers all the three. The three stands together and if it has to fall will fall together, for each comprises only the other two. I quote a part of

---

[33]BAWS, Vol.5 p.165

the speech delivered by Dr.Ambedkar on 15th October 1956 on the occasion of mass conversion to Buddhism by him and his followers:

In this country, such situation prevails that will make us unenthusiastic for thousands of years to come. Till this situation exists, there cannot be enthusiasm for our progress. In this regard we cannot do anything by remaining in this religion. There is Chaturvarna in Manusmriti. Chaturvarna system is very harmful for the progress of mankind. It has been mentioned in the Manusmriti that Shudras should do only menial service. Why do they need education? The Brahmin should take education, Kshatriya should take up arms, Vaishya should do business and Shudra should serve. Who will unfold this system? Brahmin, Kshatriya and Vaishya have some gain, but what about Shudras? Will there be any enthusiasm in other castes except these three varnas? This Chaturvarna System is not haphazardly: this not a custom; this is the religion.

There is no equality in the Hindu religion. Once I had been to Mr. Gandhi, he said, "I believe in Chaturvarna". I said, "Mahatmas like you believe in Chaturvarna! But what is this Chaturvarna and how is this? (Dr.Ambedkar expressed this by showing his hand fingers one upon another as well as keeping palm in flat position.) This Chaturvarna is whether up or flat? From where the Chaturvarna begins and where does it end? Gandhiji did not answer this question and what answer can he give? Those who ruined us, also be perished by this religion. I do not accuse this Hindu religion unnecessarily. Nobody will prosper by the Hindu religion. That religion itself is a ruinous religion.[34]

So to raise the issue of Unmarriageability equates to getting hold of both the caste system and the Hindu religion and strangulating them to the point of their death. The stigma of Unmarriageability glaringly evinces that Hindu religion is a ruinous religion. Indeed, the stigma is a whistle-blower. Hence, it all begins with the change in reference. It will be absurd

---

[34]BAWS, Vol.17 part 3 p.539

to ask anymore what is there in a name. For, everything lies in a name. It will be a greater realization if the Depressed Classes understand that they are the Unmarriageables in this society and there lies no hope for them if they continue to remain within Hindu religion. And if this much is realized, they have the potency to drive the noblest social change- the annihilation of caste.

CHAPTER 4

UNMARRIAGEABLES AND THEIR MOVEMENTS: THE PATH MADE SO FAR

I.   Introduction.

II.   Polemics.

III.   Temple Entry Movement.

IV.   The Struggle for Civil Rights.

V.   Constitutional Rights.

I
Introduction

Until the Blacks turned deviant to slavery, the seeds of its destruction were never really sown. Whenever the mankind exploited its own kindred, the path to justice had become visible only after the knees-bent and heads-bowed suppressed classes stood up and learned to act against.

Whatever space the Unmarriageables have for themselves had so far been because of their own fight against the practices that they realized to be the reason for their servileness. The issues and strategies they chose constructed not just the social movement against casteism but also its political and religious counterparts. My purpose in this chapter would be to bring into notice to what extent the flesh of casteism had been sliced off and its skeletal framework had been exposed by these movements.

In volumes are the writings written on the movements carried on by the Unmarriageables. An unhurried reading of these would throw light on the chronology, purpose, significance, impact and about the leaders who steered these movements. And also, I am sure, it would prove another crucial proposition more strong and clear- that the Dalit literature had become more of tautologies than being a literature to tackle and threaten the caste system. The writings on caste had been full of studies of the past, forgetting its annihilation in the present. The subject of casteism though volunteered or intruded by many, with the exception of very few, the alarming rest just detailed the events. The mere description of what covered the Dalit movements, writing what had already been written, like so came umpteen unauthentic, unprogressive works. The writers on caste needlessly borrowed the psyche of the newspaper reporters, got contended in just presenting the information instead of insights. They wielded the journalese sense. Eulogies on the annihilators of caste and the concern in exposing the atrocities committed against the Unmarriageables dominated their works. No denying in the requisites of such attempts. But when the inclination to perish the system of caste subsides beneath the compromise to thrive amidst the caste system, then the worrisome widening vacuum that is let to arise at the core of annihilation of caste must be accepted too. The studies on caste can move in different directions. But never should it step off from its main task and concern towards the annihilation of caste. Placing the question of possibility aside, very few good men direct their thinking on how the caste system could be eradicated. That is my contention.

Caste has been over studied in Sociology but unfortunately, the Sociologists, failing to venture even an inch outside the academic sphere, never aligned themselves as solution seekers to the caste system (though there is no need for the sociologists to be the solution seekers during their objective studies). This 'apathy' or to term it as 'study pattern' itself has led to many misunderstandings of caste in Sociology. For, I do believe that seeking solutions with regard to the problem of caste system would improve the questioning acumen of a Sociologist. The observation made by Satish Deshpande in his book 'Understanding Indian Society' is noteworthy:

> As a matter of fact, despite all its claims to expertise on caste, Indian Sociology did not have the answers, never having shown much interest in macro analysis of caste inequality. The important point, though, is that this lack of interest was itself invisible because it was so much a part of business as usual in Indian Sociology. It took a notional crisis as big as Mandal to alert us to this blind spot, and to goad us into recognizing that despite being the academic experts on this question, what we had to say on it hardly went beyond established common sense.[35]

The issue around which a movement arises and its savagery effects are not completely unrelated to each other. They both are restricted by time and space. In fact, by the accomplishment of the previous movements, it rolls further. When Mahatma Phule provided an alternate account of the texts, myths and stories contained in popular Hinduism Dr.Ambedkar chose to reject Hinduism itself in his time. When seen in retrospective, the humble progress achieved by the initial movements should not go uncredited. The significance of the initial movements, like a catalyst though minuscule in its presence plays the much vital and needed role of triggering the chemical reaction, lies in initiating a new wave towards social progress. The movements wielded by the Unmarriageables indeed had seen the facets of polemics, struggle for

---

[35]Understanding Indian Society, Sathish Deshpande, p.224

civil rights, entering into Hindu temples, burning the Manusmriti, embracing Buddhism and more importantly the relentless endeavour to win their political rights that unfolded an engrossing fight during the Round Table Conference only to eclipse under Poona Pact.

When the movement of Unmarriageables is aimed against the caste system, naturally its purpose prevails until the annihilation of caste. The onus towards its annihilation, though does not entirely rest on the Unmarriageables, the crushing hands of caste will continue to strangle their lives till it exists. Unequipped and unprivileged within the caste system, their esteem and indignation at best could resist them to remain under its clutches. They could be vigilant in claiming their rights and ensuring their own emancipation. In fact, the Unmarriageables directed their movements more in the direction of freeing themselves from the bondage of caste than towards the breaking up of caste system. But there also lies this question of who will perform the obsequies of caste system if not by the Unmarriageables. Had the kings had led their cry against monarchy and like so the Whites had been the front-runner against apartheid, then history would have been without any cogency. The exploiters to end their hold on exploitation is an improbability and the exploited to be aware of this is a necessity.

What were the methods, fundamental issues and demands of Unmarriageables' movements and to what extent the defining traits of caste system had been exposed, criticized and damned via them needs a scrutiny and my attempt from hereafter would be towards this. For this purpose, the necessity to chronicle each protest, in my opinion, serves no use except producing useless verbiage and records. Hence the space of argument would be limited to the demands made by the Unmarriageables and to what extent it destabilized the caste system.

II

Polemics

Polemics dominated all over the Dalit literature. For if it had had been ever possible to turn all the attacking words into the sharpness of a sword, the deepest roots of Hinduism would have had been chopped off at the very first swing. Such mightiness enriches the Dalit literature. Each time in their harangue against the Hindu Social Order, when the Unmarriageables asserted themselves, the articulations of great men like Dr.Ambedkar, Jotiba Phule, and Periyar provided the ideological base. The Dalit writings, speeches and orations sustained the truthful thoughts of these men in each instance of its deliverance. The slogans celebrated their polemics and the banners centred them in bold. But to what extent the Unmarriageables have imbibed the polemics and self-consciously have shed their traits of ignorance remains a crucial question to which I would like to derive a concrete answer. Let me begin with an enlightening acme found in Dr.Ambedkar's polemics that summarized his titanic works on caste:

Caste is born in religion which has consecrated it and made it sacred so that it can be rightly and truly said that Religion is the rock on which the Hindus have built their social structure.[36]

Do the Unmarriageables affirm with the above thoughts? Their lifestyle is the glaring proof. When the Hindu priests are thronged behind for each occasion to perform the rites and rituals, when donations are garnered to glorify and rally the Hindu deities on the streets, when the devotees walk miles together to get blessed with the glimpse of the Lord and his consort, when the heads are tonsured, tongues, cheeks and backs are pierced with skewers and barbs, it would be a treachery against truth to say that the Unmarriageables do not form a part in all these acts. In fact, they constitute the bigger part. Betrayal in terms of ideology is the heaviest blow a betrayer can inflict, I believe. To deceive a leader by remaining a

---

[36]BAWS, Vol.5 p.187

hypocrite had never been exhibited so flawlessly elsewhere as to the extent of the Unmarriageables' unfaithfulness towards Dr.Ambedkar. This argument would and should attract scrutiny. I urge those who do so, to centre their thoughts on the hundreds and thousands of Unmarriageables electrifying the two days, 14th of April and 6th of December each year. Who are these men and women and how much have they internalized the polemics of Dr.Ambedkar? These are the questions that never can lead to objective answers. Agreed. Facts turning to be unanimous do not exist for such questions. But supported by societal observations, normative answers could definitely be sought. I would prefer to describe the Unmarriageables as 'broken' women and men: detached from their senses to look into the social ethics of the religion they profess and departed from their identity contented to remain as 'unwanted' Hindus ever, effortlessness to understand in whole the thoughts of Dr.Ambedkar but an undying exuberance showed in erecting his busts and statues, psychological inhibitions deeply entrenched and habituated not to question every discriminatory practice happening against them but a pseudo pride in exhibiting their Dalit consciousness and solidarity, symbolic assertion in hanging the portrait of Dr.Ambedkar in their houses and at the same time the shameless vanity of placing the Hindu gods next to him and garland them, giving a voracious talk about Dalit emancipation with sacred ash gleaming on their foreheads, are not the instances suffice to hold Unmarriageables as the 'broken' women and men? Broken they are on account of two aspects. On the first one- they stand immobile on the path to emancipation[37] shown by Dr.Ambedkar, unbending to follow his way and yet simultaneously claiming themselves to be Ambedkarites. Double standard is their vice. Secondly- broken they are, unsolicited by the ruling class, underprivileged within the Hindu Social Order, unparalleled among the unprivileged, yet remaining unclear in their thoughts, unsettled in their action, undecided on their identity, unmindful of whom should be their leader, unwise in their religion, unprepared against the caste system,

---

[37] Dr.Ambedkar considered the conversion of Untouchables to Buddhism as the path to emancipation.

unable to tackle the caste Hindus, unintelligible to come out of Hinduism and uncertain about their future.

Change of mindset is the pre-requisite for change. This applies very much to the Unmarriageables both to attain social equality and to shed their servileness. In fact, their attitudinal change should occur more around the latter. To cease being the servile class is the utmost need that in its natural course would take care of the society to move towards equality of all. But then arises the real drag as the Unmarriageables here, unfortunately, happen to be the part of the problem rather than the solution. Theirs is a paradoxical mindset. They have adorned the Dalit leaders but have not accepted the Dalit polemics. The polemics connected their servileness inseparably with Hinduism and hence to shed their servileness, it concluded to shrug off their Hindu identity. The Hindu identity cunningly deceived to be their self now has become the preventive cloak against their truer self. To be peeled off their Hindu skin, the Unmarriageables find hard to accept and undergo. A bird caged long enough, if left free, will not be eager to come out of its cage to fly into the sky. Habituated to be within its cage, it loses its self to seek freedom. Sky is its home but it prefers to be doomed. In fact doomed so much and so long that even if it is thrown into the sky, it would find its way back into the cage. Birds born in a cage think flying is an illness. The Unmarriageables share similarity with such caged birds that dooms their selves even though they can rise above the horizon. Their wings are free but not their minds. Bound within the cage of Hindu religion, living the fallacious life of Hindus, never will the Unmarriageables seek their dignity and freedom.

Theory in order to be put into practise, people should have receptive minds. Minds that not just listen but also rational enough to transform its self through dialectics. It should be receptive to good ones if proven right and should weed out the old ones if confirmed to be wrong and ill. In the case of Unmarriageables, their Hindu way of living comes in between their Dalit theory and Dalit practise. The Dalit ideals they receive is poisoned completely by their Hindu beliefs and when they intend to practise it, it turns out to be the antithesis of the ideals itself. I stress again, it is their Hindu identity that separates the Dalit polemics from the utopia it dreams to attain. Clinging themselves to the Hindu religion, they have made writings of Dr.Ambedkar to be shelved in the corners of libraries instead of etching them in their minds. The Unmarriageables unashamedly have kneeled before his writings with their pseudo-identities.

Polemics are the sacred sources of social movements and the real drones in the revolutions. They are the ideological vertebrae enabling the oppressed to stand up. But unfortunately, due to unchanging affinity towards Hinduism the Unmarriageables have reduced their polemics for phrase catching purpose instead of utilizing them towards their fate changing pursuit.

Of course, there are exceptional Ambedkarites among the Unmarriageables posing the real threat to Hindu religion. No denying in that. But are not they the exceptions in their own crowd? They are the occasional shooting stars. Pry into their lives. Their own family members do not heed to the principles they believe in. Misconstrued as stones found in the rice bags, the Unmarriageables do not realize and recognize them. Hence to pick up the good exceptions and construct a positive generalization about the Depressed Classes is not fair. The scintillating polemics found in the Dalit literature in its practise is defunct and this bitter truth has to be accepted. Though the polemics should have been the leverage of the social movement carried on by the present Unmarriageables all its revolting words are locked only in their books and not in their thoughts and actions. It is action, action alone that can speak louder than voice.

III

Temple Entry Movement

The issue of Temple entry is still relevant on account of following reasons, I believe:

1) A section of Unmarriageables can be found in many Indian villages becoming jubilant and triumphant when the temples to which they are denied entry is thrown open to them because of their agitation.

2) The underlying cause for their jubilation hints about their standing that requires an examination.

Dr.Ambedkar issued to the press a statement on Temple Entry bill on 14th, February, 1933 explaining his attitude on why he did not support to the movement for Temple Entry when asked by Mr.Gandhi. The succinct extracts are:

Do the Depressed Classes desire Temple Entry or do they not? This main question is being viewed by the Depressed Classes by two points of view. One is the materialistic point of view. Starting from it, the Depressed Classes think that the surest way for their elevation lies in higher education, higher employment and better ways of earning a living. Once they become well placed in the scale of social life, they would become respectable and once they become respectable the religious outlook of the orthodox towards them is sure to undergo change, and even if this did not happen, it can do no injury to their material interest. Proceeding on these lines the Depressed Classes say that they will not spend their resources on such an empty thing as Temple Entry. There is also another reason why they do not care to fight for it. That argument is the argument of self-respect.[38]

He (the Depressed Class man) is prepared to say to the Hindus, "to open or not to open your temples is a question for you to consider and not for me to agitate. If you think, it is bad manners not to respect the sacredness of human personality, open your temples and be a gentleman.

---

[38]BAWS, Vol.9 p.110

If you rather be a Hindu than be gentleman, then shut the doors and damn yourself for I don't care to come.[39]

The second point of view is the spiritual one. As religiously minded people, do the Depressed Classes desire temple entry or do they not? That is the question. From the spiritual point of view, they are not indifferent to temple entry as they would be, if the material point of view alone were to prevail. But their final answer must depend upon the reply which Mahatma Gandhi and the Hindus give to the question namely: What is the drive behind this offer of temple entry? Is temple entry to be the final goal of the advancement in the social status of the Depressed Classes in the Hindu fold? Or is it only the first step and if it is the first step, what is the ultimate goal? Temple Entry as a final goal, the Depressed Classes can never support. Indeed they will not only reject it, but they would then regard themselves as rejected by Hindu Society and free to find their own destiny elsewhere. On the other hand, if it is only to be a first step in the direction they may be inclined to support it.[40]

If the Hindu religion is to be a religion of social equality then an amendment of its code to provide temple-entry is not enough. What is required is to purge it of the doctrine of Chaturvarna. That is the root cause of all inequality and also the parent of the caste system and Untouchability, which are merely forms of inequality. Unless it is done not only will the Depressed Classes reject Temple Entry, they will also reject the Hindu faith. Chaturvarna and the Caste system are incompatible with the self-respect of the Depressed Classes. So long as they stand to be its cardinal doctrine the Depressed Classes must continue to be looked upon as low. The Depressed Classes can say that they are Hindus only when the theory of Chaturvarna and caste system is abandoned and expunged from the Hindu Shastras. Do the Mahatma and the Hindu reformers accept this as their goal and will they show the courage to work for it? I shall look forward to their pronouncements on this issue, before I decide upon my

---

[39]BAWS, Vol.9 p.110

[40]BAWS, Vol.9 p.110

final attitude. But whether Mahatma Gandhi and the Hindus are prepared for this or not, let it be known once for all that nothing short of this will satisfy the Depressed Classes and make them accept Temple Entry. To accept temple entry and be content with it is to temporise with evil and barter away the sacredness of human personality that dwells in them.[41]

As religious minded people, still the Unmarriageables are not indifferent to temple entry. But the regrettable situation is that they continue to be so despite been and being rejected by the Hindu society. They continue to be so despite the prevailing deep-rooted social inequality within the Hindu religion, despite the doctrine of Chaturvarna structuring the every aspect of Hindu Social life. Although like a good thing happening amidst a disaster, the accomplishments of Unmarriageables in entering the Hindu temples can be taken as their effort in breaking the Established Order, their behavioural traits, when given a complete thought, it would be a wrong idea to concur with this view too. Their stance is not coherent in all the spheres. While they are not reluctant in questioning the religious denial of temple entry, nor they are provoked instinctively when made socially disadvantaged. The Unmarriageables in each Indian village live in separate settlements, not even allowed to bury their dead kinsfolk in the graveyard used by the rest of the village men. They are, at many instances, not entitled to the most basic civil rights which any person new to this country would find hard to believe and digest. A foreigner, for sure, would grasp the satire in 'Incredible India' if she looks into the caste driven social relationship among the Hindus. The denial evolves in many forms- known, unknown, imaginable and unimaginable. In no way, I am denying the fight being shown by the Unmarriageables in claiming their rights. But my contention is that their social indignation, not in any way, outweighs their religious indignation. If their outcry to worship the Hindu deities inside the denied temples, in one way or the other, leads to agitate for their social, political and economic rights, it provides a point to tolerate their spiritual aspiration, though with much agony and helplessness. But the Unmarriageables cry out with

---

[41]BAWS, Vol.9 p.112

restriction. With regard to temple entry, they are restless for not being accepted and admitted into the temples as Hindus but nor their protest is of same vigour against the inhuman treatment that they suffer because of the stigma of Untouchability over them. Which should be the issue of their concern? To not allow the existence of caste biased graveyards or to yearn for worshipping the Hindu deities that could never improve their life and worth? I believe only the former would help the Unmarriageables to retrieve their human lives.

Temple entry movement at the time of pre-independence can be understood as the initial wake up call to the Unmarriageables for their emancipation. But the attempt to enter the Hindu temples still, I consider as a grave contradiction and fault. This act does not break the Hindu Established Order. Rather, it has only evinced that the destiny of the Unmarriageables had so far been inescapable from the hold of the Hindu Established Order. It proves the stagnancy of Unmarriageables in realising the root cause for their deplorable state. Dr.Ambedkar's lifelong assertion of Hinduism as a foul religion faces a challenge here. His exposition of the Hindu religion through his writings goes in vain here. The following perspective should not be ignored:

> In some instances, the cooperative attitudes and practices of Dalit have been interpreted to mean that the Untouchables live in consensus with the established social order. Untouchables as Weber puts it, have internalized the Hindu Order. People like him have pointed out that the absence of overt rebellion as indicative of cultural consensus.[42]

To willingly embrace the religion that subdues them and desperately expecting to escape from its clutches reflects the perplexed mentality of the Unmarriageables in finding their course of freedom. Persistent in their aspiration for temple entry, the Unmarriageables have

---

[42]Seminar on Dalit movements and violence: An Analytical-Critical Approach, 19-20, November, 2012 at Indian Social Institute, Bangalore.

undoubtedly temporised with the evil and senselessly have bartered away the sacredness of human personality that dwells in them.

IV
The Struggle for Civil Rights

Not very long ago there used to be boards in club doors and other social resorts maintained by Europeans in India, which said "Dogs and Indians not allowed". The Temples of Hindus carry similar boards today, the only difference is that the boards on the Hindu temples practically say: "All Hindus and all animals including dogs are admitted, only Untouchables not admitted.[43]

The description is ample to envisage the extent of civil rights that had been left for the Unmarriageables. They had before them the daunting struggle to evince even the injustice as injustice. In the context of Mahad Satyagraha(1927), when the court granted a temporary injunction restraining the Unmarriageables from drawing water from Chawdar tank, the stand they took is noteworthy in understanding the tough fight that was in front of them to claim even the most essential civil rights:

One of the principal reasons which led the Untouchables to follow law and suspend civil disobedience was that they wanted to have a judicial pronouncement on the issue whether the custom of untouchability can be recognised by the Court of law as valid. The rule of law is that a custom to be valid must be immemorial, must be certain and must not be opposed to morality or public policy. The Untouchables' view is that it is a custom which is opposed to morality and public policy. But it is no use unless it is declared to be so by a judicial tribunal. Such a decision declaring the invalidity of the custom of untouchability would be of great value to the Untouchables in their fight for civil rights because it would seem illegal to import untouchability in civic matters. The victory of the

---

[43]BAWS, Vol.9 p.110

Untouchables in the Chawdar tank dispute was very great. But it was disappointing in one way that the Bombay High Court did not decide the issue whether the custom of untouchability was valid or not. They decided the case against the Hindus on the ground that they failed to prove that the custom alleged by them in respect of the tank was not immemorial. They held that the custom itself was not proved. The tank became open to the Untouchables. But the Untouchables cannot be said to have gained their point. The main issue was whether the custom of untouchability was a legal custom. Unfortunately the High Court avoided to give judgement on that issue. The Untouchables had to continue their struggle.[44]

Even the half favourable verdict which they eventually got happened after their prolonged persistence and patience for over a decade from the start of Mahad satyagraha.

To this time, every Unmarriageable is denied some sort of civil rights for which the prevalence of custom over law shall be sighted as the genuine reason; *the difficulty of the Untouchable does not lie in their not having civic rights. Their difficulty lies in the conspiracy of the Hindus who threaten them with dire consequences if the Untouchables dare to exercise them.*[45] *They are punished not because they do not want to mix. They are punished because they want to.*[46]

Allow me for a short time further to share the profound observation made by Dr.Ambedkar with regard to Slavery and Untouchability:

Law and public opinion are two forces which govern the conduct of men. They act and react upon each other. At times law goes ahead of public opinion and checks it and redirects in channels which it thinks proper. At times public opinion is ahead of the law. It rectifies the rigour

---

[44]BAWS, Vol.5 p.252
[45]BAWS, Vol.9 p.253
[46]BAWS, Vol.12 p.757

of the law and moderates it. There are also cases where law and public opinion are opposed to each other and public opinion being the stronger of the two forces, disregards or sets at naught what the law prescribes. Whether through compulsion arising out of convenience of commerce and industry or out of the selfish desire to make the best and the most profitable use of the slaves or out of considerations of humanity, public opinion and law were not in accord with regard to the position of the slave either in Rome or in the United States. In both places the slave was not a legal person in the eye of the law. But in both places he remained a person in the sense of a human being in the eye of the society. To put it differently the personality which the law withheld from the slave was bestowed upon him by society. There lies a profound difference between slavery and untouchability. In the case of the Untouchable just the opposite has happened. The personality which the law bestowed upon the Untouchables is withheld by society. In the case of the slave the law by refusing to recognize him as a person could do him no harm because society recognized him more amply than it was called upon to do. In the case of the Untouchables the law by recognising him as a person failed to do him any good because Hindu society is determined to set that recognition at naught. A slave had a personality which counted notwithstanding the command of the law. An Untouchable has no personality in spite of the command of the law. This distinction is fundamental. It alone can explain the paradox— the social elevation of the slave loaded though he was with the burden of legal bondage and the social degradation of the Untouchable aided as he has been with the advantages of legal freedom.[47]

... slavery was never obligatory. But untouchability is obliged. A person is "permitted" to hold another as his slave. There is no compulsion on him if he does not want to. A Hindu on the other hand is "enjoined" to hold another as Untouchable. There is compulsion on the Hindu which he cannot escape whatever his personal wishes in the matter may be.[48]

---

[47]BAWS, Vol.12 p.753

[48]BAWS, Vol.12 p.759

The denial of personality sharpened into public opinion is the rationale that fuels the Unmarriageables and them asserting their civil rights. Though the denial of personality is the direct outcome of caste system, the Unmarriageables should be clear and cautious enough to be aware of the peripheral effect the gaining of civil rights would have towards the annihilation of caste. It must be understood that the reclamation of denied rights does not happen with the dissenters perishing. The reclamation happens overpowering the dissenters' supremacy, amidst their very presence. It happens amidst the tenacity of caste Hindus. It cannot be expected that the hard-boiled caste Hindus will seek their own redemption. At least, the civil rights struggle of the Unmarriageables should not rest on such an expectation of sophist's kind.

It must be understood that the denial of civil rights to the Unmarriageables is an expression of Untouchability which in turn is an expression of caste system itself. While Untouchability is an expression strengthening the caste system, parallelly it should be kept in mind that caste system does not sustain itself via Untouchability. There are expressions which thrive the caste system and there are expressions which thrive because of caste system. In the latter falls the practice of Untouchability and the denial of civil rights. Like the guards around the fort, they guard the caste system making it practically impregnable. They confront beforehand the emancipators of Unmarriageables before the crucial aspects of the caste system could be touched. The nucleus of caste system lies far deep beneath the issue of Untouchability and civil rights, very well concealed. This must be remembered always. The tantrums sustained by these expressions succeed in serving as the armour for the basic structure of the caste system. The delay in the shift from abolition of Untouchability to annihilation of caste can be attributed to this. The annihilators of caste are forced to be preoccupied with the atrocities that the caste system generates effortlessly before they could touch the very substance of caste. Before they attempt to deal the caste system, the menaces of caste system deal them. Unmatched they fall behind defensively to find safeguards against the caste system. Though the movements of Depressed Classes have managed adequate safeguards, positive provisions and preventive measures to deal the system of caste, it must be accepted that these arrangements is an outcome of a defensive fight. The caste system was too gigantic before the Unmarriageables. The chance of facing it offensively was not an option left open to them.

Civil rights movement is one such defensive fight shown by the Unmarriageables. Though the movement evoked utter courage from the Unmarriageables to disobey the Hindu communal majority, when considered with regard to the functionality of caste system, the struggle was an outburst against what the believers of caste system had been practising as a dogma. The Unmarriageables merely reacted against a kind of denial that the caste Hindus exhibited. For sure, I would call it as a natural response as the denial of civil rights infringes the normal course of life of anyone to whom it is denied. It is not that I intend to place less significance on the civil rights movement of the Unmarriageables, for only an idle mind would ignore the social change of walking on the streets, studying in schools, entering into temples, drawing water from the wells and so on by a class of people bearing the stamp of social lepers within the Hindu society. Rather what I want to emphasize is that the accomplishment of civil rights is only a smaller step, though a crucial one, towards annihilation of caste. With the assertion of civil rights, only the surfacing symptom of the caste system had been and is being countered. Endogamy, which is the centriole of the caste system responsible for the continuity of each caste, the division and isolation of one caste from another, remains cocooned far and deep inside the system of caste. This much, the Unmarriageables should be alarmed of.

V

Constitutional Rights

The holy 'Horcrux' of the Unmarriageables- though a fictional word it is the Constitution of India that can rightly be claimed so. If it is not for the presence of this written document, the sunken humanity would have remained ever trampled under the notional barbarity of the caste

Hindus. The Constitution being the lone protector of the Unmarriageables, their political rights were not a hassle-free accomplishment. When the Unmarriageables were at the vicinity of victory, Mr.Gandhi in his mahatmian manner, placed the question of his life between them and their granted political demands. Eventually, the Unmarriageables had to make a compromise in order to save Mr.Gandhi's life that satisfied neither them nor him.[49] The repercussion can still be seen in the Indian politics as the Unmarriageables are not able to send their true representatives to the legislature every time. To let go of the separate electorates was an irreparable sacrifice the Unmarriageables had made. Still they raise their claim for separate electorates but it happens hither and thither direly in need of synergy. Time has gone and historical situations have changed. Signs and symptoms do not exist anymore for separate electorates to become a reality. Though the causes are still present, unchanged, for its introduction, going by the present pattern of caste politics, I do not see the circumstance to turn in favour of separate electorates for the Depressed Classes, at least in the near future. The observation of Marika Vicziany stands readily acceptable:

> It is difficult to categorise the Untouchable struggle in the years after Ambedkar's victories of 1930-1 in a manner consistent with that for the earlier period. This is because Ambedkar's victories were so monumental that they have dwarfed all the later achievements. At the Round Table Conferences, and only marginally pegged back later in the Poona Pact of 1932, Ambedkar was the most prodigious political athlete. Solely by virtue of his athleticism the Untouchables vaulted to centre stage, a position that they had never occupied before and have never occupied since. In an important sense the Untouchable struggle has for all the succeeding years been trying to catch up to where Ambedkar stood at that one political moment.[50]

---

[49]Refer Round Table Conference followed by Poona pact

[50]The Untouchables, Marika Vicziany, p.80

But still, the Constitution of India can be considered as the lone rope of hope holding which the Unmarriageables can come out of the trench the Hindu society has pushed them into. Each provision it holds for the Unmarriageables had been enshrined after prolonged debates and much of the finest arguments of Dr.Ambedkar that reflected the downtrodden's yearning for justice. Heroic in words and acts- slice the history and one can find it in each and every moment when the exploited stood against the tyrant. Such reasoning, I present here, when the Unmarriageables argued for their constitutional safeguards:

... there is a community economically poor, socially degraded, educationally backward and which is exploited, oppressed and tyrannized without shame and without remorse, disowned by society, unowned by Government and which has no security for protection and no guarantee for justice, fair play and equal opportunity. Such a community is told that it can have no safeguards, not because it has no case for safeguards but only because the bully on whom the bill of rights is presented thinks that because the community is not politically organized to have sanctions behind its demand he can successfully bluff.[51]

It is impossible to believe that Hindus will ever be able to absorb the Untouchables in their society. Their Caste System and the Religion completely negative any hope being entertained in this behalf. Yet there are incorrigible optimists more among the Hindus than among the Untouchables, who believe in the possibility of the Hindus assimilating the Untouchables. Whether these incorrigible optimists are honest or dishonest in their opinion is a question which cannot be overlooked. Within what time this assimilation will take place, they are unable to define. Assuming that the optimists are honest, there can be no question that this process of assimilation is going to be a long drawn process extending over many centuries. In the meantime the Untouchables will have to live under the Social and political sway of the Hindus, and continue to suffer all the tyrannies and oppressions to which they have

---

[51]BAWS, Vol.1 p.366

been subjected in the past. *Obviously no sane man will think of leaving them to the will and the pleasure of the Hindus in the hope that some day in the unpredictable future they will be assimilated by the Hindus. Long or short, there will be a period of transition and some provision must be made against the tyranny and oppression by the Hindus. What provisions should be made in this behalf? If the question is left to the Untouchables they will ask for two provisions being made: one for Constitutional Safeguards and two for Separate Settlements.*[52]

... They (the Untouchables) say that Indian social life has to be reckoned in terms of communities. There is no escape. Communities are such hard facts of Indian social life that it would be wrong to accept that communal impulse and communal prejudice do not dominate the relations of the communities. The social psychology of the Hindu Communal Majority is dominated by the dogma which recognizes not merely inequality but graded inequality as the rule governing the inter-relationship among the various communities. This dogma of graded inequality is absolutely inimical to liberty and fraternity. It cannot be believed that this graded inequality will vanish or that the Hindus will strive to abolish it. That is impossible. This graded inequality is not accidental or incidental. It is the religion of the Hindus. It is the official doctrine of Hinduism. It is sacred and no Hindu can think of doing away with it. The Hindu Communal Majority with its religion of graded inequality is not therefore a passing phase. It is a permanent fact and a menace for ever. In making a constitution for India the existence of a standing Communal Majority cannot be ignored and the problem of devising safeguards so as to reconcile it with political democracy must be faced. That is the reasoning of the Untouchables.[53]

... the only way to ensure that a sovereign and independent India will be a different India in which there will be no servile class doing duty to the governing class, is to frame a constitution which will by proper

---

[52]BAWS, Vol.12 p.731
[53]BAWS, Vol.9 p.170

safeguards, circumscribe the power of the governing class to capture government and to put a limit upon its predatory powers. This is what the Untouchables are urging and this is what the Congress is opposing. The whole controversy between the Congress and the Untouchables centres round the question of constitutional safeguards. The issue is: Is the constitution of India to be with safeguards or without safeguards for the Scheduled Castes?[54]

... the Untouchables are not opposed to freedom from British Imperialism. But they refuse to be content with mere freedom from British Imperialism. What they insist upon is that free India is not enough. Free India should be made safe for democracy. Starting with this aim, they say that on account of the peculiar social formation in India there are minority communities pitted against a Hindu Communal Majority, that if no provisions are made in the constitution to cut the fangs of the Hindu Communal Majority, India will not be safe for democracy. The Untouchables therefore insist on devising a constitution which will take note of the special circumstances of India and contain safeguards which will prevent this Hindu Communal Majority in Indian society from getting possession of political power to suppress and oppress the Untouchables and which will directly invest the Untouchables with at least a modicum of political power to prevent their suppression and exploitation, and to enable them at least to hold their own, in their struggle for existence against the Communal Majority. In short, what the Untouchables want are safeguards in the constitution itself which will prevent the tyranny of a Hindu Communal Majority from coming into being.[55]

The demand for reservation is a demand for protection against the aggressive communalism of the governing class, which wants to dominate the servile class in all fields of life and without imposing on the governing class any such ignominious conditions as was done by the Brahmins for their own aggrandizement and for the perpetuation of their

---

[54]BAWS, Vol.9 p.232

[55]BAWS, Vol.9 p.169

own domination on the Shudra, namely, to make it a crime for the governing class to learn or to acquire property.[56]

The reservations demanded by the servile classes are really controls over the power of the governing classes...The reservations do no more than correlate the constitution to the social institutions of the country in order to prevent political power to fall into the hands of the Governing class.[57]

In India the governing classes and the servile classes are divided by a bar. In other countries there exists between them only a hyphen. The resultant difference is a very crucial one. In other countries, there is a continuous replenishment of the governing class by the incorporation of others who do not belong to it but who have reached the same elevation as the governing class. In India, the governing class is a close corporation in which nobody, not born in it, is admitted. In other countries where the governing class is not a close preserve, where there is social endosmosis between it and the rest, there is a mental assimilation and accommodation which makes the governing class less antagonistic in its composition and less antagonistic to the servile classes in its social philosophy. In other words, the governing class in countries outside India is not anti-social. It is only non-social. In India where the governing class is a close corporation, tradition, social philosophy and social outlook which are antagonistic to the servile classes remain unbroken in their depth and their tenor and the distinction between masters and slaves, between the privileged and the unprivileged continues for ever hard in substance and fast in colour. In other words the governing class in India is not merely non-social. It is positively anti-social.

As to the demand for reservations by the servile classes the reason behind it is to put a limit on the power of the governing classes to have control over the instrumentalities of government. The governing classes

---

[56]BAWS, Vol.9 p.478

[57]BAWS, Vol.9 p.234

are bent on giving the reservations a bad name in order to be able to hang those who are insisting upon them. The real fact is that the reservations are only another name for what the Americans call checks and balances which every constitution must have, if democracy is not to be overwhelmed by the enemies of democracy.[58]

Now, Article 46 of the Indian Constitution envisages the State with the following duty: "The State shall promote with special care the educational and economic interests of the weaker sections of the people, and, in particular, of the Scheduled Castes and the Scheduled Tribes, and shall protect them from all social injustice and all forms of exploitation". An Unmarriageable's life, whether it is as simple as cultivating in her fields or an eminent one of raising a question in the parliament, the elevating role being ensured by the provisions in the Constitution cannot be ignored. The constitutional safeguards pervade in their lives. Whether it is a foolproof setup or not is another question to be pondered upon but my point here is, in the supreme law book of the nation, there exists enough concern towards the disprivileged Unmarriageables. Their biggest triumph hitherto is the winning of their political rights, whose magnitude of significance, could be surpassed if at all in the future, only by the occurrence of annihilation of caste.

Having said these let me discuss about the prowess of the constitutional rights which includes political rights too towards the annihilation of caste. In what way the constitutional rights of the Unmarriageables are linked to the annihilation of caste? I would regard the constitutional rights as a 'link of assumption' towards the annihilation of caste. The argument of Dr.Ambedkar in the context of temple entry could again be quoted to explain this 'link of assumption':

... the Depressed Classes think that the surest way for their elevation lies in higher education, higher employment and better ways of earning a living. Once they become well placed in the scale of social life,

---

[58]BAWS, Vol.9 p.481

they would become respectable and once they become respectable the religious outlook of the orthodox towards them is sure to undergo change, and even if this did not happen, it can do no injury to their material interest.[59]

Two things construed from the above extract can be related to the constitutional rights too. First one, the constitutional rights are meant to no longer let the Unmarriageables to live in the den of ignorance. They are to place them well in the scale of social life- with higher education, higher employment and better ways of earning a living. They are to equip and empower themselves with the essentials for a good life to the extent of caste rules becoming defunct against them. From this aspect, the constitutional rights can rightly be said as the 'safeguards' that prevents the tyranny of Hindu Communal Majority from coming into being. The second and the crucial one is, while the constitutional rights could hinder the tyranny it is only a hope that the tyrant in the course of time would not withhold to her or his religious disposition. It is only a hope because the assumption here is that the educational and economic progress of the Unmarriageables would elevate their social standing earning respect from the orthodox caste Hindus eventually changing the religious outlook of the latter towards the Unmarriageables. Can social elevation of the Unmarriageables subdue the religious outlook the caste Hindus have? A certain answer does not lie. If can be subdued, then constitutional rights could be regarded as a tool to annihilate caste. If not, a feasible alternate way to annihilate caste needs to be devised then. However, a neutral mind would accept that the Unmarriageables' social elevation had not altered the religious conscience of the caste Hindus. A few might reject the notional defilement imprinted on the Unmarriageables but when the entire Hindu society is weighed down, it is explicitly evident that the religious conviction of the caste Hindus is a too sickened phenomenon to imbibe a fair outlook. An appropriate reference to favour my argument here is the demand being made by the Unmarriageables to extend the reservation policy in promotions in government jobs. To not venture out of the

---

[59]BAWS, Vol.9 p.110

subject being discussed, the question of "Why the Unmarriageables make such a demand?" is of more relevancy than "Is the demand justifiable or not?". So, what compelled the Unmarriageables to ask for such a safeguard? I believe, theirs is an outburst of one genuine realization- that their rise in the educational, economic and social spheres making use of the constitutional rights has not altered the prejudiced religious disposition the caste Hindus have on them. Their earned merits could not amend the Hindu Established Order. Though said in a different context, the following words still fit here:

It might have been thought that this principle of equal justice would strike a death blow to the Established Order. As a matter of fact, far from suffering any damage the Established Order has continued to operate in spite of it. It might be asked why the principle of equal justice has failed to have its effect. The answer to this is simple. To enunciate the principle of justice is one thing. To make it effective is another thing. Whether the principle of equal justice is effective or not must necessarily depend upon the nature and character of the civil services who must be left to administer the principle. If the civil service is by reason of its class bias the friend of the Established Order and the enemy of the new Order, the new Order can never come into being. That a civil service in tune with the new order was essential for the success of the new order was recognised by Karl Marx in 1871 in the formation of the Paris Commune and adopted by Lenin in the constitution of Soviet Communism. Unfortunately, the British Government never cared about the personnel of the Civil Service. Indeed it opened the gates of the administration to those classes who believed in the old Established Order of the Hindus in which the principle of equality had no place. As a result of this fact, India has been ruled by the British but administered by the Hindus. A few statistics of the composition of the Civil Service will fully demonstrate this fact.

From the capital of India down to the village the whole administration is rigged by the Hindus. The Hindus are like the omnipotent almighty pervading all over the administration in all its branches having its authority in all its nooks and corners. There is no loophole for anyone opposed to the old order to escape. No matter what the Department, whether it is Revenue, Police or Justice it is manned by the Hindu. If the Established Order has continued to exist, it is because of the unfailing support it received from the Hindu officials of the State. The Hindu officials are not merely administering the affairs on their merit. They are administering them with an eye to the parties. Their principle is not equal justice to all. Their motto is justice consistent with the Established Order. This is inevitable. For they carry over into administration the attitude towards different classes in society under the Established Order. This is well illustrated by the attitude of the State officials towards the Untouchables in the field of administration.[60]

I said that the Scheduled Castes had no fear of bad laws being made to their prejudice. What they had to fear about was bad administration. This bad administration was due to the absence of men belonging to the Scheduled Castes in the administration.

The Administration was unsympathetic to the Scheduled Castes because it was maintained wholly by Caste Hindu officers who were partial to the Caste Hindus in the villages, who exacted beggar from the Scheduled Castes, and practised upon them tyranny and oppression day in and day out. This tyranny and oppression could be averted only if more of the Scheduled Castes could find places on the civil service. This can be done better by being inside the Government rather than remaining outside.[61]

Caste prejudices pervade in all the spheres of Indian social life and the civil service is not an exception. Caste ploys plot the promotions in government jobs and the Unmarriageables are its victims. Educational excellence, proved intelligence and the professional efficiency of the Unmarriageables necessarily does not elevate them to policy-making designations. The stamp of being an Unmarriageable hinders their ascent.

---

[60]BAWS, Vol.9 p.103

[61]BAWS, Vol.17, part 3 p.392

The onus is not on me to evince this. A genuine analyst would not contest my statement. But still, the data revealing the percentage of Unmarriageables served and serving in the higher echelons of the Executive[62] and the normative opinion of the Unmarriageables and the general public suffices to confirm my point. The dissenters who argue otherwise and is of the claim that the degraded caste status of the Unmarriageables is not interfering with their merit, on them lies the ugly task of overturning truth as untruth.

The gory past and stagnant present are enough to conclude the rigidity in the attitude of the caste Hindus towards the Unmarriageables. Though it should not be denied that the Unmarriageables with their social progress aided by constitutional rights expected a positive shift to occur within the collective conscience of the Hindu society, the statement should not be extended further to mean that they were very eager and expectant towards such a change to happen. As a consequence they expected but never did they yearn for it.

It is crucial and essential to understand that the constitutional rights are only loosely connected to the annihilation of caste. While the rights bring light to the Unmarriageables, it does not remove the darkness from the Hindu society. The constitutional rights and the other safeguards for the Unmarriageables is primarily an arrangement and a necessity, abundantly justified for its presence, that paves way for them to come out of the Ghettos of caste system. Mind it- the rationale of the constitutional rights is to raise the Unmarriageable slitting through the ambience of caste. In fact, the constitutional rights try to penetrate through the caste pyramid to emancipate and protect the Unmarriageables without disturbing the very structure of caste. While the constitutional safeguards partially restore them to their human stature it does not infringe the notions held by the caste Hindus. This much should be understood clearly. Allow me to

---

[62]Policy Pariahs, https://www.governancenow.com/news/regular-story/policy-pariahs-why-there-are-so-few-scst-officers-top-echelons

summarize the enshrined provisions in the Constitution that go close to the issue of caste and the rights of Unmarriageables:

Article	Safeguards
17. Abolition of Untouchability	"Untouchability" is abolished and its practice in any form is forbidden. The enforcement of any disability arising out of "Untouchability" shall be an offence punishable in accordance with law.
15. Prohibition of discrimination on grounds of religion, race, caste, sex or place of birth	(1) The State shall not discriminate against any citizen on grounds only of religion, race, caste, sex, place of birth or any of them. (2) No citizen shall, on grounds only of religion, race, caste, sex, place of birth or any of them, be subject to any disability, liability, restriction or condition with regard to— (a) access to shops, public restaurants, hotels and places of public entertainment; or (b) the use of wells, tanks, bathing ghats, roads and places of public resort maintained wholly or partly out of State funds or dedicated to the use of the general public. (4) Nothing in this article or in clause (2) of article 29 shall prevent the State from making any special provision for the advancement of any socially and educationally backward classes of citizens or for the Scheduled Castes and the Scheduled Tribes. (5) Nothing in this article or in sub-clause (g) of clause (1) of article 19 shall prevent the State from making any special provision, by law, for the advancement of any socially and educationally backward classes of citizens or

	for the Scheduled Castes or the Scheduled Tribes in so far as such special provisions relate to their admission to educational institutions including private educational institutions, whether aided or unaided by the State, other than the minority educational institutions referred to in clause (1) of article 30.
25. Freedom of conscience and free profession, practice and propagation of religion	(2) Nothing in this article shall affect the operation of any existing law or prevent the State from making any law— (b) providing for social welfare and reform or the throwing open of Hindu religious institutions of a public character to all classes and sections of Hindus.
46. Promotion of educational and economic interests of Scheduled Castes, Scheduled Tribes and other weaker sections	The State shall promote with special care the educational and economic interests of the weaker sections of the people, and, in particular, of the Scheduled Castes and the Scheduled Tribes, and shall protect them from social injustice and all forms of exploitation.
29. Protection of interests of Minorities	(2) No citizen shall be denied admission into any educational institution maintained by the State or receiving aid out of State funds on grounds only of religion, race, caste, language or any of them.
16. Equality of opportunity in matters of	(2) No citizen shall, on grounds only of religion, race, caste, sex, descent, place of birth, residence or any of them, be ineligible for, or discriminated against in respect

public employment	of, any employment or office under the State. (4A) Nothing in this article shall prevent the State from making any provision for reservation in matters of promotion of any class or classes of posts in the services under the State in favour of Scheduled Castes and the Scheduled Tribes which, in the opinion of State are not adequately represented in the services under the State.
335. Claims of Scheduled Castes and Scheduled Tribes to services and posts	The claims of the members of the Scheduled Castes and the Scheduled Tribes shall be taken into consideration, consistently with the maintenance of efficiency of administration, in the making of appointments to services and posts in connection with the affairs of the Union or of a State: Provided that nothing in this article shall prevent in making of any provision in favour of the members of the Scheduled Castes and the Scheduled Tribes for relaxation in qualifying marks in any examination or lowering the standards of evaluation, for reservation in matters of promotion to any class or classes of services or posts in connection with the affairs of the Union or of a State.
330	Reservation of seats for Scheduled Castes and Scheduled Tribes in the House of the People.
332	Reservation of seats for Scheduled Castes and Scheduled Tribes in the Legislative Assemblies of the States.
243D	Reservation of seats (for Scheduled Castes and Scheduled Tribes in the Panchayats).

243T	Reservation of seats (for Scheduled Castes and Scheduled Tribes in the Municipalities).
338. Special Officer for Scheduled Castes and Scheduled Tribes, *etc.*	(1) There shall be a special officer for the Scheduled Castes and Scheduled Tribes to be known as the **National Commission for the Scheduled Castes and Scheduled Tribes**. (5) It shall be the duty of the Commission— (a) to investigate and monitor all matters relating to the safeguards provided for the Scheduled Castes and Scheduled Tribes under this Constitution or under any other law for the time being in force or under any order of the Government and to evaluate the working of such safeguards; (b) to inquire into specific complaints with respect to the deprivation of rights and safeguards of the Scheduled Castes and Scheduled Tribes; (c) to participate and advise on the planning process of socio-economic development of the Scheduled Castes and Scheduled Tribes and to evaluate the progress of their development under the Union and any State; (d) to present to the President, annually and at such other times as the Commission may deem fit, reports upon the working of those safeguards; (e) to make in such reports recommendations as to the measures that should be taken by the Union or any State for the effective implementation of those safeguards and other measures for the protection, welfare and socio-economic development of the Scheduled Castes and Scheduled Tribes; and

<table>
<tr><td></td><td>

(f) to discharge such other functions in relation to the protection, welfare and development and advancement of the Scheduled Castes and Scheduled Tribes as the President may, subject to the provisions of any law made by Parliament, by the rule specify.

(6) The President shall cause all such reports to be laid before each House of Parliament along with a memorandum explaining the action taken or proposed to be taken on the recommendations relating to the Union and the reasons for the non-acceptance, if any, of any of such recommendations.

(7) Where any such report, or any part thereof, relates to any matter with which any State Government is concerned, a copy of such report shall be forwarded to the Governor of the State who shall cause it to be laid before the Legislature of the State along with a memorandum explaining the action taken or proposed to be taken on the recommendations relating to the State and the reasons for the non-acceptance, if any, of any of such recommendations.

(8) The Commission shall, while investigating any matter referred to in sub-clause (a) or inquiring into any complaint referred to in sub-clause (b) of clause (5), have all the powers of a civil court trying a suit and in particular in respect of the following matters, namely:—

(a) summoning and enforcing the attendance of any person from any part of India and examining him on oath;

(b) requiring the discovery and production of any documents;

(c) receiving evidence on affidavits;

(d) requisitioning any public or copy thereof from any court or office;

(e) issuing commissions for the examination of

</td></tr>
</table>

<table>
<tr><td></td><td>witnesses and documents;
(f) any other matter which the President may by rule determine.
(9) The Union and every State Government shall consult the Commission on all major policy matters affecting Scheduled Castes and Scheduled Tribes.</td></tr>
</table>

"That the State exists is like the march of God through history". For the caste conditions existing in India, this Hegelian statement comes closer to acceptance. Dialectics would interfere with Indian Communists to deal against the caste system before they go against the State. They ignoring and bypassing the question of caste will only make communism less appealing to the Unmarriageables, since the Indian State, despite the accusations holds a setup to shield the Unmarriageables from the Hindu Communal Society. However, my concern here is not to project the State as an epitome of political development but rather to sideline its catering role and bring to the forefront its limitation. Grasp the following extract:

It may well be asked how much of this Dharma of Manu now remains? It must be admitted that as law in the sense of rules which a Court of Judicature is bound to observe in deciding disputes, the Dharma of Manu has ceased to have any operative force-except in matters such as marriage succession etc.— matters which affect only the individual. As Law governing social conduct and civic rights it is inoperative. But if it has gone out as law, it remains as custom.

Custom is no small a thing as compared to Law. It is true that law is enforced by the state through its police power; custom, unless it is valid it is not. But in practice this difference is of no consequence. Custom is enforced by people far more effectively than law is by the state. This is because the compelling force of an organized people is far greater than the compelling force of the state.

Not only has there been no detriment to its enforceability on account of its having ceased to be law in the technical sense but there are circumstances which are sufficient to prevent any loss of efficacy to this Dharma of Manu.

Of these circumstances the first is the force of custom. There exists in every social group certain (habits[63]) not only to acting, but of feeling and believing, of valuing, of approving and disapproving which embody the mental habitudes of the group. Every new comer whether he comes in the group by birth or adoption is introduced into this social medium. In every group there goes on the process of persistently forcing these mental habitudes of the group upon the attention of each new member of the group. Thereby the group carries on the socialization of the individual of the shaping of the mental and practical habits of the new comer. Being dependent upon the group he can no more repudiate the mental habitudes of the group than he can the condition and regulation of his physical environment. Indeed, so dependent the individual is on the group that he readily falls in line and allows the current ways of esteeming and behaving prevailing in the community, to become a standing habit of his own mind. This socializing process of the individual by the group has been graphically described by Grote. He says—

"This aggregate of beliefs and predispositions to believe, ethical, Religious, Aesthetical, and Social respecting what is true, or false, probable or improbable, just or unjust, holy or unholy, honourable or base, respectable or contemptible, pure or impure, beautiful or ugly, decent or indecent, obligatory to do, or obligatory to avoid, respecting the status and relations of each individual in the society, respecting even the admissible fashions of amusement and recreation—this is an established fact and condition of things, the real origin of which for the most part unknown, but which each new member of the group is born to and finds subsisting..... It becomes a part of each person's nature,

---

[63]Inserted by Ed.

a standing habit of mind, or fixed set of mental tendencies, according to which particular experience is interpreted and particular persons appreciated..... The community hate, despise or deride any individual member who proclaims his dissent from their social creed..... Their hatred manifests itself in different ways..... At the very best by exclusion from that amount of forbearance, good will and estimation without which the life of an individual becomes insupportable."

But what is it that helps to bring about this result? Grote has himself answered this question. His answer is that, this is due to—"Nomos (Law and Custom), King of all" (which Herodotus cites from Pindar) exercises plenary power, spiritual and temporal, over individual minds, moulding the emotions as well as the intellect, according to the local type.... and reigning under the appearance of habitual, self suggested tendencies.

What all this comes to is that, when in any community, the ways of acting, feeling, believing, or valuing or of approving and disapproving have become crystallised into customs and traditions, they do not need any sanction of law for their enforcement. The amplitude of plenary powers which the group can always generate by mass action is always ready to see that they are not broken.

The same thing applies to the Dharma laid down by Manu. This Dharma of Manu, by reason of the governing force which it has had for centuries, has become an integral and vital part of the customs and traditions of the Hindus. It has become ingrained and has given colour to their life blood. As law it controlled the actions of the Hindus. Though now a custom, it does not do less. It moulds the character and determines the outlook of generation after generation.

The second thing which prevents the Dharma of Manu from fading away is that the law does not prevent its propagation. This is a circumstance which does not seem to be present to the minds of many people. It is said that one of the blessings of the British Rule is that Manu Smriti has ceased to be the law of the land. That the Courts are not required to enforce the provisions contained in Manu Smriti as rules of law is undoubtedly a great blessing—which might not be sufficiently appreciated except by those who were crushed beneath the weight of this "infamous" thing. It is as great a blessing to the Untouchables as the Reformation was to the peoples of Europe. At the same time it must be remembered that the Reformation would not have been a permanent gain if it had been followed by what is called the Protestant Revolution. The essential features of the Protestant Revolution as I understand them are: (1) That the state is supreme and the Church is subordinate to the state. (2) The doctrine to be preached must be approved by the state. (3) The clergy shall be servants of the state and shall be liable to punishment not only for offences against the general law of the land but also liable for offences involving moral turpitude and for preaching doctrines not approved of by the state. I am personally a believer in the "Established Church". It is a system which gives safety and security against wrong and pernicious doctrines preached by any body and every body as doctrines of religion. I know there are people who are opposed to the system of an "Established Church". But whether the system of an "Established Church" is good or bad, the fact remains that there is no legal prohibition against the propagation of the Dharma laid down by Manu. The courts do not recognize it as law. But the law does not treat it as contrary to law. Indeed every village every day. When Pandits are preaching it to parents and parents preach it to their children, how can Manu Smriti fade away? Its lessons are reinforced every day and no body is allowed to forget that untouchability is a part of their Dharma.[64]

The Dharma of Manu had never been a mere past. It is as present as though it were enacted today. It bids fair to continue to have its sway in the future. The only question is whether its sway will be for a time or forever.[65]

---

[64]BAWS, Vol.5 p.283

[65]BAWS, Vol.5 p.286

Does the Constitution dissolve the sway of Manu's Dharma? Does it remove the defects and darkness from the Hindu society? Articles 16, 29, 46 and 335 reiterate the duty of the State concerning education and employment for the Unmarriageables respectively.

Articles 330, 332, 243D, 243T guarantees political reservation for the Unmarriageables.

Article 15 and Article 25 enforces the prohibition of discrimination on the basis of caste or religion. While these two Articles resonate against caste discrimination, Article 17 concerning Untouchability enshrines the strongest substitute for the word annihilation- 'Abolition'.

Article 338 establishing for the National Commission for the Scheduled Castes and Scheduled Tribes in a way is Unmarriageables' resort to safeguard their rights. In the manner Article 32 is called as 'remedial rights' as it provides for the enforcement of fundamental rights by the Supreme Court if one or more of the fundamental rights are violated, similarly, Article 338 can be called as the 'remedial measure' to investigate and monitor all matters relating to the safeguards provided for the Scheduled Castes and Scheduled Tribes. But its efficacy remains a question.

The Scuta of Romans and Aspides of Greeks! If the functioning purpose of constitutional safeguards is understood properly, one would readily accept that they serve more like Scuta and Aspides for the Unmarriageables than like spears and swords. The Constitution at its best penetrates into the caste system via Article 17 (Abolition of Untouchability). But Untouchability must be remembered as the mere outer skin of the caste system. Caste system cannot be rooted out simply by Untouchables becoming touchables or by throwing open the Hindu temples to them. The Mahatmas who had and have been restricting their reforms only to these issues have conjured the issue of caste to the extent of annihilation of caste becoming the synonym for abolition of

Untouchability. Articles 15 and 25 of the Constitution, in their own manner, holds the State in a close proximate to deter the prejudices of caste happening within its ambit. If the constitutional provisions capable of inflicting injuries to the caste system had to be picked up, I do not see any more Articles apart from 17th, 15th, and 25th. Only they happen to be the lonesome spears and swords that outwardly are intended to pierce the dictates of caste system. They pierce but not to the deepest. The rest of the constitutional safeguards for the Unmarriageables, I would separate them as pure defensive arrangements that shield the Unmarriageables from the dictums of caste and elevates them stronger-educationally and economically. The Constitution is predominantly like Scuta and Aspides which shields and protects the Unmarriageables from the attacks of the enemy but does not retaliate the enemy's ill acts. The Indian Constitution, I would say with conviction unshakable, is direly in need of more spears and swords to offend without a spill of kindness the upholders of the caste system. The courts do not recognize the caste system as law. True. But the law does not treat it as contrary to law. True. Isn't it? *A Hindu may well say that he will not employ an Untouchable, that he will not sell him anything, that he will evict him from his land, that he will not allow him to take his cattle across his field without offending the law in the slightest degree. In doing so, he is only expressing his right. The law does not care with what motive he does it. The law does not see what injury it causes to the Untouchable.*[66]The progress of the Unmarriageables' movements lies in turning the caste system contrary to law. To take up other issues leaving behind this one would amount to suggesting for a sleeping dose to the Ogre called Caste that roams relentlessly to torment the Unmarriageables. The Monster is sure to return, again and again, to hunt the Unmarriageables, until it is slaughtered. And it should not be forgotten that the solution to annihilate caste, to start with, lies in raising the issue of Unmarriageability.

---

[66]BAWS, Vol.5 p.106

CHAPTER 5

THE WAY FORWARD: UNMARRIAGEABILITY IS THE SPEARHEAD AGAINST THE CASTE SYSTEM

I.   Indian Press- the mouthpiece of Manudharma.

II.   Issue of Unmarriageability in the Untouchables' movement.

III.   The need to raise the Social questions with regard to Caste System.

IV.   Social Inequality - Redefining the definition.

IVa. The Divine Sanctity of Caste System.

IVb. Endogamy– the synonym of Caste.

IVc. Graded Inequality- the obstacle that fortifies Caste System.

IVd. Caste System- a closed form of Stratification.

IVe. 'Social Inequality' in the context of Caste System and to the cause of studying Unmarriageability.

IVf. The peculiarity of the Social Inequality within Hindu society.

IVg. The Final Inference- the right understanding of Social Inequality in accordance with the Hindu Social Order.

V. Conclusion: Unmarriageability is the spearhead against the Caste System.

I

Indian Press- the mouthpiece of Manudharma

The caste system is not treated contrary to law. The refuters undoubtedly can be classified as ill-equipped. It is not at all a hard task to evince that the law does not prevent the propagation of caste system. The national newspapers in English and the vernacular languages serve adequate to show this. In no other societies, the Press has internalized the religious dictates and is maniacally obsessed in cherishing the differences existing among its people. Indian Press incubates the barbarian residues of the Hindu civilization. Even the open support the Press gives to the caste system mirages like a clandestine act because of the attitudinal inertness of the Hindus against the caste system. The Indians are caste addicted and the Indian press never will rip them off it. All it is doing and will be doing is to meet and promote the caste requirements of its caste minded people.

Glance at the matrimonial classifieds. The vulgarity of a casteist society could not be pointed out better than this. In no other societies, such kind of overt vulgar prejudices is thoroughly ingrained in the social behaviour of its people and is remorselessly being advertised in the national newspapers and other dailies without facing the slightest objection. In the times ahead, the present caste matrimonial columns supported by the Indian Press would be censored. Time, not just will pass but will progress and the unacceptable prejudices of caste system are bound to be left behind. The course would not be a natural one, though. The Unmarriageables should be very conscious of the Indian Press as the trumpet of Manudharma so long as the matrimonial advertisements are printed in it. Here and there, the Press brings into light the caste atrocities and accommodates editorial articles offering a critique on the system of caste. Eyewash they are and it should be understood that the Press is the breeding platform of the endogamous practices. Mind you, marriages are the genes transmitting the caste from one generation to another. And the Indian Press incubates these genes to sustain the status quo that favours the instinctive psyche of the Hindus to opt for endogamous marriages and resisting the emerging inter-caste marriages. The Indian press may not be the reason for the endogamy to exist. But definitely they are the prime factor in the better facilitation of endogamous marriages. They shamelessly tabulate the men and women jati and gotra wise and favour match-making of the brides with the bridegrooms of same caste categories. Indian Press is a realm of contradictions and double standards. And its Pressmen are the fraudulent hypocrites. In the news columns, they report of honour killings happening because of exogamous marriages and inside in their matrimonial classifieds they breed for the endogamous marriages. They are alarmingly apathetic towards caste atrocities and shamelessly generate income through matrimonial classifieds. With no hold in the news media, the Unmarriageables should be very watchful in chiselling their destiny. It would have had been a favourable ambience for them if the caste matrimonies had been outrightly perceived as the menace against the sanctity of human equality. Unfortunately, they thrive devoid of constraints not merely as any other advertisements or classifieds for profit-making purposes but also without being interpreted against the law. Under the pretext of an individual's personal liberty to choose her/his own spouse, a hardcore caste Hindu succeeds in shadowing and subduing her/his ulterior motive of caste prejudice safely and securely.

II

Issue of Unmarriageability in the Untouchables' movement

From the start to the present time, the movement of Unmarriageables has taken varied and significant courses. But it hasn't reached its zenith. This is the contention I wanted to persuade the Unmarriageables with. Their ultimate fight should be the fight against Unmarriageability but hitherto the issue has not been concretely raised. In fact, to derive from the reality, Unmarriageability is yet to be frowned upon as a stigma to be dealt against. With its sanction rooted in Hindu religion and imbibed for centuries as an unalterable custom, Unmarriageability remains too far from the perception of the Hindus as a practice that has to be annihilated.

The receptiveness of the people in their times is vital in shaping the dynamics of movements. Each movement does change the status quo of the society. But the fact that should not be missed is that the status quo of the society does play its part in kick-starting a movement and further in its spread. The ripeness of the ambience is always a factor in the success of a movement. The ambition of the movement confronts always the settled beliefs of the people. In this tussle the outcome is one of two- either the movement succeeds in altering the general psyche of the people or the belief system of the people suppresses the deviancy initiated by the movement. The movement of the Unmarriageable had been a mix of both. On one side, they have made the demeaning practice of Untouchability against the law, and on the other extreme, they have succumbed to the mental habitudes of the Hindus. The facets of Unmarriageables' movement whether it is polemic's ideological base or struggle for civil rights or breaking into Hindu temples or burning the Manusmriti or embracing Buddhism or the assertion through political rights, it has been always a struggle of constructing their ladder of liberty step by step, one above the other. Time and space do steer the pace of movements, either accelerating towards progress or being wobbled in the inertial drag of the society that is resisting to the change. Here, the prime task of the Unmarriageables should be to acquaint themselves with the limitations and the receptiveness of the present time and space and to mould their movement better by understanding and manoeuvring with the conditions of the present and pushing the movement against the foundations of caste, in the near future.

So, are the Unmarriageables in the right direction? The question seeks a thoughtful answer. No other exploited class had been so dormant to the extent of Unmarriageables in realising the real cause of their state. It is their fiasco that has to be both mocked and harshly condemned, and given a serious contemplation for not disturbing the sustaining source of the caste system. There were social movements against Untouchability and also were there political movements to uplift the Unmarriageables. But there was never a Social movement against the Caste system. It is very important for the Unmarriageables to take notice of this void, as this has been the biggest setback in their movements so far. The vacuum primarily is because of the peripheral understanding about what caste system is and ignorance of the ineffectiveness such a deficient definition could impart in a movement. What is caste system? The reply from any Indian is mostly the same and the same is reflected in the understanding of any foreigners too who is intrigued by the Indian caste system. Chaturvarna and its classification is referred as caste system. Here lies the blunder of irrationality. Caste system is said to be the four divisions or Varnas-Brahmins, the priestly class; Kshatriyas, the warrior class; Vaishyas, the trading class; Shudras, the servile class; And Depressed Classes fall outside these four Varnas as Avarna. The mistake lies here. Caste system merely does not mean the four divisions. It should actually be defined and understood by the methodology that maintains these four divisions. The four divisions are merely an outcome of this methodology. In other words, the founding principle of caste system is not the Chaturvarna but the 'Endogamy' that maintains the Chaturvarna. It is endogamy and not Chaturvarna that defines caste system. Brahmins, Kshatriyas, Vaishyas and Shudras do not define caste system. Rather, the endogamy principle that maintains the exclusivity of Brahmins, Kshatriyas, Vaishyas and Shudras defines the caste system. Endogamy is the definition of caste system. Substitute 'endogamy' for 'caste' and none of the meaning changes. The continuing mistake of focusing on Chaturvarna instead of endogamy should not be ignored. A deficient understanding would not create an efficient movement.

Anti-discriminatory actions, against Untouchability included, will fail to succeed until Unmarriageability is weeded out from the Hindu social life. Endogamy is the problem here and not merely Untouchability. The real and true notional change of the Hindu society starts with the decline in endogamous preferences and until this practice continues, Untouchability is bound to exist for sure. I, for myself, would consider no other activity that stands in short of weakening the caste system as a full-fledged movement, even if it is the Dalit political parties gaining electoral victories. Cure cannot be said to occur without the disease being destroyed. The Depressed Classes should attack the notion of endogamy, in other words, the practice of Unmarriageability. This would sow the seeds for a social movement against the system of caste. Always, the best cure is complete eradication.

III

The need to raise the Social questions with regard to Caste System

During the colonial rule, Dr.Ambedkar stressed on giving priority to the social question of caste than the political question of independence. He presented his argument with a heroic rationale and as a lone saviour of Depressed Classes that elevated him distinctly above the rest of the leaders preoccupied in the freedom struggle. At present, there is a greater need to remind the Unmarriageables about the necessity to give precedence to the social questions of caste instead of getting stranded around its essential but shallow political questions. There are critics who argue that even Dr.Ambedkar who gave so much of significance to the social sphere of caste finally had to resort through the political sphere of framing the Constitution in order to liberate, safeguard and armour the Unmarriageables from the caste system. A careless interpretation, this is. Firstly, framing of the Constitution cannot be purely construed as a political act. Secondly Dr.Ambedkar, while comparing the urgency to attain independence from British rule with the annihilation of caste from the Indian society, equated both of them to the political and social sphere respectively and arguing from this standpoint he favoured with conviction to place foremost significance to the social need of weakening the caste system instead of fighting for the political independence of a nation that never existed in a strict social sense. Thirdly, with persistent and continued indifference exhibited by the Indian leaders to exhibit their stand overtly against the caste system without limiting to Untouchability, with conscious apathy from their part to assimilate the Unmarriageables in the social, economic and political life, with the dream of free India engulfing every other social concern, and more importantly with the rigid caste Hindus drenched in their caste beliefs, the only possible working way for the Unmarriageables to free themselves from the bondage of caste system and raise with dignity was through political fight, which Dr.Ambedkar had to choose without an option. He strategically saw the political means to elevate the Unmarriageables educationally, economically and more importantly socially. In 1933, by the time the social question of caste had faded out completely, Dr.Ambedkar made the following appeal to the Unmarriageables:

You have now a way of bringing about change, an improvement in your life conditions. That way is through political action, through appropriate laws... you can make (the) government provide for you what you are now denied- food, clothing, shelter, education.... Hence instead of resorting to rosary counting or prayer, you should now depend on the political path; that will bring you liberation.... The conflict, hereafter, will not be between the British and the Indians, but between the advanced classes of India and backward classes. No borrowed or hired person who does not belong to your class can further your welfare by the least degree.[67]

On 25th April 1948, during the Fifth Conference of united provinces of Scheduled Castes Federation, Dr.Ambedkar said, *Political power is the key to all social progress and the Scheduled Castes can achieve their salvation if they captured this power by organizing themselves*

---

[67]quoted in Gore 1993;213

into a third Party and holding the balance of power between the rival political parties—Congress and Socialists.[68]

A pensive mind would affirm that Dr.Ambedkar in taking the political route eventually only has answered the social questions of caste. Like yarn is woven into a coarse fabric, the social and political part of an issue interweave over one another. The political arrangements Dr.Ambedkar made for the Unmarriageables has only improved their social standing including the educational and economic aspects.   His utmost concern for the Depressed Classes had been always in a social sense and the political and religious route (his religious conversion to Buddhism in 1956) he showed to them was only an outcome of this inclination.

With anti-reservation agitations gaining prominence and with some of the creamy layers among the Unmarriageables who have progressed making benefit of the reservation themselves now giving the most insane arguments to curb the reservation system, Unmarriageables should be ready to face the jeopardy clouding before them. Even the slightest neglect in this regard has enough potency to reverse the fate of the Unmarriageables resonating their helpless past where they were treated with defilement and rendered without the basic survival rights. If the safeguards of reservation are removed before perishing the prejudices of caste, the notoriety of caste Hindus would for sure inanimate the lives of Unmarriageables. The purpose of reservation is primarily to achieve social equality and there is no justification for its removal till the prevalence of social inequality. Hence, without any wandering objectives, the survival instinct of the Unmarriageables should shift and align their concern, agitation and movement towards the social sphere of the caste system. And it should be understood that the issue of Unmarriageability would be the piercing spear considering the social questions of Indian caste system.

---

[68]BAWS, Vol.17, part 3 p.388

IV

Social Inequality - Redefining the definition

So, the need to raise the social questions with regard to caste system is very important. At this juncture, it is important for me to connote the manner in which the phrase 'social inequality' is used all throughout in this book. First of all, the terms 'social' and 'inequality' both are very generic. Combining them both to mean 'social inequality' further widens the possible interpretations. The stratified society on gender, class, wealth, race, caste, creed, religion etc. introduces inequality. To not venture out of the argument and the Hindu society, it becomes a prerequisite to bringing into centre stage the caste criteria. I do not overlook the inimical role of other factors especially the part of gender within the Hindu society. The condition of Dalit women within the Dalit community is as much the same as Dalit community within the Hindu society. But to narrow down the much wider definition of 'social inequality' to the cause of studying Unmarriageability it is pertinent and enough to emphasis on the caste factor alone. For this, let us gather the connotation of the word 'Society' and the presence of its ideals in the Indian Society from Dr.Ambedkar's writings on the 'Prospects of Democracy in India':

Democracy is quite different from a Republic as well as from Parliamentary Government. The roots of democracy lie not in the form of Government, Parliamentary or otherwise. A democracy is more than a form of Government. It is primarily a mode of associated living. The roots of Democracy are to be searched in the social relationship, in the terms of associated life between the people who form a society.

What does the word 'Society' connote? To put it briefly when we speak of 'Society', we conceive of it as one by its very nature. The qualities which accompany this unity are praiseworthy community of purpose and desire for welfare, loyalty to public ends and mutuality of sympathy and co-operation.

115

Are these ideals to be found in Indian Society? The Indian Society does not consist of individuals. It consists of an innumerable collection of castes which are exclusive in their life and have no common experience to share and have no bond of sympathy. Given this fact it is not necessary to argue the point. The existence of the Caste System is a standing denial of the existence of those ideals of society and therefore of democracy.

Indian Society is so imbedded in the Caste System that everything is organized on the basis of caste. Enter Indian Society and you can see caste in its glaring form. An Indian cannot eat or marry with an Indian simply because he or she does not belong to his or her caste. An Indian cannot touch an Indian because he or she does not belong to his or her caste. Go and enter politics and you can see caste reflected therein. How does an Indian vote in an election? He votes for a candidate who belongs to his own caste and no other. Even the Indian Congress exploits the Caste system for election purpose as no other political party in India does. Examine the lists of its candidates in relation to the social composition of the constituencies and it will be found that the candidate belongs to the caste which is the largest one in that constituency. The Congress, as a matter of fact, is upholding the Caste System against which it is outwardly raising an outcry against the existence of caste.

Go into the field of industry. What will you find? You will find that all the topmost men drawing the highest salary belong to the caste of the particular industrialist who owns the industry. The rest hang on for life on the lowest rungs of the ladder on a pittance. Go into the field of commerce and you will see the same picture. The whole commercial house is one camp of one caste, with no entry board on the door for others.

Go into the field of charity. With one or two exceptions all charity in India is communal. If a Parsi dies, he leaves his money for Parsis. If a Jain dies, he leaves his money for Jains. If a Marwadi dies, he leaves his money for Marwadis. If a Brahmin dies, he leaves his money for

Brahmins. Thus, there is no room for the downtrodden and the outcastes in politics, in industry, in commerce, and in education.[69]

While being conscious of the ideals of the Indian Society as mentioned above, the following statement of Dr.Ambedkar also becomes relevant here:

On the 26th January 1950, we are going to enter into a life of contradictions. In politics we will have equality and in social and economic life we will have inequality. In politics we will be recognizing the principle of one man one vote and one vote one value. In our social and economic life, we shall, by reason of our social and economic structure continue to deny the principle of one man one value. How long shall we continue to live this life of contradictions? How long shall we continue to deny equality in our social and economic life? If we continue to deny it for long, we will do so only by putting our political democracy in peril.[70]

With the understandings gathered so far, let us resume to the definition of 'social inequality':

"The term social inequality simply refers to the existence of socially created inequalities. And social stratification is nothing but a particular form of social inequality. It refers to the presence of social groups which are ranked one above the other, usually in terms of the amount of Power, Prestige and Wealth their members possess."[71]

"Power refers to the degree to which individuals or groups can impose their will on others, with or without the consent of those others. Prestige relates to the amount of esteem or honour associated with social positions, qualities of individuals

---

[69]BAWS, Vol.17, part 3 p.519

[70] BAWS, Vol.13 p.1216

[71]Sociology Themes and perspectives, M Haralambos with R.M.Heald, p.24

and styles of life. Wealth refers to material possessions defined as valuable in particular societies. It may include land, livestock, buildings, money and many other forms of property owned by individuals or social groups."[72]

In the Indian society, the relevance of Power, Prestige and Wealth alone are not suffice to understand the well-established and deeply ingrained social inequality. It becomes pertinent to observe how caste system dictates, defines and distributes the Power, Prestige and Wealth to each and every caste. Understanding caste stratification not merely as a form but also as the genesis and foundation of social inequality is of great significance in defining the term 'social inequality', since defining 'social inequality' and to construe it in the right sense is crucial to the cause of studying Unmarriageability.

"Hindu society in traditional India was divided into five main strata: four varnas or castes, and a fifth group, the outcaste, whose members were known as Untouchables. Each caste is subdivided into jatis or sub-castes, which in total number many thousands. Jatis are occupational groups- there are carpenter jatis, goldsmith jatis, potter jatis, and so on. Castes are ranked in terms of ritual purity. The Brahmins or priests, members of the highest caste, personify purity, sanctity and holiness. They are the source of learning, wisdom and truth. Only they can perform the most important religious ceremonies. At the other extreme, Untouchables are defined as unclean, base and impure, a status which affects all their social relationships. They must perform unclean and degrading tasks such as the disposal of dead animals. They must be segregated from members of the caste system and live on the outskirts of villages or in their own communities in the middle of paddy fields. Their presence pollutes to the extent that even if the shadow of an Untouchable falls across the food of a Brahmin it will render it unclean. In general, the hierarchy of

---

[72]Sociology Themes and perspectives, M Haralambos with R.M.Heald, p.24

prestige based on notions of ritual purity is mirrored by the hierarchy of power. The Brahmins were custodians of law, and the legal system which they administered was based largely on their pronouncements. Inequalities of wealth were usually linked to those of prestige and power. In a largely rural economy, the Brahmins tended to be the largest landowners and the control of land was monopolized by members of the two highest castes."[73]

Unlike other forms of stratification that remain the subject matter of sociology, the stratification established and sustained by caste has to be intensively studied along with its peculiar principles and mechanisms of social control. With regard to caste system, any contemplation should be guided by the following four premises:

Firstly, caste system is strengthened by divine sanction.

Secondly, caste system is nothing but endogamy in its operation.

Thirdly, the principle of graded inequality fortifies the caste system.

Fourthly, caste system is a closed form of stratification rendering the social mobility impossible.

As my objective of defining 'social inequality' is founded on the above four premises, it becomes essential to throw proper light about them, once again with the studies of Dr.Ambedkar.

---

[73]Sociology Themes and perspectives, M Haralambos with R.M.Heald, p.25

IVa
The Divine Sanctity of Caste System

In the historical masterpiece, 'Who were the Shudras? How they came to be the Fourth Varna in the Indo-Aryan society', Dr.Ambedkar begins his proposition with the divinity and infallibility associated with the social ideal of Chaturvarna, which runs as below:

Any attempt to discover who the Shudras were and how they came to be the fourth Varna must begin with the origin of the Chaturvarnya in the Indo-Aryan society. A study of the Chaturvarnya must in its turn start with a study of the ninetieth Hymn of the Tenth Mandala of the Rig Veda— a Hymn, which is known by the famous name of Purusha Sukta.

What does the Hymn say? It says[74]:

1. *Purusha has a thousand heads, a thousand eyes, a thousand feet. On every side enveloping the earth he overpassed (it) by a space of ten fingers.*
2. *Purusha himself is this whole (universe), Whatever has been and whatever shall be. He is the Lord of immortality, since (or when) by food he expands.*
3. *Such is his greatness, and Purusha is superior to this. All existences are a quarter to him; and three-fourths of him are that which is immortal in the sky.*
4. *With three-quarters, Purusha mounted upwards. A quarter of him was again produced here. He was then diffused everywhere over things which eat and things which do not eat.*
5. *From him was born Viraj, and from Viraj, Purusha. When born, he extended beyond the earth, both behind and before.*
6. *When the gods performed a sacrifice with Purusha as the oblation, the spring was its butter, the summer its fuel, and the autumn its (accompanying) offering.*

---

[74] Muir's, Original Sanskrit Texts, Vol. I, p.9

7. *This victim, Purusha, born in the beginning, they immolated on the sacrificial grass. With him the gods, the Sadhyas, and the rishis sacrificed.*

8. *From that universal sacrifice were provided curds and butter. It formed those aerial (creatures) and animals both wild and tame.*

9. *From that universal sacrifice sprang the rik and saman verses, the metres and the yajus.*

10. *From it sprang horses, and all animals with two rows of teeth; kine sprang from it; from it goats and sheep.*

11. *When (the gods) divided Purusha, into how many parts did they cut him up? What was his mouth? What arms (had he)? What (two objects) are said (to have been) his thighs and feet?*

12. *The Brahmana was his mouth, the Rajanya was made his arms; the being called the Vaishya, he was his thighs; the Shudra sprang from his feet.*

13. *The moon sprang from his soul (manas), the sun from the eye, Indra and Agni from his mouth and Vayu from his breath.*

14. *From his navel arose the air, from his head the sky, from his feet the earth, from his ear the (four) quarters; in this manner (the gods) formed the worlds.*

15. *When the gods, performing sacrifices, bound Purusha as a victim, there were seven sticks (stuck up) for it (around the fire), and thrice seven pieces of fuel were made.*

16. *With sacrifices the gods performed the sacrifice. These were the earliest rites. These great powers have sought the sky, where are the former Sadhyas, gods.*

The Purusha Sukta is a theory of the origin of the Universe. In other words, it is a cosmogony. No nation which has reached an advanced degree of thought has failed to develop some sort of cosmogony. The Egyptians had a cosmogony somewhat analogous with that set out in the Purusha Sukta. According to it,[75] it was god Khnumu, 'the shaper', who shaped living things on the potter's wheel, "created all that is, he formed all

---

[75] Encyclopaedia of Religion and Ethics, Vol. IV, P.145

that exists, he is the father of fathers, the mother of mothers... he fashioned men, he made the gods, he was the father from the beginning... he is the creator of the heaven, the earth, the underworld, the water, the mountains... he formed a male and a female of all birds, fishes, wild beasts, cattle and of all worms." A very similar cosmogony is found in Chapter I of the Genesis in the Old Testament.

Cosmogonies have never been more than matters of academic interest and have served no other purpose than to satisfy the curiosity of the student and to help to amuse children. This may be true of some parts of the Purusha Sukta. But it certainly cannot be true of the whole of it. That is because all verse of the Purusha Sukta are not of the same importance and do not have the same significance. Verses 11 and 12 fall in one category and the rest of the verses fall in another category. Verses other than 11 and 12 may be regarded as of academic interest. Nobody relies upon them. No Hindu even remembers them. But it is quite different with regard to verses 11 and 12. Prima facie these verses do no more than explain how the four classes, namely, (1) Brahmins or priests, (2) Kshatriyas or soldiers, (3) Vaishyas or traders, and (4) Shudras or menials, arose from the body of the Creator. But the fact is that these verses are not understood as being merely explanatory of a cosmic phenomenon. It would be a grave mistake to suppose that they were regarded by the Indo-Aryans as an innocent piece of a poet's idle imagination. They are treated as containing a mandatory injunction from the Creator to the effect that Society must be constituted on the basis of four classes mentioned in the Sukta. Such a construction of the verses in question may not be warranted by their language. But there is no doubt that according to tradition this is how the verses are construed, and it would indeed be difficult to say that this traditional construction is not in consonance with the intention of the author of the Sukta. Verses 11 and 12 of the Purusha Sukta are, therefore, not a mere cosmogony. They contain a divine injunction prescribing a particular form of the constitution of society.

The constitution of society prescribed by the Purusha Sukta is known as Chaturvarnya. As a divine injunction, it naturally became the ideal of the Indo-Aryan society. This ideal of Chaturvarnya was the mould in which the life of the Indo-Aryan community in its early or liquid state was cast. It is this mould, which gave the Indo-Aryan community its peculiar shape and structure.

This reverence, which the Indo-Aryan society had for this ideal mould of Chaturvarnya, is not only beyond question, but it is also beyond description. Its influence on the Indo-Aryan society has been profound and indelible. The social order prescribed by the Purusha Sukta has never been questioned by anyone except Buddha. Even Buddha was not able to shake it, for the simple reason that both after the fall of Buddhism and even during the period of Buddhism there were enough law-givers, who made it their business not only to defend the ideal of the Purusha Sukta but to propagate it and to elaborate it.

... Many other law-givers have in parrot-like manner repeated the theme of the PurushaSukta and have reiterated its sanctity. It is unnecessary to repeat their version of it. All those, who had raised any opposition to the sanctity of the ideal set out in the Purusha Sukta, were finally laid low by Manu, the architect of the Hindu society. For Manu did two things. In the first place, he enunciated afresh the ideal of the Purusha Sukta as a part of divine injunction. He said:

> *"For the prosperity of the worlds, he (the creator) from his mouth, arms, thighs and feet created the Brahmin, Kshatriya and Vaishya and the Shudra.*[76]
> *The Brahmin, Kshatriya (and) Vaishya (constitute) the three twice-born castes; but the fourth the shudra has only one birth.*[77] *"*

In this he was no doubt merely following his predecessors. But he went a step further and enunciated another proposition in which he said:

---

[76]Manu, Chapter 1, Verse 31

[77]Manu, Chapter X, Verse 4

"Veda is the only and ultimate sanction for Dharma.[78] "

Bearing in mind that the Purusha Sukta is a part of the Veda, it cannot be difficult to realise that Manu invested the social ideal of Chaturvarnya contained in the PurushaSukta, with a degree of divinity and infallibility which it did not have before.

... What are the features of the social ideal of the Purusha Sukta, which give it the hall mark of being unique? Though the existence of classes is the de facto condition of every society, nevertheless no society has converted this de facto state of affairs into a de jure connotation of an ideal society. The scheme of the Purusha Sukta is the only instance in which the real is elevated to the dignity of an ideal. This is the first unique feature of the scheme set forth in the Purusha Sukta. Secondly, no community has given the de facto state of class composition a legal effect by accepting it as a de jure connotation of an ideal society. The case of the Greeks is a case in point. Class composition was put forth as an ideal social structure by no less an advocate than Plato. But the Greeks never thought of making it real by giving it the sanction of law. The Purusha Sukta is the only instance in which an attempt was made to give reality to the ideal by invoking the sanction of law. Thirdly, no society has accepted that the class composition is an ideal. At the most they have accepted it as being natural. The Purusha Sukta goes further. It not only regards class composition as natural and ideal, but also regards it as sacred and divine. Fourthly, the number of the classes has never been a matter of dogma in any society known to history. The Romans had two classes. The Egyptians thought three were enough. The Indo-Iranians also had no more than three classes: (1) The Atharvans (priests) (2) Rathaeshtar (warriors) and (3) the Vastrya-fshuyat (peasantry). The scheme of the Purusha Sukta makes the division of society into four classes a matter of dogma. According to it, there can be neither more nor less. Fifthly, every society leaves a class to find its place vis-a-vis other classes according to its importance in society as

---

[78]Manu, Chapter II, Verse 6

may be determined by the forces operating from time to time. No society has an official gradation laid down, fixed and permanent, with an ascending scale of reverence and a descending scale of contempt. The scheme of the Purusha Sukta is unique, inasmuch as it fixes a permanent warrant of precedence among the different classes, which neither time nor circumstances can alter. The warrant of precedence is based on the principle of graded inequality among the four classes, whereby it recognises the Brahmin to be above all, the Kshatriya below the Brahmin but above the Vaishya and the Shudra, the Vaishya below the Kshatriya but above the Shudra and the Shudra below all.[79]

IVb
Endogamy– the synonym of Caste

It is wise and critical not to lose sight of endogamy as the sustaining mechanism of caste amidst the other features of the caste system. Repeatedly, endogamy has been misunderstood as just another feature of the caste system. It is not so. Endogamy itself is caste system. It is what makes the caste system. For centuries, caste system has been sustained and is being sustained exclusively through the process of endogamy. All the features of caste and its system are purely the outcome of its basic rule- the compulsory practice of endogamy.

Understanding endogamy would enlighten the presence and purpose of certain customs within the Hindu society like sati, enforced widowhood for life, child marriage and even the 'Dishonour' killings as rampant occurrences. In this context, the lengthy replication of Dr.Ambedkar's 'Caste in India- Their Mechanism, Genesis and Development' is unavoidable considering the requirement to understand the relation between endogamy and caste.

This critical evaluation of the various characteristics of Caste leave

---

[79]BAWS, Vol.7 p.21-26

no doubt that prohibition, or rather the absence of intermarriage—endogamy, to be concise—is the only one that can be called the essence of Caste when rightly understood. But some may deny this on abstract anthropological grounds, for there exist endogamous groups without giving rise to the problem of Caste. In a general way this may be true, as endogamous societies, culturally different, making their abode in localities more or less removed, and having little to do with each other are a physical reality. The Negroes and the Whites and the various tribal groups that go by name of American Indians in the United States may be cited as more or less appropriate illustrations in support of this view. But we must not confuse matters, for in India the situation is different. As pointed out before, the peoples of India form a homogeneous whole. The various races of India occupying definite territories have more or less fused into one another and do possess cultural unity, which is the only criterion of a homogeneous population. Given this homogeneity as a basis, Caste becomes a problem altogether new in character and wholly absent in the situation constituted by the mere propinquity of endogamous social or tribal groups. Caste in India means an artificial chopping off of the population into fixed and definite units, each one prevented from fusing into another through the custom of endogamy. Thus the conclusion is inevitable that Endogamy is the only characteristic that is peculiar to caste, and if we succeed in showing how endogamy is maintained, we shall practically have proved the genesis and also the mechanism of Caste.

It may not be quite easy for you to anticipate why I regard endogamy as a key to the mystery of the Caste system. Not to strain your imagination too much, I will proceed to give you my reasons for it. It may not also be out of place to emphasize at this moment that no civilized society of today presents more survivals of primitive times than does the Indian society. Its religion is essentially primitive and its tribal code, in spite of the advance of time and civilization, operates in all its pristine vigour even today. One of these primitive survivals, to which I wish particularly to draw your attention is the Custom of Exogamy. The prevalence of exogamy in the primitive worlds is a fact too well-known to need any explanation. With the growth of history, however, exogamy has lost its efficacy, and excepting the nearest blood-kins, there is usually no social bar restricting the field of marriage. But regarding the peoples of India the law of exogamy is a positive injunction even today. Indian society still savours of the clan system, even though there are no clans; and this can be easily seen from the law of matrimony which centres round the principle of exogamy, for it is not that Sapindas (blood-kins) cannot marry, but a marriage even between Sagotras (of the same class) is regarded as a sacrilege.

Nothing is therefore more important for you to remember than the fact that endogamy is foreign to the people of India. The various Gotras of India are and have been exogamous: so are the other groups with totemic organization. It is no exaggeration to say that with the people of India exogamy is a creed and none dare infringe it, so much so that, in spite of the endogamy of the Castes within them, exogamy is strictly observed and that there are more rigorous penalties for violating exogamy than there are for violating endogamy. You will, therefore, readily see that with exogamy as the rule there could be no Caste, for exogamy means fusion. But we have castes; consequently in the final analysis creation of Castes, so far as India is concerned, means the superposition of endogamy on exogamy. However, in an originally exogamous population an easy working out of endogamy (which is equivalent to the creation of Caste) is a grave problem, and it is in the consideration of the means utilized for the preservation of endogamy against exogamy that we may hope to find the solution of our problem.

Thus the superposition of endogamy on exogamy means the creation of caste. But this is not an easy affair. Let us take an imaginary group that desires to make itself into a Caste and analyse what means it will have to adopt to make itself endogamous. If a group desires to make itself endogamous a formal injunction against intermarriage with outside groups will be of no avail, especially if prior to the introduction of endogamy, exogamy had been the rule in all matrimonial relations. Again, there is a tendency in all groups lying in close contact with one another to assimilate and amalgamate, and thus consolidate into a homogeneous society. If this tendency is to be strongly counteracted in the interest of Caste formation, it is absolutely necessary to circumscribe a circle outside which people should not contract marriages.

Nevertheless, this encircling to prevent marriages from without creates problems from within which are not very easy of solution. Roughly speaking, in a normal group the two sexes are more or less evenly distributed, and generally speaking there is an equality between those of the same age. The equality is, however, never quite realized in actual societies. At the same time to the group that is desirous of making itself into a caste the maintenance of equality between the sexes becomes the ultimate goal, for without it endogamy can no longer subsist. In other words, if endogamy is to be preserved conjugal rights from within have to be provided for, otherwise members of the group will be driven out of the circle to take care of themselves in any way they can. But in order that the conjugal rights be provided for from within, it is absolutely necessary to maintain a numerical equality between the marriageable units of the two sexes within the group desirous of making itself into a Caste. It is only through the maintenance of such an equality that the necessary endogamy of the group can be kept intact, and a very large disparity is sure to break it.

The problem of Caste, then, ultimately resolves itself into one of repairing the disparity between the marriageable units of the two sexes within it. Left to nature, the much needed parity between the units can be realized only when a couple dies simultaneously. But this is a rare contingency. The husband may die before the wife and create a surplus woman, who must be disposed of, else through intermarriage she will violate the endogamy of the group. In like manner the husband may survive his wife and be surplus man, whom the group, while it may sympathise with him for the sad bereavement, has to dispose of, else he will marry outside the Caste and will break the endogamy. Thus both the surplus man and the surplus woman constitute a menace to the Caste if not taken care of, for not finding suitable partners inside their prescribed circle (and left to themselves they cannot find any, for if the matter be not regulated there can only be just enough pairs to go round) very likely they will transgress the boundary, marry outside and import offspring that is foreign to the Caste.

Let us see what our imaginary group is likely to do with this surplus man and surplus woman. We will first take up the case of the surplus woman. She can be disposed of in two different ways so as to preserve the endogamy of the Caste.

First: burn her on the funeral pyre of her deceased husband and get rid of her. This, however, is rather an impracticable way of solving the problem of sex disparity. In some cases it may work, in others it may not. Consequently every surplus woman cannot thus be disposed of, because it is an easy solution but a hard realization. And so the surplus woman (= widow), if not disposed of, remains in the group: but in her very existence lies a double danger. She may marry outside the Caste and violate endogamy, or she may marry within the Caste and through competition encroach upon the chances of marriage that must be reserved for the potential brides in the Caste. She is therefore a menace in any case, and something must be done to her if she cannot be burned along with her deceased husband.

The second remedy is to enforce widowhood on her for the rest of her life. So far as the objective results are concerned, burning is a better solution than enforcing widowhood. Burning the widow eliminates all the three evils that a surplus woman is fraught with. Being dead and gone she creates no problem of remarriage either inside or outside the Caste. But compulsory widowhood is superior to burning because it is more practicable. Besides being comparatively humane it also guards against the evils of remarriage as does burning; but it fails to guard the morals of the group. No doubt under compulsory widowhood the woman remains, and just because she is deprived of her natural right of being a legitimate wife in future, the incentive to immoral conduct is increased. But this is by no means an insuperable difficulty. She can be degraded to a condition in which she is no longer a source of allurement.

The problem of surplus man (= widower) is much more important and much more difficult than that of the surplus woman in a group that desires to make itself into a Caste. From time immemorial man as compared with woman has had the upper hand. He is a dominant figure in every group and of the two sexes has greater prestige. With this traditional superiority of man over woman his wishes have always been consulted. Woman, on the other hand, has been an easy prey to all kinds of iniquitous injunctions, religious, social or economic. But man as a maker of injunctions is most often above them all. Such being the case, you cannot accord the same kind of treatment to a surplus man as you can to a surplus woman in a Caste.

The project of burning him with his deceased wife is hazardous in two ways: first of all it cannot be done, simply because he is a man. Secondly, if done, a sturdy soul is lost to the Caste. There remain then only two solutions which can conveniently dispose of him. I say conveniently, because he is an asset to the group.

Important as he is to the group, endogamy is still more important, and the solution must assure both these ends. Under these circumstances he may be forced or I should say induced, after the manner of the widow, to remain a widower for the rest of his life. This solution is not altogether difficult, for without any compulsion some are so disposed as to enjoy self-imposed celibacy, or even to take a further step of their own accord and renounce the world and its joys. But, given human nature as it is, this solution can hardly be expected to be realized. On the other hand, as is very likely to be the case, if the surplus man remains in the group as an active participator in group activities, he is a danger to the morals of the group. Looked at from a different point of view celibacy, though easy in cases where it succeeds, is not so advantageous even then to the material prospects of the Caste. If he observes genuine celibacy and renounces the world, he would not be a menace to the preservation of Caste endogamy or Caste morals as he undoubtedly would be if he remained a secular person. But as an ascetic celibate he is as good as burned, so far as the material wellbeing of his Caste is concerned. A Caste, in order that it may be large enough to afford a vigorous communal life, must be maintained at a certain numerical strength. But to hope for this and to proclaim celibacy is the same as trying to cure atrophy by bleeding.

Imposing celibacy on the surplus man in the group, therefore, fails both theoretically and practically. It is in the interest of the Caste to keep him as a Grahastha (one who raises a family), to use a Sanskrit technical term. But the problem is to provide him with a wife from within the Caste. At the outset this is not possible, for the ruling ratio in a caste has to be one man to one woman and none can have two chances of marriage, for in a Caste thoroughly self-enclosed there are always just enough marriageable women to go round for the marriageable men. Under these circumstances the surplus man can be provided with a wife only by recruiting a bride from the ranks of those not yet marriageable in order to tie him down to the group. This is certainly the best of the possible solutions in the case of the surplus man. By this, he is kept within the Caste. By this means numerical depletion through constant outflow is guarded against, and by this endogamy morals are preserved.

It will now be seen that the four means by which numerical disparity between the two sexes is conveniently maintained are: (1) burning the widow with her deceased husband; (2) compulsory widowhood—a milder form of burning; (3) imposing celibacy on the widower and (4) wedding him to a girl not yet marriageable. Though, as I said above, burning the widow and imposing celibacy on the widower are of doubtful service to the group in its endeavour to preserve its endogamy, all of them operate as means. But means, as forces, when liberated or set in motion create an end. What then is the end that these means create? They create and perpetuate endogamy, while caste and endogamy, according to our analysis of the various definitions of caste, are one and the same thing. Thus the existence of these means is identical with caste and caste involves these means.

This, in my opinion, is the general mechanism of a caste in a system of castes. Let us now turn from these high generalities to the castes

131

in Hindu Society and inquire into their mechanism. I need hardly premise that there are a great many pitfalls in the path of those who try to unfold the past, and caste in India to be sure is a very ancient institution. This is especially true where there exist no authentic or written records or where the people, like the Hindus, are so constituted that to them writing history is a folly, for the world is an illusion. But institutions do live, though for a long time they may remain unrecorded and as often as not customs and morals are like fossils that tell their own history. If this is true, our task will be amply rewarded if we scrutinize the solution the Hindus arrived at to meet the problems of the surplus man and surplus woman.

Complex though it be in its general working the Hindu Society, even to a superficial observer, presents three singular uxorial customs, namely:

(i) Sati or the burning of the widow on the funeral pyre of her deceased husband.

(ii) Enforced widowhood by which a widow is not allowed to remarry.

(iii) Girl marriage.

In addition, one also notes a great hankering after Sannyasa (renunciation) on the part of the widower, but this may in some cases be due purely to psychic disposition.[80]

Also, Dishonour killing is nothing but another unnatural means to curb the possibility of exogamy. It is a threat intended to maintain the rule of endogamy- a threat to every person not to transgress the caste boundary, marry outside and import offspring that is foreign and unacceptable to the caste group.

---

[80]BAWS, Vol.1 p.8

IVc
Graded Inequality- the obstacle that fortifies Caste System

The wickedness of caste system does not exhaust with the artificial chopping off of population into definite castes but in fact extends and pervades in its very structure that renders absolute impossibility of unification of subjugated and exploited lower castes against the domination and supremacy of upper castes. Permit me to reiterate again that,

... Castes are not equal in their status. They are standing one above another. They are jealous of one another. It is an ascending scale of reverence and descending scale of contempt. This feature of the caste system has most pernicious consequences. It destroys willing and helpful cooperation.

Caste and class differ in the fact that in the Class System there is no complete isolation as there is in the Caste System. This is the second evil effect in the Caste System accompanied by inequality. This manifests itself in the fact that the stimulus and response between two castes is only one-sided. The higher caste act in one recognized way and the lower caste must respond in one established way. It means that when there is no equitable opportunity to receive the stimulus from and to return the response from different caste, the result is that the influences which educate some into masters, educate others into slaves. The experience of each party loses its meaning when the free interchange of varying modes of life experience is arrested. It results into a separation of society, into a privileged and a subject class. Such a separation prevents social endosmosis.

How to put an end to the Caste System? The first obstacle lies in the system of graded inequality which is the soul of Caste System. Where people are divided into two classes, higher and lower, it is easier for the lower to combine to fight the higher, for there is no single lower class. The class consists of lower and lowerer. The lower cannot combine with the lowerer. For the lower is afraid that if he succeeds in raising the lowerer, he may well himself lose the high position given to him and his caste.[81]

IVd
Caste System- a closed form of Stratification

Micheal Haralambos in 'Sociology- Themes and Perspectives' observes the following:

> "Stratification systems which provide little opportunity for social mobility may be described as 'closed', those with a relatively high rate of social mobility as 'open'. In closed systems an individual's position is largely ascribed. Often it is fixed at birth and there is little he can do to change his status. Caste provides an example of a closed stratification system. An individual automatically belongs to the caste of his parents and, except in rare instances, spends the rest of his life in that status. By comparison, social class, the system of stratification in capitalist industrial society, provides an example of an open system. Some sociologists claim that an individual's class position is largely achieved. It results from his personal qualities and abilities and the use he makes of them rather than ascribed characteristics such as the status of his parents or the colour of his skin. By comparison with the caste, the rate of social mobility in class system is high.

> A person's position in a stratification system may have important effects on many areas of his life. It may enhance or reduce his 'life chances', that is his chances of obtaining those things defined as desirable and avoiding those things defined as undesirable in his society. Referring to Western society Gerth and Mills state that life chances include, 'Everything from the chance to stay alive during the first year after birth to the chance to view fine arts, the

---

[81]BAWS, Vol.17, part 3 p.520-521

chance to remain healthy and grow tall, and if sick to get well again quickly, the chance to avoid becoming a juvenile delinquent and very crucially, the chance to complete an intermediary or higher educational grade... Many sociologists would see these differences in life chances as a direct consequence of social stratification."[82]

The three inferences dealt in detail in the previous sections namely the divine sanction, endogamy and the graded inequality provides strong premise to conclude that caste system is a closed form of stratification. To jot down the reasons,

1. The divine sanction worn by caste system makes it unalterable and hard to question the closed form of its stratification.

Ideals as norms are good and are necessary. Neither a society nor an individual can do without a norm. But a norm must change with changes in time and circumstances. No norm can be permanently fixed. There must always be room for revaluation of the values of our norm. The possibility of revaluing values remains open only when the institution is not invested with sacredness. Sacredness prevents revaluation of its values. Once sacred, always sacred.[83]

2. Endogamy introduces exclusivity to caste thus making it a self-enclosed unit, in other words, caste system becomes closed form of stratification one and only through the rule of endogamy.

Dr. Ketkar defines caste as "a social group having two characteristics: (i) membership is confined to those who are born of members and includes all persons so born; (ii) the members are forbidden by an inexorable social law to marry outside the group".[84]

---

[82]Sociology Themes and perspectives, M Haralambos with R.M.Heald, p.26

[83]BAWS, Vol.7 p.31

[84]BAWS, Vol.1 p.7

... He speaks of Prohibition of Intermarriage and Membership by Autogeny as the two characteristics of Caste. I submit that these are but two aspects of one and the same thing, and not two different things as Dr. Ketkar supposes them to be. If you prohibit intermarriage the result is that you limit membership to those born within the group. Thus the two are the obverse and the reverse sides of the same medal.[85]

To understand clearly, Dr.Ketkar only bifurcates the concept of endogamy and presents it as the two characteristics of caste.

3. The principle of graded inequality ensures the continuity of stratification made by the caste system to remain closed. This is because no two castes are co-equals. They are simultaneously placed over some castes and below some castes with the only exception of two castes- the one at the top over which none exist and the other at the bottom below which no caste exist. Thus the principle of graded inequality binds each caste with ascending scale of reverence toward castes placed higher in order from itself and descending scale of contempt toward castes placed lower than itself, thus completely nullifying the possibility of any two castes to join hands together. Any chance of a caste to question the supremacy of upper castes has to be simultaneously met with the voluntary relinquishment of the supremacy it has over the lower castes, which no caste group would readily give up.

Thus, caste system is undoubtedly a closed form of stratification. While endogamy 'makes' it a closed form of stratification, its divine sanctity prohibits the questioning of its stratification and the graded inequality established by it ensures the continuity of its stratification in a closed form.

---

[85]BAWS, Vol.1 p.8

IVe
'Social Inequality' in the context of Caste System and to the cause of studying Unmarriageability

Statement one- Social stratification is nothing but a particular form of social inequality. Therefore, the social stratification established by caste system naturally could form the basis in understanding and exclusively defining 'social inequality' in the closer context of caste system. Such an attempt is nothing more than evaluating a substance on the basis of its properties.

Statement two- Social inequalities persist because of endogamy. So far, in the sub-chapters IVa to IVd, I have made ample arguments along with resourceful extracts of Dr.Ambedkar in support of the above two statements. And I safely assume that none would step forward to fallaciously argue that caste system does not give rise to any social inequalities or to wickedly conceal the effects of endogamy in sustaining caste. With this note, without the slightest hesitation I propose that endogamy is the genesis of social inequality, when one purposefully considers the Hindu society through the operation of caste system. I repeat. Endogamy is the sole cause for castes to sustain and thereby which caste system certainly create and sustain social inequalities. Hence a simple syllogistic reasoning is suffice to infer that endogamy does play its part in creating and sustaining social inequalities. There can be no denial in that. But to what extent it does so is a justifiable question that can be entertained.

I must be wrong if I attribute endogamy to be the sole cause for the prevailing social inequalities. Other forces like power, prestige, wealth etc. do play their part in denying equality. But that should not undermine the predominance of endogamy in dictating the structure of inequality in the social sphere of the Hindu society. Realizing caste system as the fundamental dogma of the Hindu social order would expose the function of endogamy as the 'genesis' of social inequality and not just as one among many others causes or forces. In fact, endogamy is the paramount force that dictates the power, prestige, wealth or any other force leading to social inequalities. Forget not, it is the heart beat of caste system and in it's beating flows inequality all throughout the Hindu society. Is not endogamy safeguarding the extent of power, prestige and wealth being held by each caste? Is not endogamy deterring the dilution of social inequality by averting the possibility of marital intermixing of caste? Is not endogamy maintaining an everlasting status quo of inequality within the social structure created by caste system? It would be an absolute absurdness to make a statement in negative. Forces may be multiple 'causing' inequality within the Hindu society but the inequality is 'sustained' primarily through endogamy. Each caste is socially superior to some castes but this social inequality is sustained through endogamy which is being passed on in an unaltered mode from the previous generation to the present generation and would be passed on from the present generation to the next generation and so on. The Brahmins might personify purity, sanctity and holiness but the Brahmin caste ensures the continuity of their social superiority only through the presence of endogamy and strict abidance to it. The Unmarriageables are considered impure, profane and unclean but they cannot escape from their inferior social status because of the complete arrest of the practice of exogamy in the caste determined Hindu society. Some might be intrigued by this statement. Let me to expound further.

The question of how the caste of a person is determined is an important one it is so because *Caste is still 'the foundation of the Indian social fabric'... Every Hindu (using the term in its most elastic sense) is born into a caste and his caste determines his religious, social, economic and domestic life from the cradle to the grave.*[86]

Well, the answers that come as an immediate response to the above question is that caste is determined by birth... *This Established Order is a hereditary order both in status as well as in function. Once a Touchable, always a Touchable. Once an Untouchable, always an*

---

[86]BAWS, Vol.5 p.6

Untouchable. Once a Brahmin, always a Brahmin. Once a sweeper, always a sweeper. Under it, those who are born high, remain high; those who are born low, remain low. In other words, the Established Order is based on an inexorable law of karma or destiny, which is fixed once for all and can never be changed. This destiny has no relation to the merits of the individuals living under it."[87]

The Supreme Court on 19th January 2018, in the case of Sunita Singh V. State of Uttar Pradesh[88] has held that a person's caste is determined by birth and the same cannot be changed by marriage.

Caste is determined by birth. This statement is only half-true and is not complete. In fact, it is in the illusion of the completeness of statement the required understanding that the statement is leading to is missed. When it is said that caste is determined by birth the general inference made by the scholars and sociologists is, through birth the caste of the person is determined. But the implication of the statement is not over yet. Pensiveness would further lead us to complete inference. If caste is determined by birth, what determines birth becomes the next crucial question. For sure, it is not karma or destiny. In the society driven by the rules of the caste, it is the custom of endogamy that determines birth. For whom to and whom not to marry is fixed only by the endogamous rule of caste system. A newborn baby ascribes the status of a Brahmin only from its biological Brahmin father and biological Brahmin mother. If the rule of endogamy is not complied with, the caste of the newborn would accordingly degenerate to the extent of exogamy involved in its birth. Therefore, caste is purely determined by endogamy and its rules, and not exactly by birth. Birth is just a collateral event through which endogamy ensures the continuation of castes. Hence caste is not truly 'pre' determined by birth or karma or destiny but in fact is determined by its founding principle of endogamy. It is under the misleading pretext of birth, endogamy remains cunningly concealed in its determination of caste

---

[87]BAWS, Vol.5 p.25

[88]Civil Appeal No. 487 of 2018 (Arising from SLP(C) No. 7181 of 2016)

that each and every individual should belong to. This much should not be forgotten. Thus I caution that whenever it is held that a person's caste is determined by birth, what should be remembered and regarded is the real determining role of endogamy and birth being a mere event for such determination of caste. Caste is determined by endogamy and birth is a mere event through which caste is conveyed and inherited. While endogamy determines caste, birth causes its succession and nothing more than that. Endogamy makes the caste hereditary and birth is only an event through which caste succession takes place.

Being aware of endogamy in determining caste would dispose the following misunderstandings too. Caste is a closed stratification system under which a person's position is always fixed and hardly there is a scope for social mobility. There can be no doubt with regard to this. But the misconception lies in understanding that a person's position is fixed 'by' birth. At the most, a person's position is fixed 'at' birth and not by 'birth', while the reason for the fixed position of a person should be attributed completely to endogamy. It is always the rule of endogamy that determines in what position a person should remain all through her/his life. After all, the availability of social superiority to a Brahmin is only because of the abidance to the rule of endogamy by her/his parents. Thus, it is endogamy and not birth that makes caste a closed stratification system. Hence, damaging, disturbing and diluting the rule of endogamy would naturally tend to open up the caste's stratification system.

Therefore what makes the Hindu Established Order fixed is the practice of endogamy. It is endogamy which is effecting the Established Order to be based on an inexorable law of karma or destiny which is fixed once for all and can never be changed. While the effect is not at all false the awareness that endogamy is the real cause for such effect is alarmingly required.

IVf
The peculiarity of the Social Inequality within Hindu society

Social inequalities are prevalent in every society. But the Hindu social order creates and sustains them in the manner and form that is unknown and untried in any other society. The method it devises is wickedly ingenious as the social status is primarily determined by the hymeneal relationship between a man and a woman, graded up or down, by the caste they come from. Such determination of social status is not known in any other societies. Even in the case of many tribal communities where endogamy is the norm, social status is never connected with such norm. But the Hindu society strangely does so. It connects social status with endogamy. It prescribes endogamy for the preservation of caste and thereby for the maintenance of accorded social status of each caste, while any deviation from it through exogamy would lead to degradation of social status.

Marriage and family are the fundamental institutions of a society. Moreover, marriage leads to creation of a family and families are the basic social unit in the formation of a society. While this is true to any society, the peculiarity of Hindu society lies in the adulteration of marriage and family via the endogamous rule of caste system. Endogamy introduces stratification within the institution of marriage and family of Hindu society. It is obvious that an Unmarriageable's family does not enjoy equal status with that of a Brahmin's family in the social walks of life. And the succession of this social inequality hereditarily persists and is ensured through the endogamous marriages practised by each caste. Thus the social status of each caste is preserved from generation to generation. In every society, both marriage and family create certain social status roles but the odd characteristic of Hindu society is that the status created through marriage and family is permanently fixed through endogamy. Therefore, social inequality is sustained, (1) through the institution of marriage, (2) based on principle of endogamy.

IVg
The Final Inference- the right understanding of Social Inequality in accordance with the Hindu Social Order

So far, enough reasoning has been consciously made in order to bring to the centre stage the significance of endogamy in dictating, sustaining and preserving the caste system. Endogamy exists like the invisible gravity ever exerting the divisive force of caste system on the society. The sooner its existence is realized, the quicker would arise the consciousness of it being the sustenance of caste system. And this consciousness remains the pre-requisite in rightly forming the process of annihilation of caste.

It would not be an unfair accusation to say that the intellectual class have failed to throw proper light on the Hindu institution of (1) marriage and (2) family. The Hindu institution of family is built upon the governing principles of caste system. As an inevitable consequence, its endogamous prescription governs the Hindu institution of marriage too. In return, it must be understood that the divisive force of caste system also derives its efficacy from the Hindu institution of marriage. Both operate mutually in infecting the society. This fact which is of much significance in the artificial chopping off of the homogenous population has been consciously and constantly overlooked. The institution of marriage of the Hindu society by its compliance to endogamy has provided 'permanency' to the divisions created by the caste system. By 'permanency', I intend that the created divisions are non-susceptible and resistive to any change across time and space. Independent of the passage of time and changes in space, caste system can sustain and keep its divisions intact through the institution of marriage by being in complete compliance to the rule of endogamy. Endogamy is the source and root of the divisions created by the caste system and it is imbibed in the Hindu marriages. The rationale behind the inertness of caste system to time and space and how it remains unaffected over centuries, across generation, withstanding invasions and spatial changes should be attributed to the ploy that the Hindu institution of marriage maintains through endogamy. Endogamy is the tactful fulcrum of the institution of marriage within the Hindu society. As long as it is observed in the name of custom, belief, culture or by whatever reasons, caste system would continue to exist. So long as it is conceived to be a custom, it would deceive us from the divisions it creates and maintains. The Hindu institution of marriage ensures that each caste maintains its exclusivity by not sanctioning marriage alliance across different caste groups. While marriages only among co-equals are sanctioned by it, we should remember that within caste system no two castes are co-equals as the principle of graded hierarchy governs the position of each caste with respect to the rest. Therefore marriages within the caste where its members alone remain co-equals are the only possibility. In this manner, each caste whether its falls under Brahmin, Kshatriya, Vaishya or Shudra has maintained its exclusivity through generations, resisting time. The divisions so made by the caste system are not bound to change as the modus operandi of Hindu institution of marriage does not allow it to. For the divisions to fade, intermixing of caste creating inter-caste kinship is a requisite. While marriage is the only institution through which different and unequal castes could be intermixed and the graded hierarchy of caste system could be disturbed, such possibility is completely ruled out by the Hindu institution of marriage through its fundamental rule to comply with endogamy. As a consequence, inter-caste marriages that alone can create inter-caste kinship becomes an impossibility. And by averting such creation of inter-caste kinship, the divisive potency of caste system remains as vibrant as ever. Social endosmosis is thus prevented forever. In this manner, caste never fails to ensure its succession in the lineage of every Hindu. Hence with any Hindu, irrespective of the caste she or he belongs to, on reaching the marriageable age, there arises the threat of her or him to transgress the boundaries of caste, marry outside and import offspring that is foreign to the caste, the possibility of which is effectively prevented by the Hindu's institution of marriage itself. Indeed, as regarded by Dr.Ambedkar, endogamy is the key to the mystery of caste system. And the mystery survives through the Hindu institution of marriage, transcending time and space.

The inference that endogamy ingrained in the Hindu institution of marriage sustains the caste system is irrefutable. This understanding, from another better perspective, leads us to conclude that within the Hindu society social inequality prevails through the institution of marriage. While endogamy brings into existence the caste system and caste system brings in the social inequality where no two individuals from two different castes are placed on equal footing, the functioning of Hindu institution of marriage in this should not be missed. For, the sole platform in which endogamy operates is the Hindu institution of marriage. Therefore social inequality exists and the cause for it as an institution happens to be the Hindu institution of marriage and as a rule happens to be the rule of endogamy. Targeting the rule or the institution is one and the same. To attain social equality, in other words, to break the rule of endogamy, breaking the present Hindu institution of marriage goes without any saying.

The conjugal right of any Hindu in deciding upon her or his marital partner is acutely suppressed by her or his conjugal duty to comply with endogamy. The endogamous Hindu institution of marriage takes due notice of the caste identity stamped on each and every individual. Only men and women belonging to same caste can marry each other. In other words, marriages can take place only between men and women who are conjugally equal. Bear in mind that no two castes are conjugally equal. Conjugal equality exists only within each caste and not across castes. Since conjugal equality exists only among the members within each caste and not among the individuals coming from different castes, the endogamous Hindu institution of marriage hinders any sort of marriage among conjugal unequals. The principal of descending order of contempt would not allow a conjugally superior upper caste Hindu to entertain a marital alliance with conjugally inferior lower castes.

A critical thinking at this point would make us to understand that conjugal equality maintained within each caste mechanically creates conjugal inequality among the castes thereby retaining the social inequality between the castes. Correlating social status of a Hindu to her or his conjugal status would not be so intriguing if one is able to see that social hierarchy is linked with caste hierarchy. Forget not, caste is an over-reaching ideological system encompassing all aspects of social life of Hindus, in particular, and the other communities, in general.[89] Forget not, caste is a system of social organization.[90] Forget not, the foremost structural property of caste which is endogamy has a direct linkage with social stratification.[91]

Hence when Brahmin women consider Brahmin men alone to be their conjugal equals what arises is not just the conjugal equality within the Brahmin caste but also conjugal inequality between the Brahmin caste and the rest of castes. To be specific, conjugal superiority of the Brahmin caste over the rest of the castes is established out of the desire of the Brahmins to keep themselves exclusive and pure. Let the readers be aware that when I bring in the idea of conjugal equality within a caste, all I am doing is just representing the concept of endogamy in a marital perspective. Therefore conjugal equality within each caste and conjugal inequality among the castes is nothing but prevalence of the rule of endogamy over exogamy. And the adherence to the idea of conjugal equality within a caste and simultaneously averting the martial possibility with conjugal unequals is nothing but the mechanism explaining the existence of the caste itself. In simpler terms, caste means marriage only among the conjugal equals, deterring any such marital alliance between the conjugal unequals. Dr.Ambedkar in 'Caste in India- Their Mechanism, Genesis and Development' holds that the customs of sati, enforced widowhood and girl marriage are nothing but the means available to each caste to prevent the marital import of a conjugal unequal (i.e. an individual from other castes) within its fold. His writings go as:

... In a way, but only in a way, the status of a caste in the Hindu Society varies directly with the extent of the observance of the customs of Sati, enforced widowhood, and girl marriage. But observance of these

---

[89]www.socialogydiscusion.com

[90]class and caste system of society –reatu chaudh

[91]class and caste system of society –reatu chaudh

customs varies directly with the distance (I am using the word in the Tardian sense) that separates the caste. Those castes that are nearest to the Brahmins have imitated all the three customs and insist on the strict observance thereof. Those that are less near have imitated enforced widowhood and girl marriage; others, a little further off, have only girl marriage and those furthest off have imitated only the belief in the caste principle. This imperfect imitation, I dare say, is due partly to what Tarde calls "distance" and partly to the barbarous character of these customs. This phenomenon is a complete illustration of Tarde's law and leaves no doubt that the whole process of caste-formation in India is a process of imitation of the higher by the lower. At this juncture I will turn back to support a former conclusion of mine, which might have appeared to you as too sudden or unsupported. I said that the Brahmin class first raised the structure of caste by the help of those three customs in question. My reason for that conclusion was that their existence in other classes was derivative. After what I have said regarding the role of imitation in the spread of these customs among the non-Brahmin castes, as means or as ideals, though the imitators have not been aware of it, they exist among them as derivatives; and, if they are derived, there must have been prevalent one original caste that was high enough to have served as a pattern for the rest. But in a theocratic society, who could be the pattern but the servant of God?

This completes the story of those that were weak enough to close their doors. Let us now see how others were closed in as a result of being closed out. This I call the mechanistic process of the formation of caste. It is mechanistic because it is inevitable. That this line of approach, as well as the psychological one, to the explanation of the subject has escaped my predecessors is entirely due to the fact that they have conceived caste as a unit by itself and not as one within a System of Caste. The result of this oversight or lack of sight has been very detrimental to the proper understanding of the subject matter and therefore its correct explanation. I will proceed to offer my own explanation by making one remark which I will urge you to bear constantly in mind. It is this: that caste in the singular number is an unreality. Castes exist only in the plural number. There is no such thing as a caste: There are always castes. To illustrate my meaning: while making themselves into a caste, the Brahmins, by virtue of this, created non-Brahmin caste; or, to express it in my own way, while closing themselves in they closed others out. I will clear my point by taking another illustration. Take India as a whole with its various communities designated by the various creeds to which they owe allegiance, to wit, the Hindus, Mohammedans, Jews, Christians and Parsis. Now, barring the Hindus, the rest within themselves are non-caste communities. But with respect to each other they are castes. Again, if the first four enclose themselves, the Parsis are directly closed out, but are indirectly closed in. Symbolically, if Group A wants to be endogamous, Group B has to be so by sheer force of circumstances.

Now apply the same logic to the Hindu society and you have another explanation of the "fissiparous" character of caste, as a consequence of the virtue of self-duplication that is inherent in it. Any innovation that seriously antagonises the ethical, religious and social code of the Caste is not likely to be tolerated by the Caste, and the recalcitrant members of a Caste are in danger of being thrown out of the Caste, and left to their own fate without having the alternative of being admitted into or absorbed by other Castes. Caste rules are inexorable and they do not wait to make nice distinctions between kinds of offence. Innovation may be of any kind, but all kinds will suffer the same penalty. A novel way of thinking will create a new Caste for the old ones will not tolerate it. The noxious thinker respectfully called Guru (Prophet) suffers the same fate as the sinners in illegitimate love. The former creates a caste of the nature of a religious sect and the latter a type of mixed caste. Castes have no mercy for a sinner who has the courage to violate the code. The penalty is excommunication and the result is a new caste. It is not peculiar Hindu psychology that induces the excommunicated to form themselves into a caste; far from it. On the contrary, very often they have been quite willing to be humble members of some caste (higher by preference) if they could be admitted within its fold. But castes are enclosed units and it is their conspiracy with clear conscience that compels the excommunicated to make themselves into a caste. The logic of this obdurate circumstance is merciless, and it is in obedience to its force that some unfortunate groups find themselves enclosed, because others in enclosing, themselves have closed them out, with the result that new groups (formed on any basis obnoxious to the caste rules) by a mechanical law are constantly being converted into castes to a bewildering multiplicity. Thus is told the second tale in the process of Caste formation in India.[92]

Thus the reiteration of conjugal equality within each caste is a conspirative requisite to retain the conjugal inequality among the different castes. Brahmin caste by closing themselves in via the idea of conjugal equality closed out the other castes thereby not only creating non-Brahmin castes but also infusing conjugal inequality between the Brahmin and non-Brahmin castes.

Marriage is a universal social institution and if in this institution when two individuals from two different castes are stamped to be conjugally unequals, it is nothing but one fundamental feature of social inequality that is glaringly in existence. The conjugal inequality within the caste system, no doubt divides the entire social structure. There would have arisen no concern if it is about marital selection of whom to marry and whom not to marry based on certain justifiable criteria like character, education, age, language etc. But the criterion of caste is more of marital restriction than about marital selection. Moreover, if such restriction happens to be the mechanism through which social superiority of upper castes and social inferiority of lower castes is maintained the practice is nothing short of a divisive custom leading to social inequality and degradation of human dignity.

The endogamous Hindu institution of marriage reiterates that not all Hindus are conjugally equal. It prescribes marital alliance only between the equals and condemns any among the unequals. When caste remains as a restriction within the institution of marriage, what happens is the retainment and reinforcement of social inequality within the society. The

---

[92]BAWS, Vol.1 p.20

function of the endogamous institution of Hindu marriage when wholly understood is in its precise perfection of creating a replicated new generation dittoing the exact caste structure and divisions of the preceding generation. It manoeuvres effectively in carbon copying the conjugal inequality present as caste divisions in one generation to the next generation. However, it is easy to lose sight of this replication process. The reason is- a generation does not come into existence at one go. As an average period it takes about 2 to 3 decades between the birth of parents and the birth of their offspring. Hence the abidance to conjugal equality, i.e. endogamy, in the marriage of the parents continuing to govern the marriage of the offsprings decades later would not be noticed by many as a grave process of 'biogenesis' through which caste system thrives- across generation unaffected by the passage of time. Each generation 'reproduces' the caste system through its institution of marriage which sanctions the marital alliance only between the conjugal equals. When a generation ensures that all its members have married on caste basis what it eventually creates is a new generation of offsprings born stamped with the caste identity of their parents, thereby ensuring the permanency of social structure based on caste. Thus the social damage that the endogamous Hindu institution of marriage is causing should not be overlooked just because it arises only during the brief instance of marital decisions and arrangements taken in every Hindu's life. The biogenesis of caste is ensured only during such brief marital moments. In other words, marriages happen between conjugal equals to produce (i.e. reproduce) conjugally equal offsprings. Henceforth, as a collective result of all the marriages that lead to caste biogenesis, a generation reproduces another new generation exactly with the same caste structure and divisions as its own. The damage that the Hindu institution of marriage causes is not immediate. It is not readily evident or easily visible. Rather, it is slow, steady, poignant and persistent.

Thus the final inference I wanted to put forth is this: the prevalence of conjugal inequality within the Hindu institution of marriage reflects nothing short of the social inequality as determined by the Hindu society. In simple words, the presence of conjugal inequality should be equated to the presence of social inequality. They are two sides of the same coin. Thus when attempts are made to study the social inequality within the Hindu society (perhaps the Indian society), it should centre on the dissection of concept of conjugal inequality. Because from conjugal inequality arise other forms of social inequality. Such outcomes, whether arising directly or indirectly, is of less significance. The fact of relevance is the undeniable truth that conjugal inequality is paving the way for social inequality. Remember, Indian synonym for social inequality is conjugal inequality. This is the right understanding of social inequality in accordance with the Hindu social order. And, any curious mind that is sincere and desperate to understand the 'social inequality' in the context of caste system and to the cause of studying Unmarriageability would centre her thoughts around the concept of conjugal inequality found in the Hindu institution of marriage. Eventually, redefining social inequality as conjugal inequality becomes important and inevitable.

V

Conclusion: Unmarriageability is the spearhead against the Caste System

To ignore conjugal inequality in the context of social inequality is a wilful ignorance. Any reformer or an activist trying to be the scourge and scavenger of the caste dictated Hindu society has to focus upon the issue of conjugal inequality. Any refrainment to do so would reflect only her or his apathy or wrong conception or the presence of both with regard to the annihilation of caste.

So, what does taking up of the issue of conjugal inequality means? To start with, it means bringing into the realm of discussion the issue of Unmarriageability. This would inevitably lead to confront the cause of it- the practice of endogamy. This scheme of action alone has the vigour to disturb the social inequality established by the Hindu social order in general and the caste system in particular.

Therefore, I emphasize on Unmarriageability as the spearhead to be used against the caste system. Why it should be so? A keen and conscious reader would be aware at this stage that all my efforts in the chapters so far have in some way or the other been to bring into the light that endogamy is the modus operandi of caste system. I have attempted my best, through the writings of Dr.Ambedkar, to place utmost significance on endogamy. Hence I would not venture to explain about its significance again. But all I wanted you to take notice of is this- conjugal inequality is nothing but another version of representing the prevalence of Unmarriageability. Both represent the same idea of endogamy. For instance, to say that a Shudra is conjugally unequal to a Brahmin or a Shudra is an Unmarriageable to a Brahmin are nothing but the two versions of the same concept, i.e. reflecting endogamy as prescribed by the Hindu social order. Endogamy is the genesis of social inequality within the Hindu society. Hence when conjugal inequality (endogamy) plays the primary role in the existence of social inequality within the Hindu society, the solution to attain equality lies in questioning the stigma of Unmarriageability. There can be no better conclusion than to hold on to the conviction that the stigma of Unmarriageability is the spearhead with which we can pierce the heart and soul of the caste system.

The facets of Unmarriageables' movement had been many- polemics, temple entry agitations, struggle for civil and political rights etc. Any movement gain its own momentum with the objectives it accomplishes and progresses it make. It would start with the buffer issues enveloping the main plight and the ultimate purpose of its existence would acquire vigour as it succeeds in the strategies it had devised, parallelly moulding the time receptive. The demand for proper representation making way for the declaration of Poorna Swaraj is how the Indian freedom movement waded through the colonial rule. Likewise, the Unmarriageables' movement is ripe enough to bring into centre stage the issue of Unmarriageability. Not to be stranded around, it is high time that the Unmarriageables wield the weapon called Unmarriageability to annihilate caste.

CHAPTER 6

UNMARRIAGEABILITY: WHY THE STIGMA SHOULD BECOME THE SPEARHEAD?

I. Confronting the Dissenters beforehand- the Significance of Unmarriageability.

II. Rationale One: The long hiatus of the Unmarriageables in reviving Buddhism.

III. Rationale Two: Unmarriageability has the resistance to thwart the anti- Reservation outlooks and efforts.

IV. Rationale Three: Unmarriageability exposes the present Young Generation's submissiveness before the Caste System.

V. Rationale Four: Unmarriageability would stream the activism towards Annihilation of Caste.

I

Confronting the Dissenters beforehand- the Significance of Unmarriageability

Caste Hindus hold the notion of Unmarriageability. They cherish it in their beliefs and practices and not the Unmarriageables. Therefore, it is quite natural for the Unmarriageables to think that it is not their concern to question the stigma of Unmarriageability. With the flair, only the flair and not the view, resembling the writings of their saviour, Dr.Ambedkar, they might convey to the caste Hindus that "to discard or not the practise of endogamy is a question for you to consider and not for me to agitate. If you think, it is bad manners not to respect the sacredness of human personality, leave your caste consciousness and the notion of Unmarriageability. If you rather be a fanatic caste Hindu than be a gentleman, then shut the doors and damn yourself for I don't care to come". It may be even because of this stand, the stigma of Unmarriageability has not been yet seen as a social problem. After all if it is not for the Unmarriageables, no other castes from the Hindu fold possess the necessity to drag out the issue of Unmarriageability. It must not be forgotten that the ideals of Brahminism are deep-rooted in this society. And each caste within any Varna has its own personal interest in retaining the caste system and in not annihilating it. The deceitful benefit of graded inequality would discourage each and every caste in destroying the caste system. The Unmarriageables are the only exception to it. The indignation of the Unmarriageables alone has the potential to annihilate caste. Superficially, it may not be the 'exclusive' responsibility of the Unmarriageables to annihilate caste. But they are duty-bound to express their indignation against the oppressive caste system. To revolt against the caste system and shake its foundation should definitely be their trait. In such a revolt and resistance, their efforts towards annihilation of caste would only be an inevitable fallout. And in this process, if the fading of caste begins, it is the benefit the society derives from the Unmarriageables and not the other way around. The social psychology of the caste Hindus is programmed to practise Unmarriageability. It is because of this plain reason that each caste sustains itself by imposing the stigma of

Unmarriageability on the rest of the castes. The foundation of caste system is nothing but marriageability only within each caste; in other words, Unmarriageability between the two different castes. I submit this as a reminder to the dissenters within the Unmarriageable community who share the opinion that it is not their concern to highlight the social evil of Unmarriageability. A change in their opinion could avert a blunder from being made and better the cause of social amelioration.

To those who still remain rigid in their beliefs and are not prickled by the existence of Unmarriageability as the social philosophy of Hinduism, let me remind them further that we are not dealing with the expressions of caste system like the twin-tumbler system, denial of temple entry, caste specific graveyards, the festivals exclusive for each caste etc. We are not dealing with the expressions of caste, to say, Untouchability. At present, Unmarriageability is our concern. By Unmarriageability we do not mean merely an expression of caste. Rather, Unmarriageability is what makes up a caste. To be precise and concise in defining caste, we can say caste is endogamy and endogamy is Unmarriageability. Viewed in proper light, Unmarriageability only means the custom of endogamy, the sustaining feature of caste. Replacing caste with Unmarriageability and Unmarriageability with caste would not change an iota of their meaning conveyed anywhere in any context. If the Hindu religion needs to be a religion of social equality than an amendment of its code to provide for common graveyards is not suffice. What is required is to purge the doctrine of Chaturvarna. And how to perceive this doctrine? The answer lies to the question– what sustains the Chaturvarna as four? It is the principle of Unmarriageability that retains the Varna as Chaturvarna. There is no need to use diverse terms like 'Manudharma', 'Chaturvarna', 'Endogamy', 'Caste' etc. Replace all of them with 'Unmarriageability'. I can assure you that there is no possibility for a new connotation to arise. Such is the significance of Unmarriageability as a principle, stigma and menace. Therefore, what is required to annihilate caste is the abolition of practice of Unmarriageability. Unless Unmarriageables understand this and garner their efforts towards abolition of Unmarriageability, their lonesome journey towards emancipation will not come to an end. For, as long as they allow the caste to survive, it would stand in their way towards emancipation. Maybe, the Unmarriageables are not bothered about the existence of caste. But always, there exists caste bothering about the existence of Unmarriageability in denying the inherent human personality. This being the fundamental justification, let me put forth other rationales one by one calling for the conversion of stigma of Unmarriageability into a spearhead of the Unmarriageables.

II
Rationale One: The long hiatus of the Unmarriageables in reviving Buddhism

Not long ago, Dr.Ambedkar said to Mr.Bevarali Nikolas, a Journalist from London: *the keynote of my policy is that we are not a sub-continent of the Hindus but a separate element in the national life.*[93]

And indeed, the great man of character never contradicted his words. While leaving for Nepal, on November 13th, 1956, Mr.Y.C.Shankereand Shastri very respectfully enquired at the Airport, New Delhi, "*Babasaheb, in view of your failing health how far will it be possible for you to tour India to propagate the Dhamma?*"[94] *Babasaheb felt slightly irritated but strongly asserted, for the task like propagation of Buddhism I am not at all ill. I am prepared to utilise every moment of my remaining life for the great task of revival and propagation of Buddha's Dhamma in Bharat. "I am going to administer "Deeksha" to lakhs of people in Bombay in the month of December. The kind of great revival meeting took place in Nagpur on the 14th October 1956 will also be arranged in Bombay where millions of people will be converted to Buddhism. Conversion meeting like the one which took place in Nagpur will also be organized in other cities of India...I have been struggling throughout my life to abolish this evil practise of division based on caste*

---

[93]BAWS, Vol.17, part 1 p.350 or Verdict on India, p.41
[94]Dr.Ambedkar passed away on December 6, 1956 aged 65 years

and mutual hatred. In reality, I feel guilty of starting late the work of revival of Buddhism in India. But even then I hope and believe that my people who, sacrificing their own comforts, have been faithfully following me. I hope and I trust they will continue to struggle sincerely to propagate the Buddha Dhamma in India.[95]

The leader believed that his people will sacrifice everything to establish Buddhism in India. Were his people, the Unmarriageables, been sincere followers and true Ambedkarites? Though I do not wish, I am afraid that I have to answer in negative, to the least with regard to the question of denouncing Hinduism. The census data of overall population of the Unmarriageables and the Buddhist would speak for itself. The Unmarriageables always have the greatest responsibility and duty to respond to the hope and trust Dr.Ambedkar had on them. Any person who knows well about the great revival of Buddhism that took place in Nagpur on the 14th October of 1956 would for sure pause to remark that the Unmarriageables were the most unfortunate with regard to the untimely demise of Dr.Ambedkar on 6th December of 1956. The mighty man had been a threat to Hinduism and he would have surely made the religion to tremble and stumble had his life had been as long as his achievements. His life had been unquestionably great but unfortunately not long. A misfortune, indeed, to the Sunken community he tirelessly fought for. And a massive misfortune to the Buddhism and its revival in India.

The problem is this: the Hindu religion treats the Unmarriageables as a distinct entity. And the Unmarriageables do not seem to have a thought to realize it. It would be both a blunder and burden until the Unmarriageables stop identifying themselves with the Hindu religion. Dr.Ambedkar never failed to realize the importance of the functionality of the religion. He believed that religion had been and would continue to be essential for mankind. This could be understood from the speech he delivered on 15th October 1956 on the occasion of conversion:

---

[95]BAWS, Vol.17, part 1 p.449

Religion is necessary for the poor. Religion is necessary for the Depressed People. The poor man survives on hope. The root of life lies in hope. What will happen to the life if the hope is lost? Religion makes hopeful, and gives a message to the depressed and the poor—do not be afraid, life will be hopeful, it will be! Therefore, the poor and the depressed mankind clings to the religion.[96]

Though he did not side with the communists in holding that religion is the opium of the masses, he had an unshakable conviction that the Hindu religion is the opium of the Unmarriageables. In his absence, the Unmarriageables are no more inclined to take caution of this. They no longer exhibit their zeal to come out of the Hindu religion. And that is what opium does. Though it imbalances anyone who consumes it, countless throng for it. The Hindu religion exactly does the same to the Unmarriageables. Though it imposes on them the disability of unmarriageability and brands them as Unmarriageables, the Unmarriageables are not tempted to go out of its fold. A man hardly questions the manner in which he has been brought up. He rarely escapes from the way he has been brought up. And when this collude with the area of religion, the submissiveness is much more. It becomes impossible for the rationalization to defeat the socialization. Dr.Ambedkar said in the same conversion speech: *Some people say, "Why did you take so much time to get converted? What were you doing all these days? This is the question of importance. Convincing a religion is not an easy task. That is not the mission of a single person. Any person thinking of religion will come to know this. No man in the world shoulder as much responsibility as do I. If I get a long life, I will fulfill my planned work.*[97]

Though the deviancy of denouncing the Hindu religion by the Unmarriageables is a just cause, it is also a mammoth task. It is mammoth because the Unmarriageables are born as Hindus and are accustomed to the Hindu way of life. *The Untouchables have the culture of the Hindu*

---

[96]BAWS, Vol.17, part 3 p.541

[97]BAWS, Vol.17, part 3 p.540

community. They observe the religious rites of the Hindu community. They recognize the sacred as well as the secular laws of the Hindus. They celebrate the Hindu festivals.[98]It is a tough challenge ahead for any good Samaritan to alter their religious socialization. The task of denouncing Hinduism and reviving Buddhism demands courage and perseverance. To reiterate this argument, the following thoughts of Dr.Ambedkar would not become out of context: *... whether the Buddhist way of life of reaching the goal is a lasting one, or whether the communist way of bringing about the goal is the lasting one. Because there is no use in pursuing a certain path, if it is going to lead you to the jungle, if it is going to lead you to anarchy, there is no use pursuing it. But, if you are assured that the path you are asked to follow is slow, may be devious, may be with long detours, yet if ultimately makes you reach a safe, sound ground so that the ideals you are pursuing are there to help you, to mould your life permanently, it is much better, in my judgment, to follow the slower path, and the devious path rather than to rush up and to take what we call short cuts. Short cuts in life are always dangerous, very dangerous*[99]*...the Buddha's way, as I said, is a long way, perhaps some people may say, a tedious way. But I have no doubt about it that it is the surest way.*[100]

The Unmarriageables embracing Buddhism may not lead to annihilation of caste, for the caste Hindus would be caste Hindus along with their innumerable castes to instil discriminations and divisions, with or without the Unmarriageables. But Buddhism, with its principles of equality, liberty and fraternity, can emancipate the Unmarriageables irrespective of caste Hindus' presence. So, are the Unmarriageables prepared to be their own light? No certain answer lies to sound affirmative. They no longer harangue the Hindu religion with indignation. Even if they do so, theirs remain as passing references lacking purpose and action behind such utterances. They have precariously allowed the wave of Buddhism to recede. The wave has receded. Their desire to embrace

---

[98]BAWS, Vol.5 p.133

[99]BAWS, Vol.17, part 3 p.551

[100]BAWS, Vol.17, part 3 p.554

Buddhism succumbs to their hesitation in denouncing Hinduism. They are unprepared to come out of the religion that torments them. The agenda of religious conversion is no longer the epicentre of Unmarriageables' movement. Their presence is no longer a threat to Hindu religion. Their present evinces this. As they should strive for a Buddhist movement instead of taking shortcuts, it would also be inimical, I believe, to leave their future to depend solely on a Buddhist movement to surface. What if, if such a renaissance does not arise? One who has the hindsight of the impact of Buddhism on the overall population of Unmarriageables so far would naturally be wary of such a situation. It is with this rationale, I want to remind about the significance of raising the issue of Unmarriageability.

When the Unmarriageables do not cease to be Hindus altogether, it becomes more pertinent for them to annihilate the caste system that the Hindu religion upholds. Unmarriageability has remained a mute subject and they should no longer allow it to remain so. In fact, the cry against the Unmarriageability is only an outcome of the right understanding of the teachings of Buddha. *"In his philosophy, law had a place only as a safeguard against the breaches of liberty and equality; but he did not believe that law can be a guarantee for breaches of liberty or equality".* This is true in the case of caste which is nothing but the negation of liberty and equality. *He gave the highest place to fraternity as the only real safeguard against the denial of liberty or equality or fraternity which was another name for brotherhood or humanity, which was again another name for religion.*[101] And nothing can so evidently express the blossoming of fraternity which is so far foreign to the Hindu religion except the happening of exogamous marriages which is possible only by purging the stigma of Unmarriageability. The Unmarriageables continuing to remain within the fold of Hindu religion should not evade themselves from this responsibility. If they still remain as Hindus ignoring the issue of Unmarriageability their lives share the same destiny of a goat that is under the butcher's knife. Therefore, if the Unmarriageables remain as Hindus

---

[101]BAWS, Vol.17, part 3 p.503

they should protest Unmarriageability or else they should discard their filthy Hindu identity. If they choose the former, here goes the caution: *None should misunderstand the main object of our movement as being Hindu Social Reform. The principal object of our movement is only to achieve the social freedom for the Untouchables; it is equally true that this freedom cannot be secured without conversion. I do accept that the Untouchables need equality as well and to secure equality is also one of the objectives of our movement. But nobody can say that this equality can be achieved only by remaining in Hindu religion otherwise equality will not be achieved. Before me, there are two ways of achieving the equality. The equality will be achieved either by remaining in the Hindu fold or by the conversion. If the equality is to be achieved by remaining in the Hindu fold, mere removal of polluting contact will not serve the purpose. The equality can be achieved only when intercaste dinners and marriages take place. This means that the Chaturvarna must be abolished and the Brahminic Religion must be uprooted. Is it possible? And if not, will it be wise to expect the treatment of equality by remaining in the Hindu religion? And can you be successful in your efforts? Comparatively the path of Conversion is far easy.*[102]

III

Rationale Two: Unmarriageability has the resistance to thwart the anti- Reservation outlooks and efforts

To dispel in advance any unnecessary misunderstandings, I remind the readers to bear two things in mind: firstly, the purpose of any reservation policy is to ensure representation from the marginalized sections. Therefore, though the term 'reservation' is in common parlance, the appropriate usage reflecting its purpose would be 'representation'. However, for the sake of convenience, only for the sake of convenience to converse with the adversaries and not to disturb the ongoing reservation debate by introducing a new nomenclature, I settle myself to use the

---

[102]BAWS, Vol.17, part 3 p.136

misnomer 'reservation'. For, 'reservation' is in fact a representation introduced against and to resist the centuries-old reservation system of caste determining who should belong to the privileged and the servile classes. Secondly, 'reservation' is often propagated in the mass media as a privilege given to the marginalized communities. To have reservation (i.e. representation) is not a privilege but a right of the minorities. I repeat, to have representation is their right and not a privilege.

Based on another misconception that reservation is a kind of poverty alleviation program there exist this 'creamy layer' argument that the Unmarriageables who are economically well-off should be placed outside the purview of reservation system. Though many logics have been put forth for such exclusion they lack the tenacity to be accepted upon as reasons. But despite the want of a sound rationale, the fact that the 'creamy layer' argument is garnering the majority opinion should not be ignored as this would jeopardize the prospects of social justice in India. The Unmarriageables should be wary of this development. Unlike a poverty alleviation policy which is based on the economic backwardness, the presence of reservation policy is purely and solely based on the concept of social backwardness and the prevalence of social stigmas that denies and diminishes the sacredness of human personality of the Unmarriageables. Therefore, when these stigmas continue to prevail, it becomes more crucial to safeguard the continuation of reservation system. The necessity of the medicine should not be questioned until the disappearance of the disease. It is absurd to do so. So, for how long should the reservation system continue? Till the social stigmas are eradicated, reservation would and should continue. Forget not, we live in a society that has denied, since the Gandhian times, the existence of caste and the tantrums it makes. The Indian society suffers from the Alzheimer's disease of caste system. It has selective amnesia specifically with regard to the social calamities being caused by the caste system. Being so, there is no point for the Unmarriageables to campaign for the justifications found in reservation. Their outcries for social justice could be heard by anyone but definitely not by the caste Hindus who pretend to be deaf. Only a delusionist would continue with the hope that the caste Hindus would understand the rationale behind the reservation someday or the other. Therefore, rather than reiterating again and again about the principles of reservation system what the Unmarriageable should do is to cement the reservation system with the social stigmas and reiterate firmly on the continuation of reservation system till the social stigmas cease to continue. The purpose of reservation system is the removal of social inequality and there lies no reason for its removal until the attainment of social equality. The Unmarriageables should make a strategic placement of the stigmas sustaining social inequality at the centre of reservation debate. They should coerce the adversaries of reservation to deal with the social stigmas within the Hindu society before touching upon the question of reservation. This undoubtedly would fortify the reservation system.

During the election campaign at Ramdaspur, Jullundar, Punjab on October 27, 1951, Dr.Ambedkar touched upon the connection that exists between reservation and Untouchability. He said: *The reservation of seats for the scheduled castes is for 10 years only. I wanted this reservation should remain for such time as untouchability is there, but the congress leader, late Sardar Vallabhai Patel opposed me. So the other persons who were there in the committee also had to support Sardar because they belonged to his party. Therefore, we should try to send our true representatives to the assemblies, so that they may safeguard our right and also try to secure this reservation after 10 years.*[103] It is high time to engage the destiny of reservation with the sheer uncertainty in abolition of Untouchability. In the absence of a definite endeavour to annihilate caste, any attempt to remove reservation should not see the light of the day. Till there exist the caste Hindus and the Unmarriageables, there is unquestionable social justification for the Unmarriageables to retain reservation as a matter of right.

To maintain preciseness in the argument, let me brief who is a caste Hindu followed by the realm covered by Untouchability. Clarity on both becomes essential because most of the Hindus are not ready to

---

[103]BAWS, Vol.17, part 3 p.420; The reservation dealt here was with respect to the legislatures.

accept that they are the caste Hindus too and also there is no clarity on what constitutes Untouchability. To define a caste Hindu is not a hard task. At the time of one's marriage proposals if a person is bothered or allows others to be bothered about the caste of her or his life partner, then she or he is a caste Hindu. This is the simple, short and foolproof definition of a caste Hindu. When Unmarriageability is what can be called as caste, any person who considers the members of other castes as Unmarriageables can only be a caste Hindu. Therefore, the meaning of caste Hindu is not limited to a person who practices Untouchability alone. This being so, to what extent Untouchability extends itself? *At the outset it is necessary to have a clear idea as to what is meant by Untouchability. On this point, there can be no difference of opinion. It will be agreed on all hands that what underlies Untouchability is the notion of defilement, pollution, contamination and the ways and means of getting rid of that defilement.*[104] A liberal thinking would allow us to accept that Untouchability, when expressed in the marital form, would include Unmarriageability too. Unmarriageability is simply the notional defilement of Untouchability but in the marital form. To take another perspective, when endogamy or conjugal inequality or Unmarriageability are all nothing but the synonyms expressing the very crux of the caste, it would not be wrong to conclude that Unmarriageability reiterates and reinforces the practice of Untouchability. In either way, as a source or as a derivative, Unmarriageability is inseparable from Untouchability. Therefore till there exists Untouchability, i.e., till there exists caste Hindus and the stigma of Unmarriageability, there is complete social justification for the continuation of reservation as a safeguard against all sorts of social discriminations faced by the Unmarriageables. Reservation is nothing more than the safeguard against discrimination. The relevance of it is no less significant because the problem of discrimination is no less a small problem. Hence, to understand it becomes crucial:

Government of the people and for the people cannot mean Government for the Untouchables; equal opportunity for all cannot mean

---

[104]BAWS, Vol.7 p.249

equal opportunity for the Untouchables; equal rights for all cannot mean equal rights for the Untouchables. All over the country in every nook and corner the Untouchable faces handicaps, suffers discriminations, is meted injustices to the Untouchables, the most unprivileged people in India. The extent to which this is true is known only to the Untouchables who labour under the disadvantages. This discrimination is the strongest barrier against the Untouchables. It prevents them from rising out of it. It has made the life of the Untouchables one of the constant fears of one thing or another, of unemployment, assault, persecution, etc. It is a life of insecurity.

There is another form of discrimination, which though subtle is nonetheless real. Under it a systematic attempt will be made to lower the dignity and status of a meritorious Untouchable. A Hindu leader would be described merely as a great Indian leader. No one would describe him as the leader of Kashmiri Brahmin even though he be one. If a leader who happens to be an Untouchable is to be referred to he will be described as so and so, the leader of the Untouchables. A Hindu doctor would be described as a great Indian doctor. No one would describe him as a Iyengar even though he be one. If a doctor happens to be an Untouchable doctor, he would be referred to as so and so, the Untouchable doctor. A Hindu singer would be described as a great Indian singer. If the same person happens to be an Untouchable he would be described as an Untouchable singer. A Hindu wrestler would be described as a great Indian Gymnast. If he happens to be an Untouchable he would be described as an Untouchable gymnast.

This type of discrimination has its origin in the Hindu view that the Untouchables are an inferior people and however qualified, their great men are only great among the Untouchables. They can never be greater nor even equal to the great men among the Hindus. This type of discrimination, though social in character, is no less galling than economic discrimination.

Discrimination is merely another name for absence of freedom. For as Mr. Tawney says[105]:

> *"There is no such thing as freedom in the market, divorced from the realities of a specific time and place. Whatever else it may or may not imply, it involves the power of choice between alternatives a choice which is real, not merely nominal, between alternatives which exist in fact, not only on paper. It means, in short, the ability to do or refrain from doing definite things, at a definite moment, in definite circumstances, or it means nothing at all. Because a man is most a man when he thinks, wills and acts, freedom deserves the outline things, which poets have said about it; but, as a part of the prose of every day life, it is quite practical and realistic. Every individual possesses certain requirements ranging from the material necessities of existence to the need to express himself in speech and writing, to share in the conduct of affairs of common interests, and to worship God in his own way or to refrain from worshipping him the satisfaction of which it is necessary to his welfare. Reduced to its barest essential, his freedom consists in the opportunity secured by him, within the limits set by nature and the enjoyment of similar opportunities by his fellows, to take the action needed to order to ensure that these requirements are satisfied."*

It is not my intention to add yet another catalogue of essential rights to the liberties of such lists, which already exist; but these are two observations, which apply to all of them. In the first place, if the rights are to be an effective guarantee of freedom, they must not be merely formed, like the right of all who can afford it to dine at the Ritz. They must be such that, whenever the occasion arises to exercise them, they can in fact be exercised. The rights to vote and to combine, if not wholly valueless, are obviously attenuated, when the use of the former means eviction and of the latter the sack; the right to the free choice of an occupation, if the

---

[105]We mean freedom in what labour can do? pp. 83–85.

expenses of entering a profession are prohibitive; the right to justice, if no poor man can pay for it; the right to life, liberty, and the pursuit of happiness, if the environment is such as to ensure that a considerable proportion of those born will die within twelve months, and that the happiness investments of the remainder are a gambling stock. In the second place, the rights which are essential to freedom must be such as to secure the liberties of all, not merely of a minority. Some sage has remarked that marriage would not be regarded as a national institution if, while 5 per cent of the population were polygamous, the majority passed their lives unsolved and unencumbered by husbands or wives. The same is true of freedom. Society in which some groups can do much what they please, while others can do little of what they ought, may have virtues of its own; but freedom is not one of them. It is free in so far, and only in so far, as all the elements composing it are able in fact, and not merely in theory, to make the most of their powers, to grow to their full stature, to do what they conceive to be their duty, and since liberty should not be too austere to have their fling when they feel like it. In so far as the opportunity to lead a life worthy of human beings is restricted to a minority, what is commonly described, as freedom would more properly be called privilege.

The discriminations against the Untouchables are merely the reflections of that deep and strong Hindu sentiment which is carried over in law and administration which justifies the making of distinctions between Hindus and Untouchables to the disadvantage of the Untouchables. Those discriminations have their roots in fear of the Hindus that in a free field, the Untouchables may rise above the prescribed station in life and become a menace to the Hindu Social Order the cardinal principle of which is the maintenance of Hindu superiority and Hindu domination over the Untouchables. So long as the Hindu Social Order lasts, discriminations against the Untouchables continue to exist.[106]

---

[106]BAWS, Vol.5 p.109

Reservation should be understood as the social right available to the Unmarriageables to emancipate themselves amidst the discrimination committed on them by the Hindu society. What is pertinent here is to take note of Unmarriageability as the sustaining source that is ensuring the discrimination to remain forever. As it is only through the stigma of Unmarriageability, caste Hindus continue to be caste Hindus and Unmarriageables remain as Unmarriageables. Untouchability as a form of discrimination reasons out the existence of civil disabilities only. But Unmarriageability touches the nucleus of caste system. It, as a stigma, is the explanation for the root cause of social disabilities suffered by the Unmarriageables. The horror of Dishonour killings rampant in this country is nothing but the stigma of Unmarriageability, an extreme form of Untouchability. So, never ever ignore this blatant truth while dealing with reservation. For, reservation is not a mere right against discrimination. It is the social right of the Unmarriageables against the social discrimination they face. It is an attempt to tackle the Hindu society so that the next generation does not embrace the caste system as a social heritage with the same vigour as we embraced it.

One blindfold argument for the removal of reservation is based on the assumption that the Unmarriageables have achieved enough progress. Only the caste Hindus hold such a view and it is arising out of their fear that they may lose their domination over the Unmarriageables. Dialectically there is no need to entertain the question about the progress made by the Unmarriageables because of reservation even if one fails to sense the maliciousness lying behind such a question. Because, the purpose of reservation, no doubt, is to emancipate Unmarriageables. But, it is nothing more than a safeguard and the removal of reservation has to be axiomatically anteceded by the annihilation of caste. So the subject of discussion in the context of removal of reservation is the crucial question, whether caste has been annihilated or not? Whether Unmarriageables have progressed or not is irrelevant. Unless the answer turns out to be affirmative, it would be a social injustice to deprive Unmarriageables of their right to reservation.

What is the status of annihilation of caste, at present? The non-enforcement of the Scheduled Caste and Scheduled Tribe (Prevention of Atrocities) Act, 1989 to hold the caste Hindus accountable for the atrocities they commit is one instance to show how tough the job of annihilation of caste is. The question of why even special laws become ineffective before the caste system of the Hindu society should not be ignored:

It must be admitted that the legal and the religious sanction were both powerful engines to keep caste going. But there is no doubt that the religious sanction was the primary sanction and caste has been maintained solely by the force of Religious Sanction. This is clear from two circumstances. That the legal sanction was very seldom invoked will have to be admitted. That means that the maintenance of caste was secured by other means. Secondly this legal sanction was in use only till 1850. It was lifted or rather done away with by the Caste Disabilities Removal Act passed in that year by the British Government. Although the legal sanction is withdrawn, caste has gone on without abatement. That could not have happened if caste had not in the Religious Sanction another and more powerful sanction independent of the legal sanction.

That the Religious Sanction is the highest sanction which an institution or a belief can have to support and sustain it, is beyond question. Its power is boundless in its measure and tremendous in its curb. But it is very seldom understood how and whence this Religious Sanction gets this high-grade horsepower. To appreciate this it is necessary to note that the source of authority behind the Religious Sanction is two-fold.

In the first place what is Religious is also social. To quote Prof. Durkheim:[107]

"The really religious beliefs are always common to a determined group, which makes profession of adhering to them and of

---

[107]Elementary Forms of Religious Life. pp. 37–40.

practising the rites connected with them. They are not merely received individually by all the members of this group; they are something belonging to the group, and they make its unity. The individuals which compose it feel themselves united to each other by the simple fact that they have a common faith."

In the second place what is Religious is Sacral. To quote Durkheim again: [108]

"All known religious beliefs whether simple or complex, present one common characteristic; they presuppose a classification of all the things, real and ideal, of which men think, into two classes or, opposed groups, generally designated by two distinct terms- which are translated well enough by the words profane and sacred . . . . . In all the history of human thought there exist no other example of two categories of things so profoundly differentiated or so radically opposed to one another. The traditional opposition of good and bad is nothing besides this; for the good and the bad are only two opposed species of the same class, namely morals, just as sickness and health are two different aspects of the same order of facts, life, while the Sacred and the profane have always and everywhere been conceived by the human mind as two distinct classes, as two worlds between there is nothing in common..... Religious beliefs are the representations which express the nature of sacred things and the relations which they sustain, either with each other or with profane things (while) rites are the rules of conduct which prescribe how a man should comfort himself in the presence of these Sacred objects."

From this it will be clear that the Social, Religious and Sacral beliefs are closely knit. Religious is social though all that is social is not religious. Sacral is social though all that is social is not sacral. On the other hand the religious is both social and sacral.

---

[108]Elementary Forms of Religious Life. p.43.

One source of authority behind the religious sanction comes from the fact, that is, religion is social and the religious beliefs are social beliefs. Religious beliefs are enforced on the individual by the group in the same manner and for the same reasons which leads it to enforce its other non-religious and purely social beliefs. The object is to maintain the integrity of the group and as the integrity of the group is more closely bound up with its religious beliefs, the strictness and severity with which a group punishes the breach of a religious belief is usually greater than the degree of strictness and severity it employs for the chastisement of a person guilty of a breach of a non-religious belief. Social force has an imperative authority before which the individual is often powerless. In the matter of a religious belief the imperative authority of the social force is tempered as steel is by the feeling that it is a breach of a graver kind and gives religious sanction a far greater force than a purely social sanction has.

The Sacral source of the authority behind religious sanction comes primarily from the individual and only secondarily from the group. That is the noteworthy peculiarity of the social source of religious sanction. It prepares the individual to uphold the religious beliefs. It dispenses with the necessity of the group using its social group. That is why the sacral source of its authority makes religious sanction of such high order as to supersede all other sanctions indeed to dispense with them. That is why the Religious sanction alone becomes sufficient to maintain the integrity of religious beliefs which even time and circumstances have proved powerless to affect. The way this happens is easy to follow. The Sacred inspires in the individual the sentiment of reverence and deference, which he certainly has not for the profane.[109]

This explains why laws alone do not suffice to annihilate caste. In a sickening reality like this, there sprouts a just cause for the Unmarriageables to interlock the fate of the reservation system with the responsibility of Indian society to dishonour and disgrace the stigma of Unmarriageability. Such an intermeshing is crucial. Let me explain the

---

[109]BAWS, Vol.5 p.178

why part of it. What keeps caste, that is Unmarriageability to keep going is the religious sanction. Do not forget that what is religious is social and what is religious is also sacral. The belief in caste system is a religious belief, that is, practice of Unmarriageability is clearly religious, social and sacral. To rip off from Unmarriageability its religious sanction, to make it anti-social and to degrade it to profanity is the only way to annihilate caste. The Unmarriageables not in any way can even think of coercing the caste Hindus to do so. In fact, there lies no burden on the Unmarriageables to reform the caste Hindus and cleanse the Hindu society. But there remains the survival responsibility on them to reiterate on the nexus between reservation and caste, in other words, reservation and Unmarriageability. This would inevitably offer two choices to the caste Hindus, who are restless in their demand to remove reservation, with a compulsion to pick one: "Either leave your notion of Unmarriageability or leave your demand of removing reservation. For, reservation would continue to exist till you continue to practise Unmarriageability. If you are so desperate to retain Unmarriageability and thereby allowing caste system to continue, then do not bother and fret over the continuation of reservation."

The fall of Unmarriageability and reservation should go together. If that is not happening, they would continue to coexist with the former as a menace and the latter as a safeguard from the social menace that the former actively continues to cause. More than the understanding about caste, the solution to annihilate caste has been misunderstood gravely. Striking Unmarriageability is the only way to dismantle the caste system. Till then, reservation would only serve as an interim antidote against the venom of caste.

Let me bring in the final inference of the previous chapter again: the prevalence of conjugal inequality, that is, Unmarriageability, within the Hindu institution of marriage reflects nothing short of the social inequality as determined by the Hindu society. While, Unmarriageability retains social inequality, the purpose of reservation is primarily to achieve social equality. Like Equality is the antithesis of Inequality, Reservation is the antithesis of Unmarriageability. Why the Unmarriageables should project

Unmarriageability to shield the continuation of reservation? The founding reason is this: *Social evils can have no justification whatsoever in a civilised society. But nothing can be more odious and vile than that admitted social evils should be sought to be justified on the ground of religion. The Depressed Classes may not be able to overthrow inequities to which they are being subjected. But they have made up their mind not to tolerate a religion that will lend its support to the continuance of these inequities. If the Hindu religion is to be their religion then it must become a religion of Social Equality. The mere amendment of Hindu religious code by the mere inclusion in it of a provision to permit temple entry for all, cannot make it a religion of Equality of social status. All that it can do is to recognise them as nationals and not aliens, if I may use these terms which have become so familiar in politics. But that cannot mean that they would thereby reach a position where they would be free and equal without being above or below any one else, for the simple reason that the Hindu religion does not recognise the principle of equality of social status; on the other hand fosters inequality by insisting upon grading people as Brahmins, Kashatriyas, Vaishyas and Shudras which now stand towards one another in an ascending scale of reverence and descending scale of contempt. If the Hindu religion is to be a religion of social equality then an amendment of its code to provide temple entry is not enough. What is required is to purge it of the doctrine of Chaturvarna. That is the root cause of all inequality and also the parent of the caste system and untouchability which are merely forms of inequality.*[110] But how to purge the doctrine of Chaturvarna- the parent of the caste system? The Hindu society is not interested in encouraging this question. But still, a clear cut answer has to be ascertained. Grading people as Brahmins, Kshatriyas, Vaishyas and Shudras and the operation of ascending scale of reverence and descending scale of contempt would continue till Brahmins distinctively remain as Brahmins, Kshatriyas distinctively remain as Kshatriyas, Vaishyas distinctively remain as Vaishyas and Shudras distinctively remain as Shudras. Chaturvarna is founded on the principle of distinctiveness of these four Varnas. From where does this distinctiveness arise? *A study of*

---

[110]BAWS, Vol.5 p.383

the Chaturvarnya must in its turn start with a study of the ninetieth Hymn of the Tenth Mandala of the Rig Veda— a Hymn, which is known by the famous name of Purusha Sukta. What does the Hymn say? It says:[111]

> *... 2. Purusha himself is this whole (universe), Whatever has been and whatever shall be. He is the Lord of immortality, since (or when) by food he expands.*
> *... 11. When (the gods) divided Purusha, into how many parts did they cut him up? What was his mouth? What arms (had he)? What (two objects) are said (to have been) his thighs and feet?*
> *12. The Brahmana was his mouth, the Rajanya was made his arms; the being called the Vaishya, he was his thighs; the Shudra sprang from his feet.*[112]

Thus, the Purusha Sukta Mandala being the source of distinctiveness of each Varna, how the continuation of this distinction is ensured? Nothing other than the practice of Unmarriageability sustains the distinctiveness of each of these Varna. Each Varna maintains its distinctiveness because of the notion of Unmarriageability it has over the other Varnas. Purge the practice of Unmarriageability, the Varnas would coalesce with each other eventually only to perish. Spare Unmarriageability, caste system would be spared. Annihilate Unmarriageability, caste system would be annihilated. It is up to the caste Hindus to decide what they want to do with regard to the stigma of Unmarriageability. They can continue to cherish it or reform themselves perishing it. But let it be made clear once for all that till the stigma of Unmarriageability exists to deny the equality of social status, reservation would continue to armour the Unmarriageables to claim equality in social status. When Unmarriageability, through the matrimonial custom denies the social equality to prevail among Hindus, reservation on the other hand, by improving the educational, economical and political status of the Unmarriageables tries to introduce social equality within the Hindu

---

[111]Muir's, Original Sanskrit Texts, Vol. I, p.9

[112]BAWS, Vol.7 p.22

society. Some might ask the question- how can a matrimonial custom be placed as a counter to justify reservation? My answer to this is- in the social sphere of a Hindu's life, if the institution of marriage can decide and determine one's social status, thereby pronouncing her or him as a superior or inferior being, why not the educational, economical and political aspects of progress can be the engine of change for the suppressed community to claim their social status? When the marital aspects of social life create social calamities why not the educational, economical and political aspects of the same social life be the solution to such calamities? Fire and water are not the same but is not the water that alone can extinguish fire? Further, it was not the choice of the Unmarriageables to resort to reservation. They had no other options because of the rigid caste mindset of the Hindus. When the gates of social progress remain closed to the Unmarriageables in all the directions, they had to find some sort of safeguard to their social life, which has happened through reservation. Reservation is nothing but a mere safeguard to counter the deprivation of social equality maintained in connivance by Hindu society via the principal of Unmarriageability. But it is not a complete solution to the social inequalities prevailing within the Hinduism. Reservation is only an enabling measure for the Unmarriageables to get better in their lives-educationally and economically. Political reservation available to them is only a representation arrangement to say aloud their concerns and interests amidst the Hindu Communal Majority. But still, it would be absurd to conclude that any advancements made by the Unmarriageables in any sphere would result in improvement in their social status. Till caste Hindus cling to their idea of Charturvarna, it would be absurd to conclude so. It is because *status is a dual matter, a matter inter se between two persons* (in this case, the caste Hindus and the Unmarriageables) *and unless both move from their old position there can be no change.*[113] The Hindu social order via its prescription of Unmarriageability seals tight all the possibility for the change in the status of a person to take place. For those who are perplexed, let me expound further the writings of Dr.Ambedkar: *The Chaturvarna of the Brahmins was a fixed order never*

---

[113]BAWS, Vol.5 p.470

to be changed. Once a Brahmin always a Brahmin. Once a Kshatriya always a Kshatriya, once a Vaishya always a Vaishya and once a Shudra always a Shudra. Society was based on status conferred upon an individual by the accident of his birth. Vice, however heinous, was no ground for degrading a man from his status, and virtue, however great, had no value to raise him above it. There was no room for worth nor for growth.[114]

Here, what gathers my attention is that status is conferred upon an individual by the 'accident' of his birth. If we introspect further, what is the meaning of 'accident'? It implies the Varna or to be specific the particular caste (jati) in which a person is born. But are all these births accident or the pre-determined outcomes of the practice of Unmarriageability? I would rather dissent with the former. Birth of a person in a Varna or caste is a pre-determined result of the endogamy that dictated the marriage of the person's parents. For instance, to be born as a Brahmin, both the parents- the father and the mother, must hail only from the Brahmin caste and not from any other caste, which is ensured by the custom of Unmarriageability i.e. endogamy. Therefore, one might inherit the status of her or his Varna or caste at the time of her or his birth but everyone's status was actually pre-determined by the practice of Unmarriageability by their parents through which the fusion of Varna or caste in their bloodline is effectively prevented. Once a Brahmin always a Brahmin. True. But the status succeeds to the next generation because the previous generation has imbibed to Unmarriageability. Therefore, it is the custom of Unmarriageability that makes the status of a person static and unalterable. And, in a society in which improving one's social status remains a herculean task, the presence of reservation becomes more pertinent. Till Hinduism becomes a religion of social equality, till all the Hindus acquire equal social status, the relevancy and necessity of reservation are beyond the scope of any doubt. The purpose of reservation shall end with the demise of Unmarriageability. As Unmarriageability survives, reservation shall continue to survive.

---

[114]BAWS, Vol.11 p.90

Considering the anti-reservation development in recent times, the Indian society explicitly is failing to recognize caste and reservation as an issue of problem and solution. In fact, it is committing chicanery by projecting caste and reservation as two different issues unrelated to each other. The height of fraudulency cannot extend beyond this. It must be understood that the reservation based on caste is an unavoidable arrangement to lessen the social inequalities being caused by the centuries-old reservation of status, rights and privileges as devised within the caste system. And projecting the stigma of Unmarriageability is one practical way of demonstrating how caste remains as the backbone in the social life of the Hindu society. Unmarriageability is one powerful placard against those who plot the lie that the belief in the caste system is diminishing these days. The existence of this stigma evinces clearly that the caste system is not bound by any shackles or chains and continue to prosper in an unfettered fashion as ever. Unmarriageability as a stigma reiterates the relevancy and significance of reservation. It brings to the forefront the stained mindset of the caste Hindus on one hand and the justification for reservation to remain as a safeguard for the Unmarriageables on the other hand. Contemplate from any angle- any number of times- Unmarriageability alone has the required resistance to thwart the anti-reservation outlooks and efforts. Realizing this is crucial as the stigma should become the spearhead of the Unmarriageables. This is the need of the hour, not only for the Unmarriageables but also for the Hindu society to disown the caste system.

IV

Rationale Three: Unmarriageability exposes the present Young Generation's submissiveness before the Caste System

To be aware of psyche of the present young generation is very much important. Such awareness is crucial for the following two reasons: Firstly, the future of the continuation of reservation policies and any possible amendment to it or abrogation of it would be dictated by the present generation. And secondly, the feasibility of annihilation of caste depends on their inclination to end the caste system.

The talk around any corner is that the young Indian generation does not bother about caste and the caste system would soon disappear. But that is not tantamount to the reality if one understands well what is essentially meant by not being 'bothered' about the caste and actually being 'against' the caste. To grasp the difference is important as the Indian youths profusely make this statement that they do not heed to the caste identity of the individuals they encounter in their day to day life. Is it true? Mind the following: *The caste in India is exclusive and isolated. There is no interaction and no modification of aims and objects. What a caste or a combination of castes regard "as their own interest" as against other castes remains as sacred and inviolate as ever. The fact that they mingle and co-operate does not alter their character. These acts of co-operation are mechanical and not social. Individuals use one another so as to get desired results, without reference to the emotional and intellectual disposition. The fact that they give and take orders modify actions and results. But it does not affect their dispositions.*[115] The claim of the young generation that they are not the catches in the caste's net is undoubtedly an unwarranted and objectionable claim. They carelessly connote the acts of mechanical interaction among the castes as the ascendance of castelessness. But how is their caste consciousness in the social sphere? This is the decisive question to be asked. Do they submerge under the influence of caste or express their deviancy against it? The unit of Hindu society for the purpose of marriage is family. The Hindu institution of marriage and family are the two best standards in the light of which the caste disposition of the young generation can be appropriately and adequately analyzed. One can be a hypocrite anywhere but not in the context of family and in the matters of marriage. True colours had to surface and would surface. The young generation offers no deviancy to the stigma of Unmarriageability. In fact, they lack the tenacity to knock the doors of their house with the casteless fraternity that they claim to possess

---

[115]BAWS, Vol.9 p.193

everywhere else. Their cosmopolitan benevolence does not slander the caste fellowship that they exhibit in their marriages. They see pride in their caste surnames and do not marry outside their caste group. Some are too smart, I would rather call caste-smart, to conduct the background check of caste before falling in love! With the exception of some genuine love stories that violate the boundaries of caste, the young generation is not bothered to distort the caste rules in their marriages. Glaringly, they are endogamous, and alarmingly, they reinforce the stigma of Unmarriageability. Driven by the conviction in caste or bridled by their family, it does not matter where the impetus comes from. The fact remains that the young generation conserves the custom of Unmarriageability and offer silence when it comes to annihilation of caste. And it cannot be taken as a mere silence of ignorance or innocence. To borrow the phrase of Dr.Ambedkar, theirs is a 'studied silence and cold indifference' against the stigma of Unmarriageability, which places them on an equal footing to any of the past generations' persistence in preserving and passing on the caste system. Hence, it is nothing more than a hollow statement when the young generation claims that they do not 'bother' about caste. They do bother about caste and are very much caste specific in whom not to marry and whom to marry. Till they deviate and liberate themselves from the custom of Unmarriageability, they can never be 'against' caste.

Why Unmarriageability should be a serious subject of discussion? It is because the young generation bury their heads in the sand. They refuse to be bothered about their abidance to Unmarriageability that remain as the gateway to the inheritance and perpetuity of caste based social structure. From the standpoint of the Unmarriageables, the psychology of the present young generation poses a greater challenge as compared to the well-established instincts of the conventional caste Hindus. To begin with, let me introduce what Dr.Ambedkar mentions about the psychology of the Hindus: *If you ask a Hindu, why he behaves in this savage manner, why he feels outraged by the efforts which the Untouchables are making for a clean and respectable life, his answer will be a simple one. He will say: "What you call the reform by the*

Untouchables is not a reform. It is an outrage on our Dharma". If you ask him further where this Dharma of his is laid down, his answer will again be a very simple one. He will reply, "Our Dharma is contained in our Shastras". A Hindu in suppressing what, in the view of an unbiased man, is a just revolt of the Untouchables against a fundamentally wrong system by violence, pillage, arson, and loot, to a modern man appears to be acting quite irreligiously, or, to use the term familiar to the Hindus, he is practising Adharma. But the Hindu will never admit it. The Hindu believes that it is the Untouchables who are breaking the Dharma and his acts of lawlessness which appear as Adharma are guided by his sacred duty to restore Dharma. This is an answer, the truth of which cannot be denied by those who are familiar with the psychology of the Hindus.[116] Thus, the caste Hindus have a clear stand to be an apparent adversary against those who do not want to comply with and conserve caste. And they relentlessly remain likewise in their relationship with the Unmarriageables. A caste Hindu is more desirous and comfortable in being an open enemy to an Unmarriageable. But the young generation not often acts like that. Their caste psychology never becomes conspicuous. They are more creative in concealing and camouflaging their affinity towards caste. However, their acts are not completely clandestine and are susceptible to exposure. Their fanaticism to comply with caste can be seen in all its vigour in the decisions they make with regard to their marriages. The brotherhood and friendship they boasted of everywhere instantly surrenders to the custom of Unmarriageability. Theirs is a fake claim of fraternity. Fakeness in all its glory! That is why the Unmarriageables should be even more warier of the young generation than the conventional caste Hindus. Under the cloak of modernity and unlike the caste Hindus who remain as open enemies, the young generation is succeeding smartly in dissuading the annihilation of caste. By subscribing to Unmarriageability, the young generation not only preserve the caste blueprint and import the age-old social structure founded upon caste but also backstab the genuine Mahatmas aspiring to make the Hindu society a casteless utopia. But how come they are not guilty as accused? It is for the plain reason that the general will of the

---

[116]BAWS, Vol.5 p.273

young generation does not want to remain conscious of what they practise as Unmarriageability is nothing but a filthy stigma of caste. One who understands caste would not be surprised at them for what they reflect is only the esprit de corps of the caste from which they come from. Being so, how to disgrace this young generation that is least bothered about its practise of Unmarriageability? The best the Unmarriageables could do in this regard is to project Unmarriageability as the spearhead against the caste system. It is up to the young generation to discard or not to discard the practise. Meanwhile, the Unmarriageables should not ignore the fact that the majority of the young generation also happens to be the Hindus and hence there goes a lot of similarity in their social psychology and behavior too. Therefore, the young generation is duty-bound to introspect themselves the following observation which Dr.Ambedkar has made about Hindus:

There does not seem to be much hope for the emancipation of the Untouchables, at any rate their emancipation is far more problematical and distant than the emancipation of the Primitive Tribes. The problem of the slaves was one of denial of political or economic rights. If the problem of the Untouchables was one of denial of political and economic rights, it could be solved by legal and constitutional methods. The denial of political and economic rights is the result of the social psychology of the Hindus. The problem for the Untouchables arises directly out of the social behaviour of the Hindus. Untouchability will vanish only when Hindus will change their mentality. The problem is how to make the Hindus unlearn their way of life. It is no small matter to make a whole nation give up its accustomed way of life. Besides the way of life the Hindus are accustomed to, is a way which is sanctified by their religion, at any rate they believe it to be so. To change their way of life is almost to change their religion. How can this happen? Only when it is realised that what is tragedy for the Untouchables is the crime of the Hindus. How long shall the Untouchables have to wait for this revolution in the religious psychology of the Hindus? Let those who have a gift for prophecy answer.[117]

---

[117]BAWS, Vol.5 p.144

But let it be made clear that this revolution whether in the religious psychology of the Hindus or the young generation cannot happen without discarding the practise of Unmarriageability. The young generation if wanted to change their way of life to be against caste has to purge the practice of Unmarriageability. This is the only way to unlearn their Hindu way of life that is retaining caste. Will the young generation which is restless in its demand to remove reservation and claiming itself to be casteless ready to do so? This is the test the Unmarriageables had to put for young generation. But I doubt whether the latter is even earnest enough to clear the charge against them. The problem is the young generation is not ashamed of upholding caste in their marriages. In fact, they exhibit proudness in being the bearers of custom of Unmarriageability. The proudness that is age-old and sacrosanct. Even if it is not their proudness but the parental colonialism that is binding them to practise Unmarriageability, it shall not be an excuse from their part. Till they become the change and find themselves inconsistent and unbearable to caste, the Unmarriageables should centre-stage the stigma of Unmarriageability. Unmarriageability should primarily be brought into limelight not with the intention to persuade the young generation to leave behind their caste prejudices but rather as a searing spearhead against their notoriety in camouflaging caste affinity. If Unmarriageables can emancipate themselves by embracing Buddhism, the Hindus and the young generation can annihilate caste by purging Unmarriageability. Both are intended to make a drastic change in one's way of life and also to shake the foundations of the Hindu religion. Accomplishing them, no doubt, demands the creation of a revolution in all the three realms- social, spiritual and most importantly religious.

V

Rationale Four: Unmarriageability would stream the activism towards Annihilation of Caste

The observation made by Eva-Maria Hardtmann about Dalit movement deserves attention. With regard to the organizational aspects of a movement, she finds many similarities between her own study of the Dalit movement and the study carried on by Gerlach and Hine regarding the Black Power movement and Pentecostalism in the United States. As in the case of Black Power movement and Pentecostalism, Eva-Maria Hardtmann finds the organizational structure of the Dalit movement too to be decentralized, segmentary, and reticulate. It is important to understand them because any Dalit activism that is aimed towards annihilation of caste or any other objective would be either constrained or facilitated by those characteristics. But, my interest in briefing the organizational structure of Dalit movement arises not because of this. It has a different perspective and purpose. I am thoroughly convinced that the stigma of Unmarriageability should become the spearhead of the Unmarriageables. And I equally believe that centre-staging the stigma of Unmarriageability would inherently strengthen the organizational structure of the Dalit movement since it readily places the Unmarriageables in a crucial battlefield and also providing them with the right strategy to fight and defend. If this appears unconvincing to you, allow me to elucidate but after a necessary detour briefing Hardtmann's organizational structure of Dalit movement:

> Hardmann finds the Dalit movement to be decentralized and is guided by many leaders. There is disagreement among the leaders with respect to short-range goals and methods, she notices. Though each leader possess considerable extent of influence none could be regarded as the face of the movement.

> Secondly, the Dalit movement is segmentary and there is a constant process of fission and fusion taking place because of ideological difference, personal conflict, competition between the leaders etc. However, the numerous Dalit groups having their own ideas about goals and methods may even combine and work together if the context and situation demand.

> The third feature that Hardtmann observes is that the Dalit movement is also reticulate. In the absence of a single leader and

no central headquarter, the Dalit groups and individuals are often linked through kinship, friendship and community belonging.

It is true that Dalit movement is- decentralized, segmentary and reticulate. Contrary to the general view among researchers, Hardtmann does not find any of these features to be a sign of weakness. Rather, she quotes Gerlech and Hine: "When the success of movement is reported as having occurred "because of" rather than "in spite of" organizational fission and lack cohesion, we will have come to understand the nature of movement dynamics much more clearly".[118] The organizational structure of the Dalit movement itself is a challenge to the opponents. Its structure which is flexible, constantly changing, with numerous groups each with a leader may bring frustrations to the opponents who may feel that they are facing, as put by Gerlach and Hine, 'on the one hand, a spontaneous explosion at the grass-roots level; and on the other, a many-headed hydra'.[119] However, Hardtmann is conscious to add that the Dalit activists deplore splits or tensions or even heterogeneity and consider them as inimical to their movement. They aspire to organize themselves better though it has always been a challenge. And this aspiration is nothing but one important legacy of Dr.Ambedkar that refuses to fade away.

The necessity for the Depressed Classes to become and remain united had been reiterated by Dr.Ambedkar all through his lifetime. In 1930, during the 36th anniversary of the Sant Samaj Sangh, a spiritual association of the Depressed Classes, Dr.Ambedkar pointed out in the course of his address that *his personal activities were not sufficient to bring about the redress of the grievances of the Depressed Classes who, he said, must agitate much more and organise themselves better than they were at present organized.*[120] In 1942, as a part of caring reply to the Address presented by the Chairman and Members of the Reception Committee of the All-India Depressed Classes Conference, Dr.Ambedkar writes, *You*

---

[118] Gerlech and Hine (1970a: 64)

[119] Gerlech and Hine (1970a: 65)

[120]BAWS, Vol.17, part 3 p.61

have less need of an assurance from me that I will fight for the ideal. I stand in a greater need of assurance from you. You have assured me of your love and affection. It was quite unnecessary. I want an assurance of another kind. It is an assurance of strength, unity and determination to stand for our rights, fight for our rights and never to return until we win our rights. You promise to do your part. I promise to do mine. With justice on our side, I don't see how we can lose our battle. The battle to me is a matter full of joy. The battle is in the fullest sense spiritual. There is nothing material or sordid in it. For ours is a battle, not for wealth or for power. It is a battle for freedom. It is a battle for the reclamation of human personality which has been suppressed and mutilated by the Hindu Social System and will continue to be suppressed and mutilated if in the political struggle the Hindus win and we lose. My final words of advice to you is educate, agitate and organize, have faith in yourselves and never lose hope. I shall always be with you as I know you will be with me.[121] In 1944, at Madras, he makes a similar advice to the Non-Brahmins and their party that unity is of supreme importance and the lesson should be learned before it is too late.[122] Again, in 1945, in a mass meeting at Bombay, the need for the member of the Scheduled Castes to organize themselves and stand united under the banner of the All-India Scheduled Castes' Federation for attaining social, economic and political equality with the other major communities in the country was stressed by Dr.Ambedkar.[123] In the 5th Conference of United Provinces of Scheduled Castes Federation held at Lucknow, in 1948, he said, *Political power is the key to all social progress and the Scheduled Castes can achieve their salvation if they captured this power by organising themselves into a third Party and holding the balance of power between the rival political parties- Congress and Socialists.*[124] His idea about the function of a Political Party also could be best understood from the Resolution unanimously passed by Working Committee of Scheduled Castes Federation at Bombay in 1955: *A*

---

[121]BAWS, Vol.17, part 3 p.275

[122]BAWS, Vol.17, part 3 p.321

[123]BAWS, Vol.17, part 3 p.351

[124]BAWS, Vol.17, part 3 p.388

Political Party does not exist merely for the sake of winning election. A political party exists for the sake of educating, agitating and organizing the people.[125]

My intention at this stage is to examine the finding of Hardtmann that the Dalit movement is difficult to suppress on account of its organizational structure being decentralized, segmentary and reticulate against the background of Dr.Ambedkar's reiteration on the significance and necessity of the Depressed Classes to stay united and organized. The examination is crucial as the former is more a sort of present state while the latter reflects the ideal state that the Dalit movement has to strive and reach for.

There can be no negation in holding that the Dalit movement has become difficult to suppress but the same should not be the translation for the success of the movement. For, the attainment of the objectives and achievement of the goals is what defines the success of a movement and the resistance to external suppression is only a pre-requisite for that. How organized are the Unmarriageables in ensuring the success of their movement? My concern is more about this question. By being like a many-headed hydra, as Hardtmann puts, are they successful? Never can they be. Unless the Unmarriageables organize themselves better, they can never become a strong adversary against the caste Hindus and the caste system. Until then, utmost they can remain as a chunk of pressure groups making uproar for the causes they believe in. They might receive attention for the outcry they make but that would not make the General Will of this society to heed and bend to their demands of social justice. As a keynote of his policy Dr.Ambedkar always held that the Unmarriageables are not a sub-continent of the Hindus but a separate element in the national life.[126] The separate settlements and separate burial grounds that every village has devised for them confirm this. It is unity, unity alone that can render them with hope, strength and determination. And this unity should not be a

---

125 BAWS, Vol.17, part 1 p.437
126 BAWS, Vol.17, part 1 p.350

mere outcome of community belonging but must be founded upon the indignation to reclaim the sacrosanct of human personality. Such a foundation alone would make the Unmarriageables more organized, persistent and determined in realizing their demands. It also would change the present pattern of Dalit activism from being reactive to proactive. The Dalit movement which has become more or less like a Condolence movement during the acute occurrences of Dishonour killings and caste atrocities is required to organize itself better in order to secure and safeguard the social, educational and political platforms for the Unmarriageables. In this regard, I put forward my argument that the issues of Unmarriageability could be the ideal bedrock to organize the Unmarriageables and remove from their movement the negative fallouts of being segmentary and decentralized.

I do hope and believe that the issues of Unmarriageability could effectively serve as the uniting rallying point among the segmented and decentralized Dalit groups. It potentially could infuse solidarity within the Dalit movement as a whole to move towards a definite and concurring action plan. Also, Unmarriageability being a social stigma could whistle-blow and counter the varied aspects of the problem of caste. Let me jot down the reasoning. Firstly, it places before the Unmarriageables who remain as Hindus and have no inclination to embrace Buddhism the question of questioning the practice of Unmarriageability within Hinduism. To the Dalit groups that believe Buddhism as the only way for their emancipation, Unmarriageability could be the conversing tool to question its own community that refuses to come out of Hinduism. Secondly, the stigma of Unmarriageability reiterates the relevancy and significance of reservation to continue. To the Dalit groups that are functioning as the watch-dog against the infringement of their constitutional and political safeguards, Unmarriageability could be the one prominent placard and justification against the entire anti-reservation agitations and efforts. Thirdly, it holds the young generation claiming themselves to be liberated from the clutches of caste accountable to the caste-dictated decisions to which they readily abide while choosing their life partner. To them and a certain section of Unmarriageables too who were made to believe that caste is fast disappearing, Unmarriageability is the social parameter that indicates the intactness with which caste is surviving. Adequate explanations have been made about the above three aspects in the preceding sub-chapters. But my point to remind them here is, the concern to expose and fight Unmarriageability would effortlessly unite the numerous Dalit groups that differ among themselves on the religious, social and political agendas and outlooks. Because Unmarriageability, in one way or the other becomes the justification by itself in supporting the causes that each Dalit group believe in and is working for. This being the most important functionality of exposing Unmarriageability as a stigma, it is the fourth reason to which I seek to gather your attention now: Unmarriageability would sow the seeds for annihilation of caste.

Unless casteless and classless society is created, there will be no progress in India.[127] It is one strong statement Dr.Ambedkar made and always believed in. Undoubtedly, he has become the uniting symbol of the Unmarriageables. But there can also be no denial in holding that the Unmarriageables are not yet united in scheming a unanimous and definite action plan to annihilate caste. In this context, I propose that exposing Unmarriageability is both a social and political pre-requisite to expose the freedom with which caste operates and in the long run such exposure would positively lay down the political path to annihilate caste. Unmarriageability as a stigma alone has the driving force to stream the Dalit activism towards annihilation of caste. This stigma is the bottom-most rock on which the caste structure is founded and by crushing it those above it are to be shaken for sure.

Meanwhile, I am obliged to tackle beforehand one interesting argument that the concern of Unmarriageables should be only towards their emancipation and it is a needless responsibility for them to be bothered about annihilation of caste. On February 11, 1933, Mr.Gandhi renamed his weekly newspaper 'Young India' as 'Harijan' in order to propagate the cause of the Untouchables. Dr.Ambedkar's statement on

---

[127]BAWS, Vol.17, part 3 p.495

this occasion requires attention. He stated: *The out-caste is a by-product of the caste system. There will be outcastes as long as there are castes. Nothing can emancipate the outcaste except the destruction of caste system. Nothing can help Hindus and ensure their survival is the coming struggle except the purging of Hindus faith of this odious and vicious dogma.*[128] If the emancipation of the Unmarriageables lies only in the destruction of caste system, will the Hindus be readily inclined to work for it? Certainly not. To begin with, their socialization itself would be a big hindrance. Being so, their religious submissiveness remains too for an issue to be touched upon. If at all there is a class that possesses the ideological stamina and can be relentlessly vigorous towards annihilation of caste, it is the Depressed Class- the Unmarriageables alone. Till they allow the caste to persist, the Hindus will block the way for their emancipation. If they become passive towards annihilation of caste, the Hindus will continue to be more active in deterring their emancipation. Undoubtedly, it is futile for the Unmarriageables to consider their emancipation independent of annihilation. They cannot escape from the clutches of caste without destroying it. If they ignore the existence of caste, for sure it would not result in caste to ignore their existence. Rather, caste is keen to ensure, as it always did, that the Unmarriageables remain as the sunken humanity forever. Therefore, not only as a survival instinct but also as a strategic necessity, the Unmarriageables should fight against the stigma of Unmarriageability.

When I say that Unmarriageability would propel the Dalit activism towards annihilation of caste, it is quite logical for anyone to quickly assume that the cry against Unmarriageability is nothing but only an effort to promote inter-caste marriages. Though I do not see any ill will or shortcoming behind such a motive too, I am duty-bound to make it clear that the primary purpose to purge Unmarriageability is not intended to rally for inter-caste marriages. The main reason behind the need to protest Unmarriageability is based on the founding principle that caste is endogamy. The purpose is to bring to limelight and reiterate the main idea

---

[128]BAWS, Vol.17, part 1 p.230

that caste is endogamy. I am reminding that as by the final analysis of Dr.Ambedkar, creation of castes means the superposition of endogamy on exogamy.[129] And my intention is to reiterate the extension of his idea that the destruction of caste would be the superposition of exogamy on endogamy. As the stigma of Unmarriageability is the sole deterrent towards such destruction, I intend to project it as the stigma that has to be purged. I stress against the stigma of Unmarriageability out of the urge to purge endogamy than to promote exogamy (i.e. inter-caste marriages). The rationale involved here is more an outcome of the prohibition imposed on the inter-caste marriages than about any specific intention to promote such marriages. The fight is because of the prohibition and not about promotion, though both, in the end, happen to be inevitably overlapping. If destroying endogamy is the foremost condition to annihilate caste, then exposing the stigma of Unmarriageability is naturally the first step towards it. And forget not, the attempt to purge Unmarriageability is no less a small endeavour as it would eventually make the caste sacrilege. The attempt is only a cry to reclaim the sacrosanct of human personality.

I have no hesitation to conclude that realizing the stigma of unmarriageability and fighting against it would sow the seeds of unity among the Unmarriageables. A fight against this stigma would create the required ambience and space among the Dalit groups that have become segmentary and decentralized, to concur in their action plan and function as a common front. Each might have their own reasons to fight Unmarriageability but the fight would pave the way for their unity. By borrowing Dr.Ambedkar's words for inspiration, I can only say that by marching upon the road that questions Unmarriageability, if Unmarriageables walk long enough, must necessarily lead them to Unity. Even if the Unmarriageables are not inclined to fight Unmarriageability from the point of view of annihilation of caste, they had to placard against this stigma to shield the principles of social justice from the anti-reservation progression that is clouding before them. Therefore, to take up the issue of Unmarriageability is not a step to persuade the caste Hindus but rather

---

[129]BAWS, Vol.1 p.9

a strategy to expose the caste prejudice dominant in this nation. By highlighting Unmarriageability, the Unmarriageables are not confronting the caste Hindus but the caste. It is not purely an effort concerned to handcuff the caste Hindus or the young generation from practising their caste dharma but a social justice reasoning that tries to secure the destiny of the Unmarriageables. There is no need for the Hindu society to dissect to and analyze the extent of benefits the Unmarriageables will be gaining for themselves by questioning Unmarriageability. Rather, it should move towards the realization that there lies no progress for it if the stigma of Unmarriageability remains unquestioned.

CHAPTER 7

UNMARRIAGEABILITY: HOW TO WIELD THE SPEARHEAD?

I.   Caste = Endogamy = Unmarriageability

II.   Embargoing the Matrimonies from its functioning as Caste Conclaves.

IIa. Outlook One: Confronting Manu and his Matrimonial Laws.

IIb. Outlook Two: In Support of Inter-caste Marriages.

IIc. Outlook Three: Questioning the authority of Shastras.

IId. Outlook Four: Retaliating Dishonour Killings and Khap Panchayats.

IIe. Outlook Five: Questioning the Unmarriageables within the Hindu fold.

IIf. Outlook Six: Anchoring the Reservation policy- Social backwardness stems out from Caste (Social) Stigmas and Prejudices.

IIg. Outlook Seven: The Young Generation and the Mainstream Democratic Forces- Making them Accountable.

III.   Constitutional Promulgation to Abolish Caste.

I
Caste = Endogamy = Unmarriageability

One who is concerned about caste and the annihilation of it would not be conscious about the present alone but would examine the past as well trying to understand the genesis of it. It is so because in order to ascertain a practical scheme for annihilation of caste what is equally essential is the knowledge about how caste was created in the first place. The genesis of caste holds the key in finding the path for its annihilation as well. In other words, the effort to destroy caste practically begins with the understanding about its origin. The finding of Dr.Ambedkar in 'Castes in India- their mechanism, genesis and development' that the working out of endogamy is equivalent to the creation of caste is the founding idea based on which this entire book has been constructed. And this is the basic idea which cannot be refuted by any sociologist or academician. The concept of Unmarriageability to which I am bringing the attention throughout is a mere derivative of this significant conclusion- Caste is Endogamy. Each and every argument in this book is either a nearer or distant extension of his conclusion that *prohibition, or rather the absence of intermarriage-endogamy, to be called the essence of caste when rightly understood.*[130] It is wise to remember always caste i.e. endogamy is nothing but the stigma of Unmarriageability. Endogamy is the rule preventing the people not to contract marriages outside their caste. In other words, this rule imposes

---

[130]BAWS, Vol.1 p.8

the stigma of Unmarriageability in the context of any two different castes. Therefore, if the stigma of Unmarriageability had to be wielded as the spearhead against caste, undoubtedly its target would and should remain the custom of endogamy. Minding this, to counteract the custom of endogamy that is enforcing the prohibition on inter-caste marriages, two prime objectives need to be prioritized and realized. One, an unconditional ban on caste-based matrimonies. And two, constitutional promulgation to abolish caste.

II
Embargoing the Matrimonies from its functioning as Caste Conclaves

When caste comes into the picture, hindsight becomes more important than foresight. One who has a clear hindsight about the sustaining mechanism of caste would readily harangue the matrimonial platform for its efficacy in marital segregations on the line of caste as desired by Indian population. Matrimonies emphasize on the existing caste divisions by identifying and unifying (in fact dividing) the people caste wise. It is effortlessly successful in arresting any sort of marital endosmosis or social fusion that is possible by crossing the boundaries of caste. We must not forget that the founding rule of caste is not to question Unmarriageability. Being so, the foremost requisite to annihilate caste lies in questioning it. And this questioning has to begin with the demand to ban the caste based matrimonies.

The prime argument that I am reiterating is this: what defines caste is the custom of endogamy or Unmarriageability and therefore the caste matrimony, a prominent platform where the custom freely dwells should be restrained by law. The justification calling for the ban does not end here and a proper outlook would only further question the continuance of such caste specific advertisements. In an attempt intended to persuade for this cause, allow me to brief some of these outlooks.

IIa
Outlook One: Confronting Manu and his Matrimonial Laws

To begin with, the first outlook I want to present is with regard to Manu and the matrimonial laws he laid. *It might be argued that the inequality prescribed by Manu in his Smriti is after all of historical importance. It is past history and cannot be supposed to have any bearing on the present conduct of the Hindu. I am sure nothing can be greater error than this. Manu is not a matter of the past. It is even more than a past of the present. It is a 'living past' and therefore as really present as any present can be.*[131] Consider Manu on marriage. Here are his rules governing intermarriage among the different classes. *Manu says:–*

> *III. 12. "For the first marriage of the twice born classes, a woman of the same class is recommended but for such as are impelled by inclination to marry again, women in the direct order of the classes are to be preferred."*

> *III. 13. "A Shudra woman only must be the wife of Shudra: she and a Vaisya, of a Vaisya; they two and a Kshatriya, of a Kshatriya; those two and a Brahman of a Brahman."*

Manu is of course opposed to intermarriage. His injunction is for each class to marry within his class. But he does recognize marriage outside the defined class. Here again he is particularly careful not to allow intermarriage to do harm to his principle of inequality among classes. Like Slavery he permits intermarriage but not in the inverse order. A Brahmin when marrying outside his class may marry any woman from any of the classes below him. A Kshatriya is free to marry a woman from the two classes next below him namely the Vaishya and Shudra but must not marry a woman from the Brahmin class which is above him. A Vaishya is free to marry a woman from the Shudra Class which is next below him.

---

[131]BAWS, Vol.12 p.719

But he cannot marry a woman from the Brahmin and the Kshatriya Class which are above him.

Why this discrimination? The only answer is that Manu was most anxious to preserve the rule of inequality which was his guiding principle.[132]

Well, does this discrimination exist at present? It is glaringly in existence even more than the past of the present. The rule of matrimonial inequality that Manu laid is a 'living past' and therefore as really present as any present can be. The expressions of Manu's rule – of whom to marry and whom not to marry can be found in ditto in any of the present-day matrimonies. Firstly, the matrimonies primarily function with caste as the main criteria and it is a surprise to no one to find them operating in the names of caste itself. Thus there is Reddy matrimony, Agarwal matrimony, Yadav matrimony , Patel matrimony, Iyer matrimony, Gupta matrimony, Jat matrimony, Ezhava matrimony, Kashyap matrimony, Gowda matrimony, Rajput matrimony, Arora matrimony, Bhatia matrimony, Gaur matrimony and so on and so forth. This only reflects of what Manu is opposed to- Intermarriage! Caste based matrimonies are the long-standing reality obliging to his injunction for each caste to marry within its own. These matrimonies' sole objective is to cater to the need of the Hindus in finding prospective bridegrooms and brides within their own caste. Secondly, even the case of matrimonial advertisements that open the scope for inter-caste marriages should not sway our attention. Such advertisements would not be of great appeal if we remember that even Manu recognize marriages outside the defined class but he is particularly careful not to allow intermarriage to do harm to his principle of marital inequality. Hence, even in the cases of inter-caste matrimonial advertisements, it is quite hard to find a marital preference which is not in conformity with the ascending order of reverence and descending order of contempt that is prevalent among the castes. The Hindus are very careful and caste conscious that even if they opt for inter-caste marriage they make

---

[132]BAWS, Vol.3 p.26

it a point that Manu's rule of matrimonial inequality is confirmed with. Below are some of the typical matrimonial advertisements published mostly in the well-known newspapers:

Kannada, Bharathwaja, 5'1", 43, own house, Bsc.,M.C.A., Madhwa, Iyer, Iyengar brides preferred.[133]

Telugu Brahmin Venginadu Gowsyga Poorattathi 43 yrs 170cms M.A.Business seeks Telugu Brahmin bride sub-sect no bar.[134]

Seeking Groom for Asst Superintendent of Police, State Govt, Sivaganga, RS. 50,0000 pm (own house). Gowda-Vakkliga, Rohini (Ragu/Kethu Dosham), Non-veg, 27(21.10.1986), 5.3, Fair, Expectation: Gowda-Vokkatika/Equal caste...[135]

NEOGI MAGAM 42/BE Manager differently abled on right leg seeks any Brahmin girl.[136]

Seeking 25-40, Well-Placed, Animal-loving, Vegetarian GROOM for my SON (36, 5'11') who works with an NGO Caste No Bar (though IYER Preferred).[137]

Alliance sought for Malayalee Nair girl, BTech (USA), MBA, 27yrs, highly accomplished, very fair, beautiful, 5'7" tall, Karthika Star, employed in a top tier Technology company in Management Cadre and based in Delhi. Hails from a well reputed and affluent business family in Chennai. Proposal from

---

[133] The New Sunday Express, Chennai. 15, June, 2014

[134] The Hindu Classifieds

[135] www.kmmatrimony.com June 1–15, 2014

[136] The Hindu Classifieds

[137] The Hindu Classifieds

Nair community or other upper class Hindu families of similar background will be considered.[138]

Though each of the above matrimonial advertisements appears to be opening up the scope for inter-caste marriage, none among them tries to transgress the rule of marital inequality. If looked closely, all the advertisers have specifically mentioned about their compliance to this rule. Their expectations in the form of a set of castes (Madhwa, Iyer, Iyengar), or Sub-sect no bar, or Equal caste, or Nair community or other upper class Hindu families of similar background, reflects nothing but their deep consciousness to do no harm to Manu's principle of marital inequality. Their preferences, as mentioned in the advertisement, may seem to be varying but they are all one and the same hard-core caste Hindus subscribing to the age-old Manudharma. In other words, Manu is still successful as ever in maintaining the equilibrium of inequality within the caste system amidst and despite the scope for inter-caste marriages. For those who aren't convinced, let me remind you the class-caste theory: a caste Hindu Brahmin who is at the top in the gradation of caste system could nod for the caste that comes under the same class category of her caste but would reject to have marriage alliance with the caste that does not fall under her caste's class category. In other words, there is a real chance for the marital acceptance when class similarity is felt even at the cost of caste difference. When class difference occurs, the issue of Unmarriageability arises as well. The preferences being advertised in the matrimonies in the form of a set of acceptable castes or sub-sect no bar or equal caste or caste/class with similar culture and traditions can be construed purely as an attempt to find a match at least within one's own class if there is no hope at all for finding a match within one's own caste. Thus, even if the rule of endogamy is transgressed, the class-caste theory ensures that rule of marital inequality among the classes (i.e. the 4 Varnas) is abided with. Forget not the assertion of Dr.Ambedkar: *In the first place, the idea of varna is the parent of the idea of caste. If the idea of caste is a pernicious idea it is entirely because of the viciousness of the idea of varna.*

---

[138]The Hindu Classifieds

Both are evil ideas and it matters very little whether one believes in varna or in caste.[139] This is practically possible by the mutual compromise made between the ascending order of reverence and descending order of contempt one has towards other castes. Such behaviour is best disguised in the off-quoted caste Hindu's argument: "we are not caste prejudiced as such when it comes to marriage but we are only looking at a basket of castes in the hope of finding prospective alliances with similar culture and shared traditions". Thus Manu's rule of marital inequality is confirmed within the guise of culture and traditions. And there are certain contexts in which a compromise with the notion of descending order of contempt is not at all possible. In such scenario, we find the matrimonial advertisements stating 'SC/ST kindly excuse', which is nothing but the modern representation of Manu's demarcation made between Savarna (the 4 varnas constituting the caste system) and Avarna (the Unmarriageables). Here again, his guiding principle- the rule of marital inequality is preserved. It is to be noted that even 'caste no bar' category is not free of caste prejudices. Those advertising under this tag though cannot be termed as desperate, indeed they are ostensibly hopeful in finding a match within their own caste. Certainly, 'caste no bar' category does not exclude the choice of preferences on the line of one's own caste.

Remember, the role of Manu was in limiting the Varna to be four i.e. there can be only Chaturvarna and no fifth Varna. He placed the Unmarriageables outside the fold of Varna system. In a way, the prescription for inter-caste marriage can be placed as a counter-thesis only to the principle of Chaturvarna. It may not involve the Unmarriageables. But when there is a prescription to purge the stigma of Unmarriageability, it counters the Manu's ploy of placing the Unmarriageables outside Chaturvarna. This strikes a chord in reframing Hinduism.

Caste sustains itself through endogamy (i.e. Unmarriageability) and the matrimonies are only a means for it. However, it would not be a fallacy to escalate the significance of matrimonies and holding it as a petri

---

[139]BAWS, Vol.9 p.289

dish that in reciprocation cultures and conserves the custom of Unmarriageability. No doubt, caste matrimonies are the outcome of custom of Unmarriageability. But they have become capable enough to reinforce the custom as well. Habitually, the Hindus are obedient to the custom of Unmarriageability. They are in no mood to question it. And when there exists a platform as well to effortlessly facilitate their custom via well-captioned caste labels what is the need for them to become deviants? Even an educated Hindu claiming to be liberal at heart and mind would not be interested to question the established order. She or he would hysterically resort to the reasoning of cultural and social harmony, thereby continuing to implement the caste rules. Such is the caste urge of the Hindu to confirm with Manu. Though an outcome of the custom of Unmarriageability, without an iota of doubt, the caste matrimonies reinforce the custom as well. If this much is understood embargoing the matrimonies from its functioning as caste conclaves would only be a natural corollary.

IIb
Outlook Two: In Support of Inter-caste Marriages

The second outlook that lingers in my mind is with regard to the ban on caste matrimonies as an attempt to promote inter-caste marriages. I do not wish to ignore the purview of one's common sense to consider the cry against Unmarriageability as an effort intended to promote inter-caste marriages. This could be the right juncture to elucidate why such an objective, even if held, is free from malice and has to be welcomed.

Amidst many who defend the caste system and are against the inter-caste marriages, the elucidation in itself gains significance considering the following statement coming from Mr.Gandhi, the Father and Mahatma of this Nation himself: *In India children of brothers do not intermarry. Do they cease to love because they do not intermarry? Among the Vaishnavas many women are so orthodox that they will not eat with the members of the family nor will they drink water from a common water pot. Have they no love?* The Caste system cannot be said to be bad because it does not allow interdining or intermarriage between different Castes.[140] For Dr.Ambedkar, this argument was as stupid as they were revolting. He Writes: *It is quite true the family is an ideal unit in which every member is charged with love and affection for another member although there is no intermarriage among members of a family. It may even be conceded that in a Vaishnava family members of the family do not interdine and yet they are full of love and affection for one another. What does all this prove? It does not prove that interdining and intermarrying are not necessary for establishing fraternity. What it proves is that where there are other means of maintaining fraternity—such as consciousness of family tie—interdining and intermarriage are not necessary. But it cannot be denied that where—as in the caste system—no binding force exists intermarriage and interdining are absolutely essential. There is no analogy between family and caste. Inter-caste dinner and inter-caste marriage are necessary because there are no other means of binding the different castes together while in the case of a family there exists other forces to bind them together.*[141]

In 'Annihilation of Caste', originally intended to be an address before the Hindu public at large, Dr.Ambedkar considers the question-How to bring about the reform of the Hindu Social Order? How to abolish caste? His plan of action for the abolition of caste goes as: *There are many Castes which allow inter-dining. But it is a common experience that inter-dining has not succeeded in killing the spirit of Caste and the consciousness of Caste. I am convinced that the real remedy is inter-marriage. Fusion of blood can alone create the feeling of being kith and kin and unless this feeling of kinship, of being kindred, becomes paramount the separatist feeling—the feeling of being aliens— created by Caste will not vanish. Among the Hindus inter-marriage must necessarily be a factor of greater force in social life than it need be in the life of the non-Hindus. Where society is already well-knit by other ties, marriage is*

140BAWS, Vol.9 p.276

141BAWS, Vol.9 p.287

an ordinary incident of life. But where society cut asunder, marriage as a binding force becomes a matter of urgent necessity. The real remedy for breaking Caste is inter-marriage. Nothing else will serve as the solvent of Caste.[142] So, if at all there is a reformer among the high caste Hindus, she or he should be promoting inter-caste marriage, taking the activism to impose a ban on caste-based matrimonial classifieds and websites.

IIc
Outlook Three: Questioning the authority of Shastras

The third outlook is about questioning the authority of the Shastras by bringing a ban on caste matrimonies. To the question, how to abolish caste, Dr.Ambedkar is convinced with intermarriage as the real remedy. But he does not end his solution there. His intellectual prowess and fierceness extend much beyond this prescription. In 'Annihilation of Caste' he continues: *You are right in holding that Caste will cease to be an operative force only when inter-dining and inter-marriage have become matters of common course. You have located the source of the disease. But is your prescription the right prescription for the disease? Ask yourselves this question; Why is it that a large majority of Hindus do not inter-dine and do not inter-marry? Why is it that your cause is not popular? There can be only one answer to this question and it is that inter-dining and inter-marriage are repugnant to the beliefs and dogmas which the Hindus regard as sacred. Caste is not a physical object like a wall of bricks or a line of barbed wire which prevents the Hindus from co-mingling and which has, therefore, to be pulled down. Caste is a notion, it is a state of the mind. The destruction of Caste does not therefore mean the destruction of a physical barrier. It means a notional change. Caste may be bad. Caste may lead to conduct so gross as to be called man's inhumanity to man. All the same, it must be recognized that the Hindus observe Caste not because they are inhuman or wrong headed. They observe Caste because they are deeply religious. People are not wrong in*

---

[142]BAWS, Vol.1 p.67

observing Caste. In my view, what is wrong is their religion, which has inculcated this notion of Caste. If this is correct, then obviously the enemy, you must grapple with, is not the people who observe Caste, but the Shastras which teach them this religion of Caste. Criticising and ridiculing people for not inter-dining or inter-marrying or occasionally holding inter-caste dinners and celebrating inter-caste marriages, is a futile method of achieving the desired end. The real remedy is to destroy the belief in the sanctity of the Shastras. How do you expect to succeed, if you allow the Shastras to continue to mould the beliefs and opinions of the people? Not to question the authority of the Shastras, to permit the people to believe in their sanctity and their sanctions and to blame them and to criticise them for their acts as being irrational and inhuman is a incongruous way of carrying on social reform. Reformers working for the removal of untouchability including Mahatma Gandhi, do not seem to realize that the acts of the people are merely the results of their beliefs inculcated upon their minds by the Shastras and that people will not change their conduct until they cease to believe in the sanctity of the Shastras on which their conduct is founded. No wonder that such efforts have not produced any results. You also seem to be erring in the same way as the reformers working in the cause of removing untouchability. To agitate for and to organise inter-caste dinners and inter-caste marriages is like forced feeding brought about by artificial means. Make every man and woman free from the thraldom of the Shastras, cleanse their minds of the pernicious notions founded on the Shastras, and he or she will inter-dine and intermarry, without your telling him or her to do so.[143]

But the challenge is – Is it possible to make the Hindus free from the thraldom of the Shastras and the pernicious notions founded by it? For this, it becomes essential to know about Hindu Religion beforehand, by making a distinction between principles and rules. Dr.Ambedkar again does this with flair which I am merely reproducing:

---

[143]BAWS, Vol.1 p.68

What is this Hindu Religion? Is it a set of principles or is it a code of rules? Now the Hindu Religion, as contained in the Vedas and the Smritis, is nothing but a mass of sacrificial, social, political and sanitary rules and regulations, all mixed up. What is called Religion by the Hindus is nothing but a multitude of commands and prohibitions. Religion, in the sense of spiritual principles, truly universal, applicable to all races, to all countries, to all times, is not to be found in them, and if it is, it does not form the governing part of a Hindu's life. That for a Hindu, Dharma means commands and prohibitions is clear from the way the word Dharma is used in Vedas and the Smritis and understood by the commentators. The word Dharma as used in the Vedas in most cases means religious ordinances or rites. Even Jaimini in his Purva-Mimansa defines Dharma as "a desirable goal or result that is indicated by injunctive (Vedic) passages". To put it in plain language, what the Hindus call Religion is really Law or at best legalized class-ethics. Frankly, I refuse to call this code of ordinances, as Religion.[144]

Indeed I hold that it is your bounden duty to tear the mask, to remove the misrepresentation that as caused by misnaming this Law as Religion. This is an essential step for you. Once you clear the minds of the people of this misconception and enable them to realize that what they are told as Religion is not Religion but that it is really Law, you will be in a position to urge for its amendment or abolition. So long as people look upon it as Religion they will not be ready for a change, because the idea of Religion is generally speaking not associated with the idea of change. But the idea of law is associated with the idea of change and when people come to know that what is called Religion is really Law, old and archaic, they will be ready for a change, for people know and accept that law can be changed.[145]

Now let us consider the possibility of liberating the Hindus from the thraldom of the Shastras bearing in mind what the Hindus believe as

---

[144]BAWS, Vol.1 p.75

[145]BAWS, Vol.1 p.76

their religion is nothing more than an old and archaic law. In this regard, there is one such archaic law, resonating the very pulse of the Hinduism, which is the well-known 'Law of Caste'– the law that pervades the length and breadth of the Hindu society. It is this law of caste whose perniciousness unfolds by enforcing the stigma of Unmarriageability and thereby maintaining endogamy and gradation among the castes. If the modern law, by which I mean the absolute supremacy of regular law, replaces the archaic law of caste, will it lead to destroying the belief of the Hindus in the sanctity of the Shastras? Will it cease the Shastras from moulding the beliefs and opinions of the people? The onus lies on the Hindus alone to answer this question. Only they know how deep-dyed casteist are they and what kind of reforms would be required to change their hardened notions. But one thing is for sure. If the modern law is made to counter the archaic law of caste, the effect it would produce on the general conscience of this Nation would be reforming– immensely reforming. It would bring to the forefront the need for realization that the law of caste is a mere part and parcel of the code of ordinances which the Hindus have misconceived as religion. It other words, it would undermine the significance of Hinduism as a religion.

Well, the above argument could give rise to another question- hasn't the modern law ever before countered the archaic law of caste? Yes, it has. For instance, there is Article 15 and 17 in the Indian Constitution itself. The former prohibits the State from discriminating its citizens on the basis of caste. The latter is concerned with abolition of Untouchability. There are special laws as well providing penalties for practising Untouchability. While all these constitutional and statutory provisions apparently function as a shield they are not the sword against casteism. Hitherto the modern law hasn't countered the governing principle of caste. It continues to remain a silent spectator with regard to the stigma of Unmarriageability- the vicious custom of endogamy. It would not be wrong to say that amidst the inertness of modern law, the Hindus thrive caste.

So, how to wield the modern law against the archaic law of caste? My answer is, by imposing a ban on caste matrimonies and websites. With a peripheral sight, the remedy might appear to be so remote to the problem. But it is indeed a frontal attack targeting the foundation of caste system. My reasoning would make an appeal if one remembers that the pre-requisite of Brahminism is endogamy. There might be many reasons, of wickedness and unfairness, for the Brahmins to occupy the highest place in the social hierarchy of the Hindu society. But if a reason has to be made out on how they continue to derive the privileges till now, unspilled and unscattered, by virtue of being at the top of social hierarchy, it is exclusively because they continue to be endogamous. Brahmin Class– the father of the institution of caste is exclusive. And it remains exclusive by being endogamous. *Endogamy or the closed-door system, was a fashion in the Hindu society, and as it had originated from the Brahmin caste it was whole-heartedly imitated by all the non-Brahmin sub-divisions or classes, who, in their turn, became endogamous castes. It is "the infection of imitation" that caught all these sub-divisions on their onward march of differentiation and has turned them into castes. The propensity to imitate is a deep-seated one in the human mind and need not be deemed an inadequate explanation for the formation of the various castes in India.*[146] Arguing further, in order to strengthen his explanation, Dr.Ambedkar presents the two conditions for imitation: *(1) that the source of imitation must enjoy prestige in the group and (2) that there must be "numerous and daily relations" among members of a group. That these conditions were present in India there is little reason to doubt. The Brahmin is a semi-god and very nearly a demi-god. He sets up a mode and moulds the rest. His prestige is unquestionable and is the fountain-head of bliss and good. Can such a being, idolised by scriptures and venerated by the priest-ridden multitude, fail to project his personality on the suppliant humanity? Why, if the story be true, he is believed to be the very end of creation. Such a creature is worthy of more than mere imitation, but at least of imitation; and if he lives in an endogamous enclosure, should not the rest follow his example? Frail humanity! Be it embodied in a grave philosopher or a*

---

[146]BAWS, Vol.1 p.18

frivolous housemaid, it succumbs. It cannot be otherwise. Imitation is easy and invention is difficult.[147]

In my opinion, there might be many different ways to question the authority of Shastras but one effective way to do so would be by nullifying the founding principle of caste itself. This can be achieved by banning the caste matrimony in all its forms– classifieds, websites, centres or whatsoever. In other words, an embargo should be imposed on the matrimonies from functioning as caste conclaves. Caste being a notion gives shape to itself via the custom of endogamy. Grappling the custom would mean grappling the caste itself. The ban would be an attempt to disrupt the Shastras from teaching the religion of caste. *There is a strong belief in the mind of orthodox Hindus that the Hindu Society was somehow moulded into the framework of the Caste System and that it is an organization consciously created by the Shastras. Not only does this belief exist, but it is being justified on the ground that it cannot but be good, because it is ordained by the Shastras and the Shastras cannot be wrong.*[148]

Unfortunately, no one can assert with conscience that the mind of Hindus is receptive to progressive changes. At least the Hindus do not offer any hope in this regard. Casteist they are and casteist they would be. Whatever they are, it is crucial for the law to contradict caste. It is crucial for the law to bring forth the tenets of the Hindu religion and subject it to legal scrutiny. If these tenets continue to lay only the caste rules and the Hindus continue to prefer only the caste matrimonies, let it be so but not under the blanket of law. It is up to the Hindus to conjugally be open only to their caste but if it has to be so let the law inflict on them the bearing of a thief stealthily evading from its clutches. Let they practise caste knowing they are off the tracks of law. It is quite true that the Hindus would ensure their custom to prevail over the law. But while their custom prevails, let the

---

[147]BAWS, Vol.1 p.19

[148]BAWS, Vol.1 p.16

law make the Hindus as legal offenders. Let the law ban the caste matrimonies!

IId
Outlook Four: Retaliating Dishonour Killings and Khap Panchayats

So, in order to destroy the authority of Shastras and Vedas, the very first step is to make it incompatible with the authority of law. If the prescription of Shastras and Vedas is to prohibit exogamy, then the law has the obligation to prohibit such prescription. If Dishonour killings are the grave outcome of the exogamous marriages, then the law is duty-bound to question the Khap Panchayats' insistence on abidance to endogamy.[149] The nature of this discourse thus inevitably leads to the fourth outlook-retaliating Dishonour killings and Khap Panchayats by imposing a ban on caste matrimonies.

Khap Panchayats- the inglorious institution of the Indian villages are nothing more than the reminder of what Dr.Ambedkar wrote: *What is the village but a sink of localism, a den of ignorance, narrow-mindedness and communalism?*[150] Self-proclaimed conscience keepers of the society, these caste councils convene Kangaroo Courts to dissolve the marriages that violate caste rules and sanction Dishonour killings. What makes them so audacious and unapologetic? Understanding the concept of prayaschitas would bring in more clarity: *The Hindus have a system of Prayaschitas which are penances and which a man who has been expelled from caste must perform before he can be admitted to caste fellowship. With regard to these Prayaschitas or Penances certain points must be remembered. In the first place there are caste offences for which there is no Prayaschita. In the second place the Prayaschitas vary according to the offence. In some cases the Prayaschita involves a very small penalty. In other cases the penalty involved is a very severe one.*

---

[149]In some parts of India, Khap Panchayats are opposed to same gotra (Sagotra) marriages too.
[150]BAWS, Vol.13 p.62

The existing of a Prayaschita and its absence have a significance which must be clearly understood. The absence of Prayaschita does not mean that any one may commit the offence with impunity. On the contrary it means that the offence is of an immeasurable magnitude and the offender once expelled is beyond reclamation. There is no re-entry for him in the caste from which he is expelled. The existence of a Prayaschita means that the offence is compoundable. The offender can take the prescribed Prayaschita and obtain admission in the caste from which he is expelled.

There are two offences for which there is no penance. These are (1) change from Hindu Religion to another religion, (2) Marriage with a person of another caste or another religion. It is obvious if a man loses, caste for these offences he loses it permanently...

... The surest clue to find out what are the fundamental rules of caste and what caste consists in is furnished by the rules regarding Prayaschitas. Those for the infringement of which there is no Prayaschita constitute the very soul of caste and those for the infringement of which the Prayaschita is of the severest kind make up the body of caste...

... In the matter of marriage the regulation lays down that the caste must be endogamous. There can be no intermarriage between members of different castes. This is the first and the most fundamental idea on which the whole fabric of the caste is built up.[151]

The Khap Panchayats exist exactly to preserve this fundamental idea: there can be no intermarriage between members of different castes. And when the transgression happens, the transgressors are eliminated in the name of caste honours. It is vital to understand that the Khap Panchayats sanction Dishonour killings because there is no prayaschita provided for violating endogamy. They evaluate the occurrence of inter-caste marriages as a grave violation of the founding rule of caste itself and

---

[151]BAWS, Vol.5 p.158

regard the elimination of deviant couples as the only remedy. When Khap Panchayats claim themselves to be the conscience keepers of the society, their precise contention is that caste is endogamous and there shall be no violation with regard to this rule, whatsoever and howsoever.

There is one proposed legislation, Prohibition of Unlawful Assembly (Interference with the Freedom of Matrimonial Alliances) Bill, 2011, which deserves attention. The bill which has long been pending in parliament seeks to declare Khap Panchayats unlawful. The statement of objects and reasons detailed by the Law Commission of India in this regard is noteworthy:

There has been a spurt in illegal intimidation by self appointed bodies for bringing pressure against Sagotra marriages and inter-caste, inter-community and inter-religious marriages between two consenting adults in the name of vindicating the honour of family, caste or community. In a number of cases, such bodies have resorted to incitement of violence and such newly married or couples desirous of getting married have been subjected to intimidation and violence which has also resulted into their being hounded out of their homes and sometimes even murdered. Although such intimidation or acts of violence constitute offences under Indian Penal Code, yet, it is necessary to prevent assemblies which take place to condemn such alliances and to prescribe more severe punishment for such intimidatory or violent acts or acts imperiling the liberty of individual. This Act is, therefore, enacted to nip the evil in the bud and to prevent spreading of hatred or incitement of violence through such gatherings. The Act is designed to constitute special offences against such assemblies and is in addition to other offences under the Indian Penal Code.[152]

---

[152]In Annexure I, draft Bill as proposed by the Law Commission of India.

Does creation of special offences alone is adequate to secure freedom of choice to matrimony? What must not be neglected at this juncture is that within the Hindu society which by default epitomizes the custom of endogamy and whose family unit is fundamentally casteist, rarely an individual realizes her freedom of choice to matrimony. Even if she realizes, she is unable to exercise her choice outside her caste because of the family's acute addiction and abidance to the custom of endogamy. Hence, prohibition of unlawful assembly alone does not suffice. The mischief here is Unmarriageability. Dishonour killings are the direct outcome of Unmarriageability. What the Hindu families believe in is the stigma of Unmarriageability. What the Khap Panchayats believe in is the stigma of Unmarriageability. Khap Panchayats merely reiterate the belief of Hindu families. Naturally, the prohibition should be on the stigma of Unmarriageability.

The West Bengal National University of Juridical Science, in its suggestions and recommendations to 'The Prohibition of Unlawful Assembly (Interference with Freedom of Matrimonial Alliances) Bill 2011' has rightly pointed out that the target demographic of the Bill is the family units, and this being so, there is a real chance for less reporting of offences since the individuals will not be always ready to report against the members of their family or persons in the neighbourhood.[153] On the other hand, the Law Commission of India is hopeful that creation of substantive offences and its criminalization would have a deterrent effect on the Khap Panchayats and similar groups. In the matters of contradiction between the custom and the law, the Hindu society has shown exemplary resistance to change, thereby allowing the custom to prevail over the law. Therefore, the Bill should be ambitious enough to go beyond criminalizing unfair assemblies. It should be wary of the interferences with the freedom of matrimonial alliances, and at the same time, should strive to secure freedom of choice to matrimony and right to family. For this, the Bill

---

[153]The Prohibition of Unlawful Assembly (Interference with Freedom of Matrimonial Alliances) Bill 2011- Suggestions and Recommendation, submitted by. The West Bengal National University of Juridical Science, 2nd para.

should retaliate the stigma of Unmarriageability. It should retaliate the custom of endogamy. And this retaliation should begin with the banning of caste matrimonies that facilitate, glorify and reiterate the endogamous custom. If one's mind is sensible enough to admit that *caste without endogamy is a Fake*[154] the argument so far done would not fail to make an appeal. When seen from any front, banning the caste matrimonies is the strongest way to retaliate Dishonour killings and Khap Panchayats. And it is the surest way to secure freedom of matrimonial alliances and right to family of one's choice.

IIe
Outlook Five: Questioning the Unmarriageables
within the Hindu fold

What could be the height of ignorance and idiocy? It could be the Blacks endorsing Slavery or the Jews accepting Nazism or the Unmarriageables following Hinduism. But none had been suctioned into such a dystopian reality except the Unmarriageables. This also discloses why Hinduism is more wicked and pernicious than Slavery or Nazism or any other institutionalized oppressions. Unlike the Slaves, the Unmarriageables are unaware about their true conditions:

A deprivation of a man's freedom by an open and direct way is a preferable form of enslavement. It makes the slave conscious of his enslavement and to become conscious of slavery is the first and most important step in the battle for freedom. But if a man is deprived of his liberty indirectly he has no consciousness of his enslavement. Untouchability is an indirect form of slavery. To tell an Untouchable 'you are free, you are a citizen, you have all the rights of a citizen', and to tighten the rope in such a way as to leave him no opportunity to realize the ideal is a cruel deception. It is enslavement without making the Untouchables conscious of their enslavement. It is slavery though it is

---

154BAWS,Vol.1 p.14

untouchability. It is real though it is indirect. It is enduring because it is unconscious. Of the two orders, untouchability is beyond doubt the worse.[155]

... the Untouchables unlike the slaves are owned by the Hindus for purposes which further their interests and are disowned by them, when owning them places them under burden. The Untouchables can claim none of the advantages of an unfree social order and are left to bear all the disadvantages of a free social order.[156] But still, they are the Hindus hitherto, enslaved by the tenets of the Hindu religion.

In the course of general discussion on the draft of the Hindu Code Bill, Dr.Ambedkar remarked: *So far as I am concerned I am a very conservative person: Although some people may not accept that fact, I am indeed very conservative. All I say is that I am a progressive conservative and I should like to tell the House one important fact which I think every one of us must bear in mind, particularly the conservative members of this House. The great political philosopher Edmund Burke who wrote a big book against the French revolution because of its radicalism and revolutionism did not forget to tell his own countrymen who were very conservative, one very important truth. He said that those who want to conserve must be ready to repair and all I am asking of this house is this: that if you want to maintain the Hindu system, the Hindu culture, the Hindu society, do not hesitate to repair where repair is necessary.*[157] Are the Hindus ready for this? Not at all. They are conservative as far as maintaining the status quo of the Hindu system. And without any doubt the Hindu system is eternally regressive. Thus the Hindus are only regressive conservatives and never can they become progressive to repair the faults of their religion. Does this place needless and abundant burden on the Unmarriageables? If they continue to be Hindus, then the answer is in affirmative. The appeal of Dr.Ambedkar to his people is: *If we are to*

---

[155]BAWS, Vol.5 p.15

[156]BAWS, Vol.5 p.18

[157]BAWS, Vol. 14, part 1 p.283

die in our struggle for freedom, what is the use of fighting at wrong place? To reform the Hindu society is neither our aim nor our field of action. Our aim is to gain freedom for us. We have nothing to do with anything else. If we can gain our freedom by the conversion, why should we shoulder the responsibility of reforming the Hindu Society?[158]

Hence, the leaders of the Unmarriageables should no longer ignore their twin responsibilities- One, to question the Unmarriageables' way of life as Hindus; and two, to work for the renaissance of Buddhism. It is, in view of these twin responsibilities, exposing the stigma of Unmarriageability parallelly gains significance. The prevalence of Unmarriageability is nothing but a blatant exposition that Unmarriageables are not a sub-continent of the Hindus but a separate element in the national life. All the more, Unmarriageability whistle-blows the cause of their enslavement. It brings to the fore the functioning mechanism of caste. Undoubtedly, the stigma is the crucial catapult of self-realization that would strike the consciousness of the Unmarriageables within the Hindu fold. Therefore, whatever the choice of Unmarriageables is- to remain within Hinduism or to come out of it, they cannot shun the task of exposing Unmarriageability. If they despicably continue to be Hindus, they had to expose Unmarriageability in order to question the tenets of the religion which they ignorantly follow. If they choose the path of conversion, then again Unmarriageability in itself becomes one prime justification for them to discard the filthy Hindu religion. To begin with, the Unmarriageables should presently focus their efforts to ban the matrimonies from functioning as caste conclaves, thereby bringing to the fore- the stigma of Unmarriageability. They have to begin their fight with a successful ban on caste matrimonies. The strategy is nothing but a lethal attack on the foundation of Hindu religion but in disguise.

---

[158]BAWS, Vol. 17, part 3 p.136

IIf
Outlook Six: Anchoring the Reservation policy- Social backwardness stems out from Caste (Social) Stigmas and Prejudices

As argued in the previous chapter, the Unmarriageables should strategically placard the stigmas sustaining social inequality to resist and counter the dilution of reservation rights. They need to reiterate that the purpose of reservation shall continue until the demise of Unmarriageability. Reservation is a tool for the removal of social inequality and there lies no reason for its removal until the Indian society reconstructs its structure based on social equality. It has the responsibility to start its reform process with the ban on caste matrimonies.

Will banning caste matrimonies sermonize the Hindus about the notion of marital equality? Will it purge the determination of status based on caste? None would hope much in this regard. Legal ban at best could make the caste matrimonies unlawful. It cannot be a complete deterrent to the functioning of such caste conclaves. The Hindu society which is, by and large, endogamous, would not heed to the strokes of law that hinders the practice of endogamy. But still, the imposition of such a ban should be regarded significant. It is because caste matrimonies should be understood and remembered as one resemblance of ant colony optimization. The behavior of ants which live only in colonies is more associated with the purpose of colony survival rather than the survival of the individual. In the scientific world, the ant colony optimization refers to the foraging behavior of the ants- the behavior they adopt to find the shortest paths between food sources and the ant hill. The ant colony optimization is an inspiration to the scientific and industrial world situations[159] in finding approximate solutions to discrete optimization problems, and loosely, caste matrimonies can be considered to follow the technique of ant colony optimization. To the discrete caste requirement of each Hindu in the context of her marriage, caste matrimonies optimize the best possible alliances along with the default requirement of same language, region,

---

[159]"Ant Colony Optimizations: Introduction and recent trends" by Christian Blum.

status etc. always considered and also complementing the individual's specific expectation relating to education, profession, income, complexion, habits etc. Caste matrimonies are successful in meeting all the odds without contravening the caste rules. At the outset, the caste matrimonies might appear to satisfy the caste urge of the prospective brides and bridegrooms. But it goes beyond that and when given a complete thought, what it has promoted and is promoting is the successful continuation of the age-old custom of endogamy. The caste matrimonies are primarily guided by the purpose of sustaining endogamy though they address the other marital expectations of each individual. This explains why banning the caste matrimonies is crucial. The ban would be tantamount to disturbing an ant colony thereby dislodging an army of ants nesting in it. It introduces perplexity among the Hindus, as in the case of ants. If caste matrimonies are declared unlawful, the Hindus would instinctively become desperate to find a detour to accomplish their endogamous custom. Exposing this detour is important. And likewise, understanding their desperation is necessary. The detour they architect would expose the limitation of law in annihilating caste. While the desperation they exhibit would bring to the light the much ignored truth: caste stigmas and caste prejudices are the root cause of social backwardness prevalent in the Hindu society.

Whatever progress that a marginal section of Unmarriageables has managed can be attributed only to the reservation safeguards. The destiny of Unmarriageables inseparably travels with the right of reservation. Of late, the meaning of social justice has been largely tampered by the Indian State itself. The 10% reservation for economically weaker section in the general category which came into effect on 14th, January 2019 has severely mutilated the concept of social justice. It has revealed the legislatures' apathy and hostility towards Unmarriageables. The dilution of 'Scheduled Caste and Scheduled Tribes (Prevention of Atrocities) Act, 1989' by the Supreme Court of India on March 20, 2018, is a warning to the Unmarriageables that the Honourable Courts can also close the doors of justice. It is needless to mention about the inimical role being played by the Indian media in this regard. It has a notorious history against the Unmarriageables. It is presently notorious and will be so tomorrow as well. This is the time of darkness for the Unmarriageables as the concept of reservation based on social backwardness is receding. The 10% reservation for the general category based on economical backwardness is nothing but the grand mausoleum that has been constructed to put the principle of social justice to eternal rest. The remark by the Noble laureate economist Amartya Sen should not be taken lightly: "If the whole of the population is covered by reservation then that would be removal of reservation".[160]

The need of the hour at present is to retrieve the principle of social justice and the concept of reservation based on social backwardness. The reservation policy has been reduced to the logic of poverty alleviation program. 'Poverty' has replaced 'social backwardness' as the rationale for reservation. The Unmarriageables are required to become resilient swiftly. To bring a ban on the caste matrimonies and turn the spotlight on the stigma of Unmarriageability and the caste prejudice of the Hindus abiding to endogamy would, to an extent, bring to the fore the deep-dyed casteist mindset predominant in this society. The exposure is required to reason out how caste stigmas and caste prejudices pave way for the social inequality and the social backwardness of the Unmarriageables. A ban on caste matrimonies is nothing but a strategic justification on why reservation should be based on social backwardness and why economical backwardness can never become the basis for it whatsoever. It is a strategic coercion on the Hindus to deal with their caste prejudices first instead of being so persistent to usurp an unjustified and underserved claim in reservation on the pretext of economic backwardness. The ban would be an attempt so that the half-baked scholars and policy makers might concede that the introduction of economic backwardness in the concept of reservation is against the principle of social justice. Reservation is a social justice mechanism against the social subjugation and discrimination met by the Unmarriageables. Chances are high that the repercussion of ban on caste matrimonies would glaringly exhibit much of the social stigmas and prejudices oozing out from the Hindu society. Highlighting the caste based

---

[160] as told to PTI in an exclusive interview

reservation in matrimonies is definitely not an unrelated or distant justification to continue the reservation policy for socially unprivileged. Reservation in education, jobs, and legislatures etc. has its root in the reservation in marriages. Reservation is simply an antidote to caste system. The latter has caused the problem while the former is an arrangement trying to seek a solution. Remember, the justification for reservation is not social backwardness per se. Rather, the rationale arises from the fact that social backwardness stems out from social (caste) stigmas and prejudices. Therefore, if at all reservation is desired to be removed, it has to be preceded by the removal of caste stigmas, prejudices and disparities.

There lies another reason for the need to associate caste matrimonies with the issue of reservation. The Unmarriageables' effort to annihilate caste is usually seen by the Hindus as a humorous endeavour. In fact, they would continue to perceive so. Hindus have nothing to fear from the Unmarriageables, nor have they anything to gain by the abolition of caste.[161] To take the efforts of annihilation of caste lightly in itself is a blend of their wickedness. If the wicked need to tremble, then the Unmarriageables should juxtapose the stigma of Unmarriageability with the issue of reservation. They should succeed in banning the caste matrimonies and its repercussion should be relied to reiterate on the relevancy of reservation. Reservation is to attain social equality. Till then, the existence of Unmarriageability should be a factor in assessing the social inequality prevailing in this society.

IIg
Outlook Seven: The Young Generation and the Mainstream Democratic Forces- Making them Accountable

In 'Annihilation of Caste', the Doctor writes: *To put it in plain language, what the Hindus call Religion is really Law or at best legalized*

---

[161]Dr.Ambedkar had the same view with regard to abolition of Untouchability; BAWS, Vol. 9 p.195

class-ethics. Frankly, I refuse to call this code of ordinances, as Religion. The first evil of such a code of ordinances, misrepresented to the people as Religion, is that it tends to deprive moral life of freedom and spontaneity and to reduce it (for the conscientious at any rate) to a more or less anxious and servile conformity to externally imposed rules. Under it, there is no loyalty to ideals, there is only conformity to commands. But the worst evil of this code of ordinances is that the laws it contains must be the same yesterday, today and forever. They are iniquitous in that they are not the same for one class as for another. But this iniquity is made perpetual in that they are prescribed to be the same for all generations. The objectionable part of such a scheme is not that they are made by certain persons called Prophets or Law-givers. The objectionable part is that this code has been invested with the character of finality and fixity.[162] If the Hindu religion is so, what is equally noteworthy is how this code of ordinances have given caste a perpetual lease of life: *It must be a source of silent amusement to many a Non-Hindu to find hundreds and thousands of Hindus breaking Caste on certain occasions, such as railway journey and foreign travel and yet endeavouring to maintain Caste for the rest of their lives! The explanation of this phenomenon discloses another fetter on the reasoning faculties of the Hindus. Man's life is generally habitual and unreflective. Reflective thought, in the sense of active, persistent and careful consideration of any belief or supposed form or knowledge in the light of the grounds that support it and further conclusions to which it tends, is quite rare and arises only in a situation which presents a dilemma—a crisis. Railway journeys and foreign travels are really occasions of crisis in the life of a Hindu and it is natural to expect a Hindu to ask himself why he should maintain Caste at all, if he cannot maintain it at all times. But he does not. He breaks Caste at one step and proceeds to observe it at the next without raising any question. The reason for this astonishing conduct is to be found in the rule of the Shastras, which directs him to maintain Caste as far as possible and to undergo prayaschitta when he cannot. By this theory of prayaschitta, the Shastras by following a spirit of compromise have given caste a perpetual lease of life and have*

---

[162]BAWS, Vol. 1 p.75

smothered reflective thought which would have otherwise led to the destruction of the notion of Caste.[163]

Even the young generation that is boasting about its casteless fraternity is not an exemption to this rule of the Shastras. Typically, like the Hindus, they too break caste on the occasions of railway journey and other travels. But do they ignore caste beyond these mechanical occasions? Do they exhibit a state of castelessness in their social interactions? Do they reflect on their thoughts when it comes to the abidance of endogamy? Do they disregard the stigma of Unmarriageability? In all these matters, what the young generation has followed is an exemplary spirit of obedience as demanded by the Shastras which has, as usual, given caste a perpetual lease of life. They have failed collectively to discard the practice of Unmarriageability which would have otherwise led to the destruction of the notion of caste.

Unmarriageability is the mould in which the Hindu Social Organization has casted itself so far. And out of this same mould, each generation is casting its succeeding generation with the much peculiar shape and structure of caste system- unaltered and uncompromised in its entirety. What cannot now be refused is that the present young generation offers no reluctance in getting themselves casted in the caste mould. They overlook the fact that marriage eventually forms a generation. In fact, marriage is the beginning step in the formation of a new generation.

At the same time, in the Indian context, whatever kinds and forms of social inequality that is in existence has its root in the prevalence of marital inequality. This being so, banning the caste matrimonies would be a heuristic strategy to initiate a social dialogue for a social change. The ban would bring compulsion on the young generation, whom can be considered as the present marriageable units, to discuss about the stigma of Unmarriageability and disown their belief in caste in the matters of their marriage. It is nothing more than a social appeal pressing the present

---

[163]BAWS, Vol. 1 p.73

young generation to come out of the caste mould and denounce and discard the custom of endogamy. There must occur marital endosmosis which is possible only in a casteless society. And if the young generation needs to prove their claim of castelessness to be true, they should first realize that the sincerest form of social amalgamation is possible only via inter-caste marriages. Meanwhile, the youths who fret over reservation should understand that reservation is not only to uplift the socially backward but also a reminder to each and every one to hoist castelessness in this society.

The Unmarriageables are casteless and only they can 'initiate' the effort towards a casteless society. But, at the most, they can only centre-stage the stigma of Unmarriageability by demanding a ban on caste matrimonies. It is the moral duty of the young generation and the mainstream democratic forces to take up the course of annihilation of caste. The democratic forces functioning in the political and social arena should realize that *Brahmins, the chief and the leading element in the governing class, acquired their political power not by force of intellect—intellect is nobody's monopoly—but by sheer communalism.*[164] The Brahmins are very conscious that in order to establish their communalistic hegemony, even more than rejecting the non-Brahmins what is essentially important is to maintain the assimilation of Brahmins intact. They are aware that the consolidation of their community would, by default, aid in the rejection of non-Brahmin communities. This explains why abidance to endogamy is stricter in the Brahmin class. In fact, Brahminism exists exclusively via endogamy. Undoubtedly, the Brahmins continue to maintain their superior status by their strict practise of custom of Unmarriageability giving rise to the deadly combination of casteism and nepotism deciding the seats of power, prestige and money.

The young generation and the mainstream democratic forces should contemplate on the questions raised by Dr.Ambedkar: *How are you going to break up Caste, if people are not free to consider whether it*

---

[164]BAWS, Vol. 9 p.230

accords with reason? How are you going to break up Caste if people are not free to consider whether it accords with morality? The wall built around Caste is impregnable and the material, of which it is built, contains none of the combustible stuff of reason and morality. Add to this the fact that inside this wall stands the army of Brahmins who form the intellectual class, Brahmins who are the natural leaders of the Hindus, Brahmins who are there not as mere mercenary soldiers but as an army fighting for its homeland and you will get an idea why I think that breaking-up of Caste amongst the Hindus is well-nigh impossible. At any rate, it would take ages before a breach is made.[165] But, one thing is for sure. Until the mainstream democratic forces take serious efforts to politically question the foundation of caste system, a legal ban on the caste matrimonies would remain a mute subject as ever. If left to the will of the Hindu communal majority, there would be no scope for progress in this direction. I believe, banning the caste matrimonies and questioning the stigma of Unmarriageability would be a breach. It would be a breach made into the caste system. It is too early to ascertain whether the ban would produce the effect of dynamite applied to the Vedas and the Shastras. But definitely, it would question the casteist decision in the marriages which deny any part to reason. It would question the conjugal inequality based on castes which deny any part to morality.

There is another revelation that the ban would serve to highlight. The Unmarriageables have become precarious in choosing their allies-both ideologically and politically. Identifying the allies is as important as identifying the adversaries and the Unmarriageables are strangely ignoring this which is suicidal. The stealthy manner in which the Communists have allowed and endorsed the 10% reservation for general category based on economical backwardness to come into effect is one recent warning that has illustrated how there can be no difference between the allies and adversaries of the Unmarriageables in politics. It has evinced how the so-called leftist comrades even can doom the destiny of Unmarriageables. In the present political times where the vote bank politics have left no scope

---

[165]BAWS, Vol. 1 p.74

for the ideologies to be the guide, the struggle to ban caste matrimonies could be the litmus test in marking apart the allies and the adversaries of the Unmarriageables. The political and social turnouts in meeting the demand for the caste matrimonial ban would not only educate the Unmarriageables in differentiating the allies and the adversaries but would also critically dissect the sincerity of their allies in genuinely working for the cause of annihilation of caste. It is stupidity manifold if the Unmarriageables continue to place the trust on their allies purely on ideological nexus. The allies are disowning the Unmarriageables in the matters of reservation. The Unmarriageables are already in solitude in the matters of their emancipation. Hence it would be futile if the Unmarriageables do not keep a check on their allies with regard to the cause of annihilation of caste. It would be the beginning of dystopia, if reservation is taken away while caste continues to exist. The struggle to ban caste matrimonies is a litmus test that would glaringly and unapologetically reveal the caste pH of all the participants- whether it be the young generation or the mainstream democratic forces or the Communists or the Dravidian parties. The Unmarriageables should take note of this test results for it would disclose their enemies who are in the guise of friends and well-wishers.

I have tried so far to present few outlooks as a justification to bring a ban on caste matrimonies. Though I have listed them one by one, the list is not comprehensive or complete. Is such a detailed justification even required is another question that deserves to be entertained. Yet, bearing in mind that the larger section of this society happens to be the subjects of Hindu religion, I believe the effort could be validly utilized to confront the tenets of Manudharma, inch by inch. We are the only nation notoriously unique in stamping its people caste wise and also continuing to advertise such classification in the matrimonial classifieds of national dailies without any remorse. Nowhere else is the sanctity of humanity been publicly denounced to such a shameless extent. To sustain casteism so perfectly with changing times reflect the rigidity of the people. We must not forget that we can be a nation only through social amalgamation and to bring a ban on caste matrimonies is only a beginning to realize such an ambition.

III

Constitutional Promulgation to Abolish Caste

All are slaves of the Caste System. But all the slaves are not equal in status. To excite the proletariat to bring about an economic revolution, Karl Marx told them: "You have nothing to lose except your chains." But the artful way in which the social and religious rights are distributed among the different castes whereby some have more and some have less, makes the slogan of Karl Marx quite useless to excite the Hindus against the Caste System. Castes form a graded system of sovereignties, high and low, which are jealous of their status and which know that if a general dissolution came, some of them stand to lose more of their prestige and power than others do. You cannot, therefore, have a general mobilization of the Hindus, to use a military expression, for an attack on the Caste System.[166]

In the war against caste system, understanding its genesis and mechanism becomes crucial. A system which, despite its perniciousness, reigns for more than two thousand years, undisturbed by the harangues of reformers relentlessly attempting to perish it, is nothing short of an ill-inspiration before which even warlords and dictators would sit cross-legged with folded arms to learn its strategy of eternal suppression and subjugation. The revolting strategy of caste system is very unique. And it is not only unique but also hard to be devised or replicated by any of the adversaries, making them eventually perplexed and powerless. Many military strategists believe that the best defence is a good offence. While few others are attracted to the idea that the best offence is a good defence. Caste system does not pick and choose either of the two strategies. Rather, it covertly combines them both, thereby making itself formidable. The

---

[166]BAWS, Vol. 1 p.72

offensive setup of caste system is numerous– Religious sanctity, Khap Panchayats, Dishonour killings, Ostracization, Social and Economic boycott etc. Even the customs of Hindu religion are an outcome of its offensive setup. Child marriage, enforced widowhood, sati all have the singular purpose of sustaining caste by deterring the members to go outside their caste group. While these offensive arrangements serve as the best defence what makes the caste system even more formidable is its defensive mechanism. In fact, caste has remained the most offensive system only through its defensive built up, namely, the custom of Unmarriageability. The argument is foolproof if we bear in mind that the purpose of graded inequality forming the structure of caste and enshrined by the principle of ascending order of reverence and descending order of contempt, is exclusively intended to maintain stigma of Unmarriageability. Without an iota of doubt, the best offence of caste system happens to be its defence- the custom of Unmarriageability viciously promoting endogamy. Therefore, the only way to confront caste, all in a worthwhile fashion, is to be more offensive specifically against the custom of Unmarriageability. Wielding the stigma of Unmarriageability is the only offensive strategy to collapse the defensive structure of the caste system. Purging this stigma, as a chain reaction, would collapse all the fortresses guarding the caste system. This is the only way to infiltrate into the system and destroy it from within, which is otherwise impregnable.

There is another floating argument one sometimes comes across. The basis of the argument is that Untouchability is a vanishing thing and therefore there is no use recognizing the Untouchables as a separate element in the national life of India. Everything is vanishing and there is nothing that is permanent in human history. The point may be considered when Untouchability has gone root and branch. Until that state arrives, it is unnecessary to pay any regard to it. We must all hope for the disappearance of Untouchability. But we must be careful not to be misled by people who boast of being incorrigible optimists. An optimist is a good companion to cheer up when one is in a state of depression. But he is not always a truthful witness of facts.

This argument is no argument at all. But since some people may be allured by it I wish to expose it and to show how futile it is. Those who raise this point do not seem to make a distinction between Untouchability as a touch-me-not-ism and Untouchability as a mental attitude manifesting itself in social discrimination. The two are quite different. It may be that Untouchability as a touch-me-not-ism may be gradually vanishing in towns, although I am doubtful if this is happening in any appreciable degree. But I am quite certain Untouchability as a propensity on the part of the Hindus to discriminate against the Untouchables will not vanish either in towns or in villages within an imaginable distance of time. Not only Untouchability as a discriminating propensity will not disappear but Untouchability as touch-me-not-ism will not disappear within a measurable distance of time in the vast number of villages in which the vast number of Hindus live and will continue to live. You cannot untwist a two-thousand-year-twist of the human mind and turn it in the opposite direction.[167]

As prevised by Dr.Ambedkar, Untouchability as a touch–me-not-ism itself is a common sight in today's Indian villages. The separate settlements, separate graveyards, separate temples, separate festivals etc. labelled for the Unmarriageables is only a stark reflection of Untouchability as a touch–me-not-ism. In this unchanging and unprogressive scenario, even incorrigible optimists would not hope for the quick fading of social discrimination resulted by Untouchability. Thus the caution though is not direct is however real- the path to annihilate Unmarriageability would be a long and tedious one. This is because of the simple fact that Untouchability as a mental attitude manifesting itself in social discrimination is a mere corollary of the stigma of the Unmarriageability. While Unmarriageability is the disease, Untouchability is only a symptom of it. And it is futile to expect the symptom to disappear without even attempting to cure the disease. The analogy is only an explanation as to why Untouchability is and will continue to be deep-rooted despite Article 17 of the Indian Constitution proclaiming "Untouchability is abolished and its practice in any form is forbidden".

---

[167]BAWS, Vol. 9 p.194

Article 17 is not only a fundamental right but also an absolute right i.e. no reasonable restrictions can be imposed on it. But still, the constitutional provision of abolition of Untouchability exists only in form and not in practise. How can Untouchability be abolished without annihilating Unmarriageability? The makers of our Constitution placed on us the responsibility to reform and we are yet to respond. Untouchability will exist till the existence of Unmarriageability i.e. Caste. The propensity to discriminate socially should cease first in order to remove its effect of touch-me-not-ism completely. In other words, Unmarriageability should cease in order to remove Untouchability root and branch. Abolition of Unmarriageability should precede if we want to succeed with abolition of Untouchability.

The crux of my argument is this- annihilating Unmarriageability is the only way to annihilate caste. And to annihilate Unmarriageability we must not solely rely on the demand to ban caste matrimonies. Rather there should be constitutional promulgation for abolition of caste itself. Constitutionally, caste must be recognized as Unmarriageability and conscious efforts must be made to abolish this stigma. Unmarriageability should be deciphered as the root cause of Casteism and Untouchability. To achieve this, a new Article 17A which reads as 'Abolition of Unmarriageability' should be introduced into the Constitution.

The expeditious manner in which 'The Constitution (One Hundred and Third Amendment) Act, 2019' amended Article 15 and Article 16 of the Constitution to include the criteria of 'economic backwardness' in admission to educational institution and reservation in government jobs is a wake-up lesson to the Unmarriageables who have so far availed with deficiency the provisions of Constitution especially the one pertaining to abolition of Untouchability under Article 17. If the Unmarriageables fail to wield Article 17 in their struggle for social equality, sooner or later, without any doubt, the noble principles of social justice would be wiped out without any traces from Article 15 and Article 16 of the Constitution in the similar fashion of 'The Constitution (One Hundred and Third Amendment) Act, 2019'. The Unmarriageables, therefore, should succeed in bringing in Article 17A as 'Abolition of Unmarriageability'. They should enlighten the world that annihilating Unmarriageability is the only way forward to annihilate caste.

The constitutional amendment to bring in 'Abolition of Unmarriageability' would definitely coerce the Hindu public to speak about the problem of caste alongside their institution of family and marriage instead of conveniently continuing to restrict caste to the aspect of reservation alone. Even if the Hindus remain deaf and dumb, the rest of the public opinion for sure would not ignore the justifications that exist in questioning the stigma of Unmarriageability. It would be an interesting attempt to construct imaginarily how the judiciary might respond to the custom of Unmarriageability. Let's say that the question of banning the caste matrimonies comes before the court of law. What would the learned counsels argue or on what basis the honourable judges would adjudicate upon? It is sensible to hold that the issue of concern would centre on the presence or absence of caste discrimination revealed in the caste matrimonies. If it is proved with relevant facts that caste discrimination is practised in the matrimonial advertisements, the legal consequence of it would be the ban on such caste matrimonies from practising discrimination. An example to share in this regard is the accusation against Shaadi.com- United Kingdom's largest marriage site catering to the Indian community, for reinforcing caste discrimination with an option for the Scheduled castes to be left out of its algorithms.[168] Chris Milsom, a barrister, who led the first successful charge of caste discrimination in the United Kingdom in 2015 remarked: "Restricting matches by caste could be contravening the Equality Act. By forcing users to state their caste, the sites are either discriminating themselves or knowingly aiding discrimination by users". Taking this as a precedent, the numerous matrimonies whose advertisements include 'Except SC/ST' or 'SC/ST Excuse' should be constitutionally challenged by the progressive forces in India. At this juncture, I want to persuade that even these efforts are not

---

[168] https://economictimes.indiatimes.com/news/politics-and-nation/indian-matrimonial-site-shaadi-com-under-fire-in-uk-over-caste-based-matches/articleshow/73872898.cms

suffice. At best, they could lead to prohibition of matrimonial advertisements that openly discriminate or exclude the Unmarriageables. But there would be no hindrance on the matrimonies from functioning as caste conclaves. They would continue to connect the prospective brides and bridegrooms on caste terms. They may not be operating under the tags of 'Except SC/ST' or 'SC/ST Excuse' but would continue to evade the law by quoting their requirements in a much nuanced and subtle manner like 'Same Caste', 'Sub-sect no bar', 'Equal castes', 'Madhwa preferred', 'Iyer preferred' etc. By this, the caste matrimonies make themselves available with better defences. To elucidate in the context, Shaadi.com has maintained that its "Community" question "works as an important proxy to determine lifestyles fitment". It is crucial to realize how these matrimonies successfully camouflage their caste prejudices under the fancy pretext of 'lifestyle fitment' or the standard excuses like culture, tradition, custom etc. What they call as community matrimonies are nothing but caste matrimonies. The term 'Community' has become the sugarcoating or euphemism for caste. So, how to deal this evasion?

I am of the opinion that we are failing to see the larger picture in connection with caste matrimonies. What we are focusing on is the ban on caste matrimonies from practising discrimination. This restricts us to the realm of just proving the presence of element of discrimination in the matrimonial advertisements. This perspective does not lead us to realize that caste matrimonies itself are a form of discrimination. The burden to prove should not be about the presence of element of discrimination alone. Rather, the caste matrimonies that are in line with endogamous custom itself are an outcome of discrimination. Endogamy or Unmarriageability by itself is discrimination. Whistle-blowing this should be our burden and responsibility. To single out the Unmarriageables in the matrimonial advertisements demands judicial scrutiny. No denial in this regard. But the much more important task before us is to constitutionally challenge the functioning of caste matrimonies or what is referred in disguise as community matrimonies.

Accomplishing the constitutional amendment to abolish Unmarriageability would strikingly aid the banning of caste matrimonies. But will the Indian society progress itself by bringing in such a reform? It will if it is no longer a residue of ancient Society.

Why is it that in modern times societies seem to progress continuously without many difficulties except those which wars give rise to? Why was it not so in the ancient society?

The difference between ancient society and modern society lies in the fact that in ancient societies law-making was not the function of the people. Law was made by God or by the law-giver. The function of the Society was merely to obey law that was made either by the divine power or the law maker. This was the fundamental reason for ancient societies not having any continuous civilization.

The true function of law consists in repairing the faults of the society. Unfortunately ancient societies never dared to assume the function of repairing their own defects; consequently they decayed. One of the reasons for the decay of Hindu society is that it was governed by law which had either been made by Manu or Yajnavalkya. Law that has been laid down by these law-makers is divine law. The result was that Hindu society was never able to repair itself.

In Europe after a course of time, jurisdiction of ecclesiastical law was challenged by secular law with the result that today law in the West was purely secular and the jurisdiction of the Church was confined merely to the priest.

Unfortunately many writers who have carried on researches into India's past, including the great scholar Prof. Max Muller, have given currency to the motion that Indian law has not changed at all. This is in conformity with what the orthodox pundits maintain. But from such study as I have made I can say that it is a complete fallacy.

There is no country in the world which has undergone so many revolutions as this country. This country has been in a conflict between ecclesiastical law and secular law long before the Europeans sought to challenge the authority of the Pope. Kautilyas's Arthshastra lays down foundation of secular law. In India unfortunately ecclesiastical law triumphed over secular law. Why did it happen? In my opinion, it was one of the greatest disasters in this country. The unprogressive character of Hindu society was due to the notion that law cannot be changed.[169]

This unprogressive character of Hindu society will confront every effort that tries to bring in constitutional amendment to abolish Unmarriageability. It is because the idea of abolition of Unmarriageability will be seen by the Hindus as a counter-thesis to the idea of Chaturvarna that they have so far believed in. But if at all we are inclined in repairing the faults of the society, then the cause of abolishing the stigma of Unmarriageability should be taken up. Undoubtedly, introducing 'Abolition of Unmarriageability' into the Constitution will serve more effective than bringing in the phrase 'Abolition of Caste'. Because when we peruse 'Abolition of Unmarriageability', it not only includes the complete aspect of 'Abolition of Caste' but also goes a step ahead by constitutionally recognizing and defining caste as the custom of Unmarriageability i.e. endogamy. We should not leave caste to be undefined in the Constitution as we erred in the case of Article 17 in which Untouchability has not been constitutionally defined hitherto. Defining caste as Unmarriageability is very important constitutionally. Because that would enlarge the scope and application of Article 15, Article 16 and Article 17. In the case of Article 17, Untouchability would then mean to include Unmarriageability as well. Considering Article 16, 'The Constitution (One Hundred and Third Amendment) Act 2019' only reiterates how the concept of reservation has been reduced to the likes of poverty alleviation program by bringing in the criteria of 'economic backwardness' to accommodate the 'General category" or to say otherwise the 'privileged castes'. When the principle of

---

[169]BAWS, Vol. 17, part 3 p.386

social justice suffers a back door burial like this, it is high time that we at least make it relevant till the removal of stigma of Unmarriageability.

To open up the subject of Unmarriageability would not be an easy exercise, I expect. It is because it would mean voluntary disclosure of caste prejudices that we have believed and practised in our private lives, in our marriages, and also as family affairs. Despite this challenge always existing, it is pertinent to progress the public opinion towards purging the stigma of Unmarriageability. This book is purely an appeal to the people in this direction. It began with the selected works of Dr.Amedkar to ensure the needed clarity among the readers before introducing the concept of Unmarriageability. The concept is introduced in chapter 2 by terming the Depressed Classes as the true Unmarriageables within Hindu social order, though in a rudimentary sense, each caste group is Unmarriageable to the rest of the castes. By arguing about the significance to popularize the reference 'Unmarriageables' in chapter 3, what has been precariously claimed as a custom i.e. Endogamy, has been exposed and degraded to the level of stigma i.e. Unmarriageability. While chapter 4 establishes that this stigma has not been dealt by any movement so far, chapter 5 proceeds to persuade that Unmarriageability should become the spearhead against the caste system in the present and future movements. Chapter 5 is important in the sense that it reveals the ploy of Unmarriageability and how this stigma ensures the social inequality based on caste to remain eternal. Chapter 6 provides for four rationales holding which the same stigma of Unmarriageability can be wielded as the spearhead against the caste system itself. So what has been valued as a custom is demeaned to become a stigma eventually turning it as a spearhead against its own existence. Finally, the plan of action is prescribed in chapter 7 to achieve what has been argued at length and theorized with vigour- the annihilation of caste.

Not only the subject of Unmarriageability but also the idea of bringing in 'Abolition of Unmarriageability' into the Constitution itself is bound to create new perspectives, dialogues, debates, discussions and uproars in favour of it and against it. Whatever the turnout of the events might be, a proper public opinion should be arrived at in order to accomplish such a bold constitutional amendment. I hope that this book would be the first step in that direction. What I have tried is to provide a new and sensible perspective not only to look at the caste system but also to find a practical way to make its annihilation a reality.

The subject of Unmarriageability though is not altogether new, yet can be considered to have been left in the shadows for a very long period. Hence, to talk about it and its aspect is bound to create for sure numerous differences of opinion. Whatever the differences might be, I hope none of it would go to the extent of denying the existence of stigma of Unmarriageability itself. I hope, only hope, that the society we live in is not so ancient, is not so primaeval.

The fact remains that there is no legal prohibition against the
propagation of the Dharma laid down by Manu.
The Courts do not recognize it as Law. But the Law does not
treat it as contrary to Law.

-Dr.Ambedkar in BAWS, Vol. 5, p.285.